Praise for *The Anatomy of Prison Life*

"Just got through the first chapter . . . I am hooked!"

—Christina Calabria, Social Advocate

"Just read first chapter. Riveting!!!"

—Jan Prichett, Attorney at Law

"I just finished reading your book. I asked for the *truth* of prison life, and you give it in all of its unadulterated form—straight with no chaser. I will tell anyone who wants to know what it is truly like to be in prison, to read your book!"

—Thomas Rush, writer and author

"As it pertains to the IL DOC it is insightful and factually true as it corresponds with my personal experience between the years 1991 and 2000."

—Herman Moore, former chaplain in Illinois Department of Corrections

"I could not help but think of one word: Suburb!!!

—Richard Vance, from a perspective of personal experience

"Interesting, informative, and fascinating!

—Anita Francois, a professional clinical social worker

THE ANATOMY OF
PRISON LIFE

The Anatomy of
PRISON LIFE

Behind the Walls
of the Illinois
Department of
Corrections

CHARLES L. HINSLEY

Linguistic Freedom Publications
Greensboro, NC

This book is dedicated to the memory of my good friend and former colleague Jim Page. His 30-plus years of commitment and dedicated service to the Illinois Department of Corrections will forever be appreciated and remembered.

Cover and Interior Design by Imagine! Studios, LLC
www.ArtsImagine.com

Published by Linguistic Freedom Publications
Greensboro, NC

Articles appearing in the Appendices were previously published and are reprinted with permission from their orignial publishers.

ISBN 13: 978-0-9895873-0-3

Library of Congress Control Number: 2013911669

First Linguistic Freedom Publications printing: July 2013

TABLE OF CONTENTS

Foreword   *ix*

Acknowledgments   *xv*

Introduction   *xix*

About the Author   *xxiii*

1 Welcome to Prison   1

2 Surviving in Prison   11

3 How It All Began   23

4 My Road to Prison   39

5 Entering the Illinois Prison System   47

6 Thrown into the Lion's Den   59

7 Problems in Segregation   69

8 The Gang Influence   83

9 Maximum Security   97

10 The War on Gangs   103

11 The Rise of Illinois' Supermax System   115

12 Dealing with Racism and Surviving the Pressures
of Prison Life   133

13 The Death Penalty in Illinois   143

14 Taking the Life of a Human Being   153

15 Ongoing Challenges   169

16 Managing Inmate Protests   179

17 A Different Perspective   191

18 Super Maximum Security Prison   203

19 Politics and Vying for Power   211

20 What Does This All Mean?   233

Appendix I: The Illinois Department of Corrections   243

Appendix II: Menard Correctional Center   255

Appendix III: Tamms Correctional Center   273

Appendix IV: Personal   293

FOREWORD

CHANCES ARE YOU have heard, read, or seen the prison movie, *The Shawshank Redemption.*

Made in Hollywood by the usual Hollywood standards, *Shawshank* is widely considered to be one of the best movies ever made about life behind prison bars, a special place of human confinement often isolated, whether or not by design, from the public consciousness.

As a movie, it is a pretty good tale of man's inhumanity to man, an entertaining, heartwarming saga of eventual triumph over abject adversity, where in the end of every conceivable misfortune, the good guys always emerge victorious. Movies, you know, must always end on a high note. They are made to make you feel good, refreshed with a good feeling so that you will purchase another ticket and come visit again.

. . . and also to tell your neighbor.

This is hardly the case with Charles Hinsley's masterfully written and painstakingly documented, "Anatomy of Prison Life", a riveting, straight-from-the heart account of real life, *crime and tragedy* behind the walls of a real prison—the Illinois Department of Corrections.

If you have ever made a visit, be it to a jail or a prison, you left, I know, with a sigh of supreme relief, grateful that your stay was temporary, and nothing you would ever want recorded on your bucket list.

Freedom takes on an entirely new meaning once you say your goodbyes to the people you went to visit. Whether temporary or permanent, men locked up like caged animals, leaves a pungent odor in one's consciousness, a smell unlikely never to be eliminated, erased, glossed over, or wiped clean.

Though his educational background includes both a Bachelor and a Master's degree, largely in the field of psychology, Hinsley writes with the passion, style, wit, and fluidity of a trained journalist, a skill not easily mastered even by the best of the best.

Such a skill-set, in my view, is nothing short of a sanctified anointing because nothing else makes sense. College degrees and professional training, notwithstanding, can only take one so far. After that, it becomes a case of divine intervention.

Instead of giving us a regurgitated, statistically laden documentary, Hinsley deliberately and succinctly presents the unvarnished facts, and just the facts, mind you, much like an old fashion Perry Mason TV whodunit drama. With his gripping, tell-all account of life on the inside, you'll have no trouble separating the good guys from the bad guys, and yet, unwittingly identify with the humanity of inmates whose dignity languishes in a perpetual state of degradation.

Hinsley's sharply-written prose and analytical mindset captures the essence of prison life in such mesmerizing detail that you are easily misled to assume that you are watching a made-in Hollywood movie, not reading a book.

Actually, his reporting rivals, matches, surpass, or complement, anything you would see on *60 Minutes*, *Nightline*, or any network evening news program. *The Anatomy of Prison Life* is an irresistible page-turner.

For 20 years, as a correctional professional, and being an Assistant Warden and Warden for over half of his 20 year career, Hinsley sat in the cat bird's seat, overseeing, documenting, fact-checking, administrating, and managing the activities of some of the nation's most notorious inmates. His take on prisons known as Super Max or maximum security prisons, is a walk down a road less traveled, and you definitely don't want to go there, even if accompanied by armed security.

He watched, up close, how some inmates lived; and how some of them died. Watching a man take his last breath on Death Row, for example, is not a pleasant sight to behold. It sends a chill that freezes the brain cells.

But Hinsley was there; he saw, learned, and heard everything—and probably some things you may not want to hear, see, or know anyway. It's hard to miss the action on the field when you're sitting in the cat bird's seat.

As a movie, *Shawshank* will entertain you; on the other hand, Hinsley's mesmerizing narrative will inform you, inspire, educate, and yes, disturb your Hollywood view of prison life because it captures and presents a prospective that no movie or TV program could ever match or duplicate.

This view from his ring side seat is the real deal, or what the old folk would call, the "real McCoy". In short, this is grown folk stuff.

Even if you have relatives or friends in prison, *even* if you have visited prisons, and *even* if you have been locked up yourself, it will be hard, nearly impossible to match or grasp the totality of prison life in the grand sweep so eloquently captured by Hinsley's analytical description.

This book will not fully explain why so many people, especially why so many African American males comprise well over half of the nation's prison population, an emerging trend that shows no sign of changing, at least not any time soon. His book was not written to do that. It will provide, however, an inside look at prison culture from a seasoned professional whose major aim is to forge a greater understanding of our complex criminal penal system, and the dry rot that has now settled in—both outside and inside the walls.

For most Americans, real prison life is reflected in Hollywood-made movies. Of course, movie theaters don't let you exit with hung down heads and frayed nerves because you may never come back. So they lace your arsenic with heavy doses of cream and sugar, and if given enough Novocain, you will never experience the agony of real pain.

But it strains my spirit to see so many young Black males locked away, many of them for a lifetime. Even as this is being written, more billion dollar prisons are on the drawing board awaiting the arrival of a new generation of young Black males who are not yet born.

There's hardly a Black family in America that has not had a friend, family member, relative, co-worker or knowledge of someone who's done time in our nation's jails and prisons. Today's, two million-plus prison population is mostly young, mostly poor, and mostly Black, a reality that should cause all of us to seriously ask ourselves this probing, gut-checking question; Why and how much more are we willing to tolerate?

The stark reality of prison life is a phenomenon not easily understood by the masses. And unless you have had an encounter with the system or found yourself standing in a courtroom, chances are you could probably care less about the millions of young Black and Brown faces now languishing in overcrowded jails and prison cells.

There's no denying the fact that race plays a major role in the mass incarceration of so many prison-bound Black males. The same racism that many of us confront on the outside on a daily basis is the same kind of racism present behind prison walls today.

But this is nothing new. This unfortunate social disease has been, and always will be a *strain* and a *stain* on the nation's consciousness. However, we who are conscious and blessed with a knowledge of *self*, know full well how to rise above, even conqueror this debilitating disorder. And we have a duty and an obligation to help those who have been stricken by its crippling and self-destructive effects.

With personal knowledge and accurate, factual information, Hinsley gives us reasons to hope and reasons to believe that in spite of the darkness of the hour, morning will come again.

This then, is what I surmise to be the major purpose of his book. Enlightening us with a knowledge rarely shared and for us to embrace this knowledge for the purpose of changing how we treat our fellow human being. Knowledge is the great sledgehammer of emotional maturity and the precursor to obtaining psychological freedom. But knowledge has no value, no power, until it is applied. The time to apply such is now.

So brace yourself. This is not the Twilight Zone. In this chilling, tour-de-force of prison life, Hinsley has given us an abundance of proper knowledge—a place where the rubber must meet the road. Thus, our focus must now incorporate the wisdom and actions of the late Baba Hannibal Afrik who declared,

> *"If we are incorrect, reality will correct us; but if we are serious, we will correct ourselves".*

The signs and symptoms are very clear. All indicators point to a Code Blue. But there is still time, if we are serious, to change the code and correct ourselves. So read on—the challenge is yet to come!

John Raye
Entrepreneur, author, motivational speaker, renaissance man
Kernersville, North Carolina

ACKNOWLEDGMENTS

FIRST AND FOREMOST, all praise and honor is given to my Heavenly Father. Without His tender mercy and benevolent grace, this moment would never be, and without Him, there would be no me.

Arriving at this point of accomplishment, for which I had never dreamed of achieving until now, makes this tribute an exceptionally special honor for me. The private and intense labor of commitment that it took, the hundreds of arduous rewrites that were required, the frustrating struggle to overcome writer's block, the battle against self-doubt, the challenging times spent isolated from family, the lack of understanding of my need to write by family members, and the many solitary moments spent searching for my truth as a writer have all culminated to bear fruition through the pages of this book.

I simply have no words that could ever express the sincere and heartfelt gratitude for all of those who believed in me, encouraged me, offered their critiques—both positive and negative—and those who were there as a sounding board as I struggled to find my way along this journey of possible dreams. And to those of you who do not see your name among the noted few, please accept my humble apology and know that your omission is not one of insignificance, it's simply that there are not enough pages in this book to account for each and every one of you.

Having championed the highs and lows of writing, I wish to deeply thank my wife Lori, my son Nicholas, and my daughter Olivia for standing by me in the shadows of my private literary world when at times I'm sure it seemed that I was so, so far away from them. Thank you for your enduring patience, and know that I love you!

To my sisters Gail and Gwen, who allowed me to vent my moments of frustration upon them when I needed so badly to scream out loud! Thank you both for your unconditional support and belief in me.

I wish to thank, most sincerely, Dr. John Raye. His unprecedented spirit of encouragement, uplifting inspiration, and voice of reason is unlike any form of guidance I have ever experienced. He is truly one of my living heroes and respected mentors. I will always have maximum respect and love for you, sir!

I wish to thank several of my prison colleagues for the advice and insight that they shared with me to ensure that my account of events was indeed accurate. Special thanks are given to George Welborn, Tom Page, Roger Cowan, and Austin Randolph. Your professional acquaintances and personal friendships added an invaluable element to the creation of this book.

To Sage Smith, for our unique bond and respected friendship that has transcended the boundaries of our different walks in life. You helped enlighten my perspective on what it means to endure the long suffering of hard prison time with supreme dignity. You demonstrated what a true indomitable spirit is when governed by faith and conviction. You helped bring clarity to my sense of divine humanity. I love you, my brother, for the truth of your spirit.

I give special thanks to Randy Kassebaum for designing the cover of my book. His extraordinary vision added an element of provocation to my work that speaks directly to the human spirit. He was able to elicit a surreal, gut-level connection that relates to the injustices of the human condition of prison life. Thank you, my friend, for sharing your creative talent and giving my book a unique identity.

And finally, I wish to offer a very special thank you to my mom Juanita Tutt and my step-dad Isaiah Tutt who have always supported me in everything I set out to do. I love you both dearly. And to Jamison Adams, Herman Moore, George "G-Man" Galbreath, Malcolm "Big Money" Pharr, Donna Price, Dr. Cynthia Hunter, Joan Brown, Charles Turner, Eric Leggett, Ellis "Bossman" Griffin, Reginald "Jap" Chiles, Larry "Cool Mo-D" Eubanks, Alvin "A. P." Pearson, Grover "P-Funk" Alexander, Donald "Earl" Buie, Kenneth "Fuji" Rice, Antonio Logan, Albert Maybin, Derrick Hennessy, Patricia Baxter, Niece Eubanks, Debra Briggs, Linda Proctor, The Asheville High School Class of '76, Ricky Morgan, Jimmy Hinsley, Dennis "Disco" Wilson, Anthony "Bass Man" Griffin, Greg Irby, Larry Grant, Harold Burton, Angelo Quentin Reid, Howard Saffold, Claude Julian, Sharon Tindell, Carol Willis, Greg Commander, Karen Kassebaum, Marge Holly, Charles Holly Sr., Maurice Holly, Lynette "Sister Soldier" Miller, Brother Ezra Miller, Yolanda Arrington, Lynn Byrd, Judson Chiles, Tom Bell, Charles "Bonnie" Green, Diane Woods, Wesley Woods, Virgil "Skip" Walton, Sherry Harper, Vernon Bailey, Steven Plair, Tony "T-Harp" Harper, Terrell Harper, Kimberly Bailey, William "Billy" Harper Jr., Lawrence Gilliam Jr., Clarissa Gilliam, Gloria Gilliam, Lawrence Gilliam Sr., Vernell Bailey, William Bailey, Thomas Harper Sr., Nancy Hughes, Walter Hughes, Kevin Smith, Linda Smith, Ian Oliver, Edwin Lewis, Rick Cotton, Richard Vance, Jerry Skenes, Ann Davies, Stacey Clutter, Kenneth Fairbanks, Donna Fryer, DeWayne Clark, P. A. Severs, Mark Pierson, Larry Hopkins, Donna Howell, my white soul brother Donald "Froggy" Young, Bruce Davis, Thomas Rush, Veronica Johnson, Paulette Snyder, Gale Murphy, Arlene Brown, Milton Grady, Otis Robinson, Clinton Thomas, Lamar Deloatch, Bonnie Dingman, Janet Mitchell, Charlotte Mans, Teshuna Dubose, Nikeata Walker, Drury Underwood, Sharon Mangum, Latonia Williams, Sam Kwarteng, Christina Calabria, Jan Pritchett, Dr. James Mayes and many, many others for offering their words of support and encouragement over the years and throughout this most private and personal journey. I realize that I didn't accomplish this on my own. All of you have expressed a genuine belief in me that helped bolster my confidence in seeing this through. I cannot begin to tell you how much that has meant to me. May God continue to bless you all and thank you so very much for your support!

INTRODUCTION

THE EFFORT CONTAINED within these pages is not an attempt to provide a new and unarticulated perspective regarding the complex issues that face our criminal justice system, for these issues have all-too-well been examined and re-examined by many great leaders and experts in the field. However, I do feel that my experience within this field of work can add to the discussion and offer a perspective that is not normally heard from, and certainly not heard from through the form of a published text by a former prison administrator. I worked in the Illinois Department of Corrections for close to 20 years, and during the last 11 years of my career, I obtained the positions of assistant warden and warden in a maximum security and a super maximum security prison. I am confident that I can share a respected perspective on this subject. The aim of this book is to shed some light into the reality of prison life as experienced in the Illinois prison system and to bring attention to the systemic and paralyzing issues that govern our overall correctional system.

The idea to write this book came to me after reading the book *Fighting for Your Life: The African-American Criminal Justice Survival Guide* by John V. Elmore. He chronicled his experiences as a state trooper, a prosecuting attorney, and a defense attorney into an instructional handbook designed to help African Americans deal with the criminal justice system more effectively. He related how the criminal justice system disproportionately impacts the African American community from the time of an arrest, through the process of adjudication, and ultimately to imprisonment. What he left out, in my opinion, was the story of what happens once a person is confined behind the walls of our nation's prisons. It is also my belief that he did so, in part, because he lacked the direct experience of working in a prison setting to articulate with first-hand knowledge what this experience is actually like on a day-to-day basis.

However, I do have that experience! My experience includes working in a minimum security facility, a prison boot camp facility, a high-medium security facility, a maximum security facility, and a super maximum security facility. This experience represents every level of custody that has been designated for the adult male adjudicated population.

Hence, the idea was created in my spirit to set out and try to relate this experience in the most honest, objective, and unbiased manner that I could. And in doing so, I hope to generate a more earnest and critical dialogue toward *solution thinking* about the issues that adversely impact the well-being of so many Americans, and particularly the African American community. What follows is a semi-autobiographical account of my perspective regarding our prison system in America. The details of my childhood and early adulthood are chronicled only for the purpose of sharing how those periods have significantly influenced my perspective about our criminal justice system. The backdrop for much of those times is centered in my hometown of Asheville, North Carolina. Asheville today, however, is vastly different from the Asheville I knew when growing up. Segregation played a major role in my formative years in Asheville, and it is from this context of discrimination and prejudice that my insights about America's idea of *justice* have been profoundly affected. My accounts of dates, times, and events are offered with the complete integrity of my fragile memory and with the short-sightedness attributed to Father Time. But at no point have I purposefully exaggerated or misrepresented the truth of my experiences, and I stand by my personal observations.

Contrary to common belief that inmates have no control over their lives in prison, I submit that there are a few aspects of an inmate's life that he does have control over. Despite the immense pressures that prison life presents for inmates, inmates control their choice to conform to the rules of authority or to conform to the code of prison culture. Sadly, most conform to the code of prison culture. But, more concerning than that, there are far greater aspects of their lives that they do not control. For example, the politics of mass incarceration, the intentional design of the prison industrial complex, legislatively biased court rulings, economical disenfranchisement, and the institutionalization of a discriminatorily biased system all have an influence in the management of prison life of which inmates have no control. These and other collateral aspects of our criminal justice system contribute to the larger themes and competing issues of public safety, control and order, rehabilitation, and prison re-entry.

I submit that an egalitarian democratic society is viewed as the preeminent form of government that embodies the idealistic goals of liberty and freedom for all its people. This libertarian concept of social order and sovereign independence is promulgated upon principles of governance that operate based upon a formalized structure of laws and regulations. These laws and regulations are designed to ensure fair and equitable administration of judicial jurisprudence for the *just* treatment of its citizens. Equally germane to this core principle of governing is for its citizens to be able to obtain social and economic prosperity without fear of discriminatory reprisals. Regrettably, America's criminal justice system as it has been practiced up until our contemporary times has not lived up to this ideal standard of social equity. If this does not change, our social structure of democracy will implode.

My aim is to share some insights into the complex world of managing our nation's prisons while bringing attention to the collateral issues that impact upon it. I seek to evoke genuine debate between the ardent advocates of judicial punishment versus the vigilant seekers of fair and equal justice. I hope that you find the stories and perspectives in this book as compelling for you to read as they were for me to write. *The Anatomy of Prison Life* is a symptomatic warning of a societal infection, and the extent to which this infection goes untreated will be the extent to which it will consume our society.

Prison life ... the good, the bad, and the ugly!

ABOUT THE AUTHOR

CHARLES HINSLEY IS a retired warden from the Illinois Department of Corrections with 28 years of combined correctional management and human services experience. He currently works for the North Carolina Department of Corrections in their Community Corrections Division assisting probationers in connecting with community service agencies. In addition to this, he is an Adjunct Instructor for North Carolina A & T State University in their Criminal Justice Department. After his retirement in 2004, Hinsley took a short hiatus before accepting offers to work in both the private and nonprofit sector. He first served as the Program Administrator for a private company that provided job training and employment placement services for recipients of the Department of Children and Family Services in Middle Georgia. He managed this program until he relocated back to his native state of North Carolina in December 2007.

In 2008, Hinsley was hired by Goodwill Industries of Central North Carolina in Greensboro, NC to design and implement a job training and job placement program for the ex-offender population. The program received notable success for assisting ex-offenders with employment opportunities, as well as, assisting them with other transitional support services. While managing this program, Hinsley was appointed Co-Chairman of The Guilford County Prison Re-entry Coalition and became an active member in several other community coalitions; The Fatherhood Coalition, Partners Ending Homelessness, The Greensboro Safe Community Coalition, The Greensboro Housing Coalition Committee—HPRP, The Lord's Table, a faith-based organization servicing the homeless and ex-offender population; The East Market Street Merchant Association, and served as an Advisory Board member for the Department of Human Resources and Rehabilitation Counseling at North Carolina A & T State University.

Most recently in late 2012, Hinsley became a founding member of the 15th affiliate chapter of the national organization, The National African American Drug Policy Coalition of which former Superior Court Judge; Arthur L. Burnett, Sr. is the National Executive Director. This organization is a coalition of pre-eminent African American professional organizations united to promote drug policies and laws that embrace the public health nature of drug abuse and provide a more effective and humane approach to address the chronic societal problem of drug abuse. Hinsley devotes much of his time supporting groups and organizations whose mission is designed to empower individuals through social, economic, and real-life needs. He is committed to the emerging movement to end the mass incarceration of African American males for which Michelle Alexander so succinctly describes in her book, *The New Jim Crow*. And he is also engaged in efforts to help reprogram the consciousness of the Black Inferiority complex perpetrated against African Americans through the indoctrination of slavery as articulated in Tom Burrell's book, *Brainwashed*.

Hinsley is an honor graduate of Winston-Salem State University and a Master's level graduate of Southern Illinois University-Carbondale. *The Anatomy of Prison Life* is his first book; however, he has several other books of different subject matter pending future publication and he is available for speaking engagements. For more information, visit www.theanatomyofprisonlife.com.

WELCOME TO PRISON

IT WAS MONDAY, January 4, 1993, my first day as a unit superintendent at the Menard Maximum Security Correctional Center in Chester, Illinois. I had been at Menard once before, but that was ten years earlier as a graduate school practicum student. At that time, I certainly didn't have any idea that I would be back here directly involved in managing its day-to-day operation. It didn't look physically different than before, but there was definitely a different feeling in the atmosphere that seemed much more ominous. A few days prior to my arrival, I had heard about an assault on a correctional officer. This was certainly not a comforting thought as I drove up to the facility. The three large sandstone buildings that serve as your first point of contact with the facility emitted an eerie sense of tension that seemed to penetrate from behind their thick, crusted walls. And the Death Row Unit that sat high on a bluff overlooking the prison added an element of suspense and intrigue that was incredibly daunting.

Menard is an antiquated 19th century-style prison that was built in 1878 with the labor of American Indians and prison inmates. It is situated in the southernmost part of Illinois in a predominantly white rural community on the banks of the mighty Mississippi River. Menard is the largest correctional facility in the Illinois Department of Corrections, and it houses one of the largest maximum security inmate prison populations in the nation. The day itself was a bright, unseasonably warm winter morning. I arrived exactly at 7:30 a.m. I pride myself on being early for any appointment, and I viewed this appointment as a jump start to a profoundly different aspect of my prison career. I wanted to make my first impression a good impression, and being half-an-hour early gave me the air of confidence that I wanted to project.

As a new administrator, it was customary to meet with the warden and his administrative staff. I met with Warden George Welborn, his two assistant wardens, Tom Page and Al Frentzel, as well as their five unit superintendents and two majors. Warden Welborn and his staff were seasoned prison officials with over 120 years of combined experience.

As I entered the main foyer of the warden's office, I was immediately confronted with a huge wall display of pictures that represented every warden who had managed Menard since its inception, which at that time was 115 years. When walking into the main lobby area, this display of pictures instantly projected an impressive historic legacy of this unique prison facility. While I waited in the foyer to meet with Warden Welborn, I took a few moments to contemplate the legacy of the facility, and I carefully studied the faces of each warden. Strikingly, but not surprisingly, they were all Caucasian men. But just as striking, the thought of becoming the first person of color to share in their distinction immediately registered in my mind. I imagined my picture being on that wall as the period at the end of a sentence and a new sentence would then begin with my legacy. Although this was a fleeting thought, the genesis of its conception was more prophetic than I realized at the time.

A short while later, Warden Welborn came out from his inner office and greeted me. His reputation as a stern, no-nonsense warden preceded him, and from my first impression, he lived up to his reputation. He stood about 6 feet 3 inches tall and projected an air of confidence and imperial leadership. He had a strong but tempered voice, and I got the impression that he took his work extremely seriously. He escorted me into his conference room where I met his other staff. The room was a large, spacious area aligned with oak wood bookshelves expanding three-fourths of the way around the room. The shelves stood only a few inches shy of touching a 15-foot ceiling. They were adorned with hundreds of trophies that the facility had received over the years from competing in various events and obtaining other honors. It was quite an impressive room. I confess; I was mentally pinching myself, wondering how I had arrived at this point.

After the warden formally introduced me to the group, he proceeded to give me an extensive overview of the history of Menard. He gave me an in-depth analysis of the pervasive gang presence that existed within the facility and a very candid account of the violence and disruption that was almost an everyday occurrence. Trying to control the gang problem was the biggest challenge that faced the day-to-day management of this facility, and although we shared the same challenges with other maximum security facilities in the agency, Menard was a far greater challenge because of the size of its population, which in 1993 housed over 2,600 inmates.

During the meeting, I paid close attention to the interactions of his staff with one another, as well as their observations and reactions to me. I wanted to get as clear of a sense as I could of what kind of connection we would have with one another, and to detect, if possible, any resentment that may or may not exist. Menard had a dubious reputation as being a staunchly racist facility. Since I was considered an outsider, as well as a person of color, this aspect of my working relationship would be critical to my acceptance or non-acceptance, and this element had to be astutely and decisively fettered out. Gratefully, and I'll admit to some surprise, his staff welcomed me with great respect and genuinely expressed their willingness to teach me their collective experience on how to manage a highly volatile prison. I felt extremely honored by their reception of me, but I was still guarded for any dubious acceptance by them. After all, I had only just met the administrative staff; I had not yet met the rest of the 1,000-plus employees.

Superintendent Roger Cowan and Superintendent Larry Hopkins stood out a little bit more than the other superintendents. They had a certain demeanor about them that communicated an unpretentious and open sense of trust about what kind of people they were. It wasn't exactly what they said, but how they came across when we interacted, and it gave me an intuitive sense that they could be trusted. We had a warm and respectful engagement. The following year, Superintendent Cowan and I were appointed as the assistant wardens of Menard, an accomplishment not foreseen by either of us when we first met. Superintendent Hopkins became a close confidant during the course of my career. Their relationships, as well as those with the other administrative staff, developed into very respected and loyal friendships that remain to this day.

After the meeting was over, I was given an extensive tour of the facility to familiarize myself with the enormous size of the facility's physical layout. The prison sat on over 2,400 acres of land. This tour was also intended to give me a true sense of the complexity involved in managing the state's largest correctional facility and most dangerous inmate population. Would I be prepared for the task?

We toured several housing units where the inmates lived, and, much to my surprise and dismay, the living conditions were quite deplorable. Inmate graffiti and gang symbolism was written on the walls of almost every cell. Almost every cell door had bedsheets covering the cell bars to prevent the officers from seeing inside, and trash and debris were strewn all over the galleries. This made for a very unsettling feeling, and an extremely unsavory smell permeated the air. Many of the inmates were loitering around the cell houses as if they owned the facility, and, needless to say, I didn't get the sense that we, the prison officials, were in control of much of anything. As the ensuing days passed, I quickly found out that we weren't really in control at all. We were just buying time day-by-day.

As we continued the tour, I was amazed at the number of inner perimeter gates and fences that were constructed throughout the facility. I learned that they were constructed to reduce large numbers of inmates from congregating together as they moved from one point to another or participated in certain activities. The gates also helped control their movement to and from designated areas. Equally as important, they served as a protective barrier or safe haven for staff in the event a disruptive situation occurred. The gates and fences were intended to provide a place of refuge for staff should a threatening situation develop.

In order to get from the two main cell houses at the front entrance of the prison to the other cell houses and support buildings in the back of the facility, you had to cross a street-like area that ran through the center of the facility in an east/west direction. This partial street was used for cargo trains to bring supplies into the facility when it was first built. Railroad tracks once ran the length of this area but had long since been covered with concrete pavement. A gun tower, designed to provide armed coverage for all movement that occurred throughout the day and night, was positioned in the center of this walkway. In all, there were eight outer perimeter gun towers strategically positioned at various points along the walls and inside grounds of the facility.

Several support buildings, such as the school building, the inmate laundry house, the health care unit, the inmate dining hall, and the prison chapel, were all situated in the middle portion of the prison compound. They were a makeshift barrier between the cell houses in the front of the prison and the two cell houses in the back of the prison. Traveling from the front cell houses and support buildings to the cell houses in the back of the facility took approximately three to four minutes, however, waiting to get clearance to travel through the different gated areas added extra time.

During our tour, we approached an area where the inmates were allowed to gather for their outdoor and indoor recreation. We had to go through a double-gated fence area to gain access to this portion of the facility. A multipurpose gymnasium was situated in the middle of two large outdoor recreational areas that we referred to as the East Yard and the West Yard. The inmates were allowed to go to the gymnasium for various indoor activities. Although this building was designed to provide a common place for inmates to engage in positive activities and respectable socialization, the inmates used it to conduct their gang business and to engage in gang activities.

As we were approaching the entrance of the building, we were confronted by a small group of inmates rushing toward us in a very aggressive manner. However, as it turned out, they were not attempting to attack us. They were reacting to a fight that had broken out inside the gym that had begun to spill over to the outside of the building.

When the inmates rushed out of the gym engaged in what could have turned into a major disturbance, an officer in the gun tower who had been monitoring our movement noticed the incident and began firing warning shots to get the inmates to stop. When the warning shots were fired, all the inmates immediately dove to the ground and lay motionless. This was an automated, learned response of prison life for the inmates. When warning shots are fired, inmates know that the next shot could be at them. They knew that they had just come perilously close to having deadly force used against them.

While all of this commotion was occurring, ranking security staff in our group began radioing for additional backup in order to get assistance to help ensure control was established and to contain the disturbance from spreading. A cavalry of security officers arrived in a very short time and began securing the inmates in handcuffs. Other officers rushed inside the gym to assess what was taking place and to establish control and order. A show of force is a mandatory and life-saving prerequisite for gaining control of any violent or potentially violent situation in prison. Officers are trained to respond quickly and decisively in these situations in order to lessen the chance of someone getting seriously injured, but unfortunately their responses are not always quick enough.

While the officers were bringing order to the situation, a few of us went inside the gym. The others stayed outside to ensure that the incident was controlled safely. Warden Welborn, Superintendent Bonnie Gross, and I went inside. Once inside, Warden Welborn made a call to our central office and reported the incident to our executive directors. It is mandatory for wardens to report any incident that becomes a major security concern, and the use of deadly force is always a reportable incident.

Upon contacting the directors and informing them of the incident and advising them of his plan to continue normal operations of the facility once the situation was under control, we continued the tour. This incident was just a typical occurrence in the daily throes of prison life.

I was later escorted to the medium and minimum security unit located on the outside of the prison compound. This unit sat on the hill where the Death Row Unit was located and overlooked the general prison. We had to drive approximately half-a-mile up a winding road to get to this site. Once there, the view overlooking the general prison compound provided you with a clear visual perspective of just how immense Menard was. To witness the mighty Mississippi River flowing uncontested in front of the facility, only being held back by a railroad berm that tenuously prevented her majestic strength from overtaking the entire facility, was indeed a humbling experience. But it's noteworthy to mention, that later in that same year when the Great Flood of 1993 occurred, the power and strength of the mighty

Mississippi reminded Menard that she was not at all safe from her wrath.

With Menard being built on a sandy gravel foundation, the floodwaters found its way into the prison's underbelly and flooded much of the facility's primary compound. And needless to say, the railroad berm that served as a barrier between the Mississippi and Menard's prison sanctuary was no match for the rise in water level. The resulting effect was like a dam that had uncontrollably burst open. We had to evacuate the bottom two galleries of our first two cell houses because the flood crest level reached over 49 feet. We had to bring in 100 port-a-potties just to provide inmates a means to relieve their body functions. We had to knock out a hole in the west side of our outer perimeter wall near the back of the facility in order to bring in food, water, and other supplies for the continued operation of the facility. It was an extremely challenging administrative task that we overcame with tremendous teamwork and cooperation from all involved.

Getting back to the tour, this unit overlooking the Mississippi River housed our medium and minimum custody inmates as well as our condemned inmates. The inmates who were housed in this unit, except those on death row, had earned their placement there based upon good behavior. They were in transition of being transferred to other facilities throughout the state, and their compliant behavior warranted consideration for a transfer to a reduced security setting.

Upon completing the tour of this unit, Warden Welborn had to return to his office. He had to submit an electronic incident report as follow up to his verbal report earlier that morning. As the fighting incident was unfolding, and throughout my tour, I frequently asked myself if I was cut out for this. Did I have what it took to help effectively manage this kind of prison? How would I survive? But yet, even amongst my doubts, the one thing that continued to surface to the forefront of my mind was the dominating thought that I was not about to shy away from the challenge.

After the incident in the gymnasium was under control and order was established, the inmates that were involved were taken to segregation. Segregation is a separate housing unit within most prisons that prison officials commonly refer to as a jail house inside the prison. Inmates who disobey and violate the facility rules are placed there for various lengths of time to be separated from the rest of the general population. The inmates involved in this incident were taken to segregation pending a formal disciplinary hearing while awaiting the completion of a thorough investigation by our Internal Affairs Division.

When Internal Affairs completed their investigation, they concluded that there was an internal power struggle amongst members of the Mickey Cobra street gang, a very small and less organized gang within Illinois' prison system. Ten of their members were placed in segregation for the rule violations of fighting and dangerous disturbance. They all received a year in segregation confinement, one year loss of good conduct credits, and one year demotion to "C" grade status. This meant that they would be confined to a cell for approximately 23 hours a day and they would not be allowed to participate with the general population inmates in any activities for at least one year. They would also have one year added to their minimum custody release date, which would require them to stay in prison one year longer than their original minimum release date. And lastly, they would not be allowed to receive certain privileges for one year because of their demotion in grade status.

This gang incident occurred on the very first day of my new assignment, within three hours of being on duty. And this was my indoctrination into the life and death struggle for survival by inmates and staff living behind the walls of a maximum security prison. The warning shots only served to underscore the reality of how deadly violence could erupt at any moment and how the sanctity of life could be snuffed out in a mere instant for both staff and inmates.

As the day progressed, there were several other less dramatic incidents, but they all had the same potential for causing a major disturbance. A deadly sense of intense explosiveness was a pervasive feeling throughout the prison every day, and you could virtually cut the tension with a knife.

The following day was just as intense, but there was an added variable that made the day equally memorable. An inmate committed suicide in his cell by hanging himself, and this incident became the first of many suicides that I would encounter throughout my career. After getting a first-hand, up close glimpse of the violence that could erupt at any moment, I was now about to face the realities of life and death behind the walls of a real prison.

SURVIVING IN PRISON

IT WAS MID-MORNING and I was in Assistant Warden Page's office, along with a few of the other superintendents, when Assistant Warden Page received a call on his radio. The caller instructed him to go to our private channel. Major Pierson was calling to inform Assistant Warden Page about a suspected suicide that had been discovered. After getting some preliminary information, Assistant Warden Page notified Warden Welborn and we headed to the cell house where the body was located.

I recall a deep sadness coming over me when we arrived at the inmate's cell and I saw his lifeless body lying on the floor. It wasn't a feeling of sadness that you experience from the loss of a family member or a personal friend, because he was neither of those to me. It was more of a sadness that comes from experiencing the face-to-face reality of sheer helplessness. We, the prison officials, could not prevent his death nor save his life. I grappled with the daunting reality of how miniature my role was with respect to the daunting pressures of prison life for many inmates. His death was the outward result of the intense hopelessness and despair that so many inmates feel from being incarcerated and having no sense of worth. Such intense feelings of worthlessness literally cause inmates to kill themselves. These inmates are not crazy nor do they suffer from any clinically diagnosed mental health malady. They simply suffer from an unrelenting, life-choking grip of an overwhelming sense of insignificance and hopelessness.

This incident became an eye-opening and personally defining moment for me. It made me more cognizant of the immense suffering that many families, and particularly black families, experience over and over and over again due to the collateral consequences of prison life. This suicide was a symptomatic sign of an acute underlying illness that was not being effectively treated and had no cure. The gross maladapted conditions of prison life that led to this inmate's death were enabled by society's treatment protocol of throwing away the key. It became very clear to me at that precise moment that my new responsibilities were going to challenge me in ways that I had never been challenged before and probably would never be again.

As with many hangings in prison, this inmate hanged himself with his bedsheets tied to his cell bars. He had been assigned to our Protective Custody Unit for protection against the intimidation and threats of the gangs. However, the irony of this incident, as with many others, was that we could not protect him from himself, so he took his life even though we were doing our best to protect it. The stark reality of life in prison is that it is hard, brutal, and oftentimes unforgiving.

A Reality of Prison Life

As a result of this inmate's death, I experienced my first autopsy. I went to the local coroner's office with another administrative official to observe the coroner's examination of the inmate's body. An autopsy is required in order for an official cause of death to be documented. Witnessing an autopsy is not something that you would want to see on a regular basis, but it was considered a necessary part of my development to become a well-rounded and effective administrator. It was vital for me to have as broad of an understanding of the intricate dynamics of my new responsibilities as I could because death is commonplace in prison. Natural deaths, suicides, homicides, and state sanctioned deaths (the execution of an inmate) would all become an intimate part of the next 12 years of my life, but at that time I didn't have a clue as to how intimate that would actually become.

While dealing with my first inmate death, I learned the protocol for reporting a death through our chain of command. Wardens and/ or their designees have the unwelcome responsibility of contacting various executive officials as well as the inmate's family member(s) when a death occurs. We must contact several executive staff such as the director, our deputy directors, our Internal Affairs Division, the agency's public relations coordinator, the local coroner, and the inmate's next of kin. Reporting a suicide is no different than reporting a homicide, except that in a homicide the state police are required to investigate the murder as though it was a crime committed on the streets. The same investigative process that occurs in the civilian community for a homicide also takes place in a prison when investigating a suspected homicide. The area where the body or bodies are found is treated as a crime scene, evidence collection is conducted, witnesses are interviewed, and a profile for a suspect or suspects is developed. If a suspect or suspects are identified, charges are filed and the inmate or inmates are taken into custody to await the process of their new criminal charges, and the judicial process for them is initiated all over again.

During the course of my career, I dealt with a few inmates who had been sentenced to death for either killing another inmate or killing a correctional staff person. These episodes of violence against staff and inmates, as well as other acts of criminal behavior that jeopardize the safety of prison life, are played out to some degree every day in prison facilities across the country. The Menard Maximum

Security Correctional Center was no exception. If the truth is ever shared with the public, it is my opinion that it is just as hard, if not harder, to protect the innocent person from being victimized and preyed upon in prison than it is to protect the innocent person from being victimized in free society. True prison life in our maximum security prisons is ugly, mean, and dangerous.

The most unpleasant duty for any warden is to inform an employee's family member or significant other that their loved one—a father, mother, husband, wife, brother, sister, cousin, aunt, uncle, etc.—has been killed in the line of duty. Although this is an extremely rare incident, and I am thankful that I never had the unpleasant task of delivering this form of traumatic news to an employee's family member, it does happen. I have, however, had the unpleasant duty of notifying a family member that their loved one was found dead in an employee restroom due to natural causes—he had a heart attack. Sobering as that was, it comes nowhere close in comparison to reporting the death of an employee from the result of inmate violence. Inmates have historically killed correctional officers and other correctional employees, and due to the inherent nature of how we incarcerate people, this will continue to happen. I am just thankful that it did not happen on my watch.

It is also less than desirable for wardens to inform an inmate's family member that their son, father, brother, husband, uncle, nephew, or grandfather has either committed suicide, died naturally, been killed due to inmate violence, or died due to staff negligence. During the last 12 years of my career, I made several such calls to family members. It was my experience that in all cases of a homicide and in most cases of a suicide, and even with some natural deaths, the family members seem to have a suspicious attitude about the death of their loved one. This seemed to be more prevalent among family members of the African American community, and given our historical experience with the criminal justice system, this is a valid suspicion. However, the sad reality of prison life for many black inmates is that black-on-black crime is just as prevalent behind prison walls as it is in many black neighborhoods.

I highlight black-on-black crime simply because the majority of our prison populations are black, and black inmates hurt other black inmates more often than they hurt non-black inmates. Many young black males come into the prison system with the conditioned street mentality of manipulation, retaliation, and mistrust. They harbor the anti-establishment attitude of being against the "system" and against anybody that they perceive to be a threat to their misguided way of claiming what they believe is their entitlement to the American dream. And yes, they do have an entitlement to pursue the American dream, but not by way of their illegitimate and illegal criminal behavior. More often than not, acts of aggression and violence by black inmates are inflicted against other black inmates. They bring with them their long-standing rivalries with other street gangs, and they continue their adversarial disputes inside our prisons. Most often these disputes have some connection with the manufacturing of, the selling of, and the distribution of drugs. But to put it simply, they senselessly hurt and kill one another in prison for the same pseudostatus of maintaining their reputation as hardcore street gangsters. Sadly, this is a mentality and a way of life that, if continued, will surely lead many African American men to prison in ever-increasing numbers or it will lead them to an early grave.

Does the overall criminal justice system play a significant role in disproportionately incarcerating black males? The answer is an emphatic *yes!* But do we as an ethnic group contribute to the opportunity for the system to continually take advantage of us by locking us behind prison walls? The answer is also an emphatic *yes!* Please do not misunderstand my criticism against the Black community for what may seem like an attack against our lack of cultural or social accountability. For I am not overlooking, nor minimizing, nor excusing away the fact that the system of racism has played and still does play a major role in this equation. It is well-known and documented that acts of racism, both systematically and physically, have been perpetrated against black folks by white law enforcement officials, white judicial officials, and white correctional officials throughout the history of this country's criminal justice system. The reality is that this is still America, and where you have a unilaterally bias and discriminatory system such as our criminal justice system, there will continue to be acts of racism ranging from false arrests to wrongful convictions to false imprisonment and even to murder under the guise of legal homicide (the death penalty). Once an individual gets caught up in the unrelenting penal system of dehumanization and criminalization, all minority inmates and particularly men of color will be confronted with many degrading and demeaning acts perpetrated by correctional officials solely because of the officials' racist attitudes against them. The Illinois Department of Corrections, for which I had the privilege to work for virtually 20 years, was no exception to this rule.

However, with that being said, do we as black men and black women have some responsibility in our choice to offend or not offend? The answer is also an emphatic *yes!* But unfortunately, once in prison, a human life—and particularly a black life—is devalued to such a low, substandard level that whether you are black or white you may be victimized, and not much of anything will or can be done about it. Black men make up more than 65 percent of all prison populations in this country. Because of this fact, black families and their communities are the predominant recipients of this victimization and therefore experience the greatest loss in human dignity, human worth, and human suffering. This again is the cold reality and tragic consequence of prison life!

During the weeks that followed the inmate's suicide, I encountered several other incidents that depicted one of the everyday stressors that inmates deal with and one of the everyday challenges that prison administrators have to contend with. One such incident involved a non-gang-affiliated inmate who was stabbed several times on a stairwell in the cell house that I was assigned to manage. He was stabbed with a homemade knife, commonly referred to as a shank, by members of the Latin Disciples street gang for his un-willingness to give in to their intimidation and threats. He survived the stabbing and was assigned to our Protective Custody Unit for his safety.

Homemade weapons are a common element of prison life. Weapons are created from all types of crude materials scavenged from different places and different sources inside the prison. Mun-dane items such as paint rollers, plastic eating utensils, and ink pens are routinely used by inmates to make weapons. On rare occasions, a manufactured weapon such as a store-bought knife is smuggled into the prison, but 99 percent of all weapons found in prison are made from ordinary material taken from sources inside the prison. Most weapons are carried for protection and are used only in self-defense, but others are purposely made to be used to inflict serious or fatal injuries to staff and other inmates. Searches of cells, housing units, and common areas within and outside the prison are done routinely to look for and remove these items from the facility. However, the creativity and ingenuity that inmates demonstrate makes it virtually a no-win situation for prison officials. Crude homemade weapons will always be available inside prisons.

There were two other stabbing incidents in the first month of my assignment at Menard. Although neither one was fatal, these stabbing incidents represent everyday life for many inmates. Their whole existence is reduced to the primitive instincts of survival. The proverbial question that each inmate privately asks himself is, "Will I stay alive and go home to my family in one piece?" The thought of whether or not they will live to see freedom again or whether they will die in prison is the unspoken but-ever present question on every inmate's mind. And this same question, however suppressed it may appear to be, is just as much on the minds of each correctional officer regarding their own safety and well-being. The untold stress of this mental challenge is more than the average person can relate to.

The Power of Gangs

As a unit superintendent, I was responsible for ensuring that all of the custodial, clinical, educational, medical, and mental health services that were required to be provided for the inmates assigned to my unit were delivered. Because I was new and inexperienced in my position, I was assigned to the unit that was considered to be the least problematic in the facility. This was done so that I could gradually learn the dynamics of managing this prison without being ill-prepared and thrown into the lion's den. However, considering that an inmate was stabbed several times in this unit that was considered to be the least problematic unit in the facility, you can imagine what took place in all of the other cell houses—some form of aggressive and violent behavior virtually every day.

Each unit in the facility was given a specific name, and my unit was called the South Uppers Cell House. It housed slightly over 300 inmates at the time. The entire facility housed approximately 2,750 inmates, but over the course of my career this number increased to over 3,500 inmates on an average day. During my first tour of duty at Menard, which was from January 1993 to September 1997, we operated a Death Row Unit that housed approximately 56 inmates, a Segregation Unit that housed approximately 350 inmates, a Protective Custody Unit that housed approximately 300 inmates, a Medium & Minimum Security Unit that housed approximately 200 inmates, a Specialized Housing Unit that housed approximately 150 inmates, and four General Population Housing Units totaling approximately 1,700 inmates.

As I mentioned earlier, Warden Welborn talked very candidly to me about the pervasive influence that the gangs had developed within our prison system and their impact at Menard. Warden Welborn was a very serious and tough-minded administrator. He had worked in several facilities throughout his career and had held several positions of responsibility within the agency. He was a very seasoned correctional administrator, having over 20 years of experience. As he would describe issues related to the influence of gang activity to me, I could sense the experience that he had mastered in understanding how to deal with the problems they created. The validity of his descriptions about the gang's influence and disruptive nature became very evident to me around my third or fourth day at Menard.

Warden Welborn, Assistant Warden Page, Assistant Warden Frentzel, the other unit superintendents, and I were sitting in Warden Welborn's office one morning during my first week at Menard. We were discussing various concerns about the prison. However, our primary concern was focused on a gang-related issue that had come to our attention by Internal Affairs. As we were discussing this concern, Warden Welborn received a phone call from our chief of security, or the major as he was most commonly referred. The major was the highest ranking uniformed security personnel in the facility and was responsible for managing the frontline correctional staff that consisted of captains, lieutenants, sergeants, and officers. When the major called the office, he informed Warden Welborn that there was a group of inmates in the South Uppers Cell House, the one that I was assigned to manage, refusing to lock up, and he emphasized the point that they were not going to lock up until they spoke with him.

Warden Welborn, Assistant Warden Page, the other unit superintendents, and I all got up and proceeded to the South Uppers to assess what was going on. Assistant Warden Frentzel stayed in the office in order to set up a command post operation in the event that this situation became problematic. And true to form, when we arrived at the cell house and walked to the entranceway of the gallery, there were approximately 40 to 50 inmates standing together at the back end of the gallery. In order to gain access to the gallery, we had to go through a gated doorway that was manually operated by a correctional officer. The officer had to grip a handle on the side of the door and pull the door open. As the officer opened the gate to let us through, another officer was positioned inside an inner perimeter gun tower to provide armed coverage for us in case the situation turned south and became violent. As we walked down the gallery, three inmates maneuvered their way from among the inner circle of the group and began walking toward us. We came to a meeting point about halfway in the middle of the gallery, and Warden Welborn proceeded to speak to them very candidly, but in somewhat of a guarded tone.

He told them in no uncertain terms that if they did not lock up now there would be no discussion of any kind and he would do whatever it took to secure the gallery. One of them turned around toward the group of inmates who were standing at the back of the gallery and gave them a short nod of his head. When he did that, the entire group simply walked into their cells and locked up without an incident. At that moment, I instantly conjured up images from Spike Lee's movie *Malcolm X* when Malcolm allegedly gave his mythical command to members of the Nation of Islam to stand down and not become violent after confronting the police regarding one of his members being beaten and unjustly put in jail. The difference, however, in our situation than that of Spike Lee's movie is that this was no movie. This was real life!

I had just witnessed the overwhelming power and influence that gang organizations had developed within our prison system and the depth of their grip on prison officials. Had that inmate not given his approval for the other inmates to lock up with the simple nod of his head, there is no doubt in my mind that we would have had a major situation to deal with. The inmates knew it and we knew it, but what was even more interesting to me was witnessing the fact that the inmates knew that they had the power to dictate a given situation to their advantage and were prepared to use violence to do so. Intimidation, threats, violence, and fear were the order of the day for the gangs. Prison officials oftentimes negotiated with gangs just so that they could have a non-problematic day. This form of grandstanding by the gangs was par for the course and was designed to send a clear message not only to the prison administration but to the other gangs as well to let them know just how powerful and influential they were in determining how the prison would be run.

The end result of this encounter concluded with a meeting between Warden Welborn and a couple of the gang leaders from that organization. An understanding was reached that temporarily caused the tensions to subside so that the unit activities could resume normal operations. I emphasize *temporarily* because there was always another issue to deal with that was equally as threatening to the safety and security of the facility.

The issue in this case centered around one of their gang members being locked up in segregation and them wanting him out. They were claiming that the inmate was issued a bogus disciplinary report by staff, and they wanted some form of justice to be done in correcting the situation. Locking up a gang member in segregation, and particularly a ranking gang member, was a constant issue that created much tension between staff and inmates.

This incident served as an early lesson for me. It showed me just how critical my understanding of managing this population had to be and how the real world of prison life behind the walls of our maximum security facilities had drastically shifted to the inmate's advantage.

HOW IT ALL BEGAN

WORKING IN A Correctional Agency was not my intended career choice. It started out only as a means to an end when I had finished the coursework for my Master's degree but had not written my thesis paper. The financial stipend that I was receiving had ended, so in order for me to stay and complete my degree, I needed to find a job to pay for my remaining schooling. I was attending Southern Illinois University in Carbondale, Illinois, majoring in Special Education with an emphasis in Correctional Education. I was able to find a part-time job as an overnight attendant at a drug rehab program called Hill House. I was responsible for the supervision and custodial care of the residents who were in the program, and I worked the night shift from 11:00 p.m. until 7: 00 a.m.

While working at Hill House, I learned that a new prison in the area was hiring for several counselor positions. Since I had a bachelor's degree in Psychology and wanted to be a counselor anyway, I thought that this would be a good fit, and besides, I could use the higher paying salary. I found out where I needed to take the examination that was required to qualify for the position, and I took the exam. Upon receiving a qualifying grade, I contacted the facility for an interview. I received an interview a couple of weeks later and was subsequently hired for the position. I only intended for this job to be a stop gap and a way for me to pay my remaining way through graduate school. It was not my intention to make this a career endeavor; however, it didn't turn out quite like I had planned. And this is how I began my career with the Illinois Department of Corrections.

But long before then, there was another beginning that set everything into motion that led up to that life-changing moment. I was born in Atlanta, Georgia, in Grady Memorial Hospital on October 21, 1957, to James Jay Hinsley II and Juanita Frances Harper Hinsley. I was the fourth of four children. My sisters and brother were Gail, Jimmy, and Gwen. Regrettably for us, my mother and father were experiencing some serious marital issues when I was born, and those issues caused my mother to leave my father when I was only nine months old. I never saw him again!

When my parents separated, my mother moved back to her hometown in Asheville, North Carolina. It was in Asheville where I was raised and grew up as a young man. My mother only had a high school education, but she always encouraged and supported her children to get as much education as we could achieve. She initially moved in with her mother and father along with several of her siblings. My grandfather had a very large home, and it reasonably accommodated all of us at the time. He owned a two-story house that had a huge front porch and was situated on a corner lot in a predominantly black neighborhood. It had a big front yard with nice green hedges about knee high running along the front edge of the lawn. A concrete walkway separated the lawn into two halves, and the walkway went right up to a set of concrete steps about ten rows high leading up to the porch and the front door. My grandfather had an old rocking chair that sat off to the right side of the porch where he would sit many times watching my cousins and me play in the yard. He seemed to have delighted in those private moments.

There were two large maple trees in the front yard, with one situated on either side of the walkway that led to the steps of the porch. There was a large apple tree on the west side of the house situated close to the sidewalk that ran adjacent to the street. Kids would oftentimes knock down an apple or two as they walked along the sidewalk going about their care-free lives. There was also a small grape vineyard situated directly behind the apple tree. In the back of the house, an old weather-beaten garage set off to the east side of the house. A gravel driveway about 30 yards long led from the front of the house to the entrance of the garage. The backyard was also fairly large, or at least it seemed that way to me at the time. It had a pear tree and a cherry tree sitting close to the garage, which made it easy for us to climb into and pick the pears and cherries that grew on them. An L-shaped set of green hedges about six feet tall ran along the backside of the yard separating our house from our neighbor's house and provided a natural barrier between our yard and the pedestrian traffic that traveled on the sidewalk.

This backyard was a playground haven where my sisters, brother, cousins, and many neighborhood friends had so much fun growing up. I can remember when one of my cousins and I set the hedges on fire and got our butts tore up. I was in the third grade and had learned about photosynthesis. I learned how green plants supposedly wouldn't burn, so when I got home from school I was eager to show my cousin what I had learned. I found some matches lying around the house and took my cousin out back to show him that green plants don't burn. Well, when I lit those bushes, they burst into flames like wildfire. We were scared as you know what, and we ran and hid in the garage. When the fire was eventually put out, my grandmother and my cousin's mother made sure that we knew what a switch was. We quickly learned that green plants do burn and that green switches will set your butt on fire!

My grandfather was a Pullman Porter for the railroad, and on a few occasions he would take my cousins and me to the train depot for a short ride on the train. That was pretty cool and we thought our grandfather was pretty important. My grandmother was a house-wife, and she was very instrumental in rearing us. She looked after us when we would come home from school while our mother did domestic work in the homes of white families and other part-time work. We grew up in the company of many aunts, uncles, and cous-ins, which made for a very lively and oftentimes interesting family dynamic. The joys, the sorrows, the happy times, and the not-so-happy times were all a part of my growing up in a large extended family. The way I grew up was no different than how most kids in my neighborhood grew up because large extended families were a natural part of our everyday lives. It was the dynamics of this cul-tural upbringing combined with the many special moments of my family and my extended community family that helped shaped the character I am today.

My mom's family was an old Southern Baptist, God-believing family, and they made church a very important part of our lives. Like many black families in the late '50s and early '60s during the high-lighted years of the civil rights movement, a sense of family pride and community pride was essential to our existence. This great sense of pride was instilled within us because of their Christian faith and their belief in the value of doing right by one another. When times would get really tough, my mom would often say, "Children, where there's a will, there's a way and always try to do your best." From this simple statement we came to learn how profoundly spiritual my mother truly was. She wasn't the type of mother who would beat you over the head with religion, but in her own quiet soft-spoken way she made us understand that the love of Jesus Christ was the most important thing in life. Her words reverberate with me to this very day.

When I was around six years old, my mother remarried and my siblings and I were now confronted with the nuances of having a stepfather. Shouldering the responsibility of a new marriage and the task of raising four children, my mom moved out of my grandfather's house into a two-story apartment just a few houses up the street from where my grandfather lived. We lived on a street named South French Broad Avenue. This was a long and hilly street that ran the length of the south side area of town in a north and south direction. As kids, we loved when it snowed in the wintertime because we could experience some of the best sleigh rides ever on this street. There were lots of kids in my neighborhood, and we created plenty of things to do to have fun. We lived there for about seven years before we moved to another area of Asheville called Shiloh. At that time, Shiloh was transitioning from being an all-white community to becoming a predominantly black community. I never really cared too much for living there, but I didn't have much of a choice. I liked the new house we moved into, but I missed all of my friends that I had grown up with back on the south side of town. I wanted to hang out and be with them so bad that for much of the time that I lived in Shiloh, I would go stay with my cousin Stevie or with my best friend, Bossman.

My stepdad also only had a high school education, but he served in the military and received an honorable discharge. He was a proud man, and as I grew older, I came to learn that his upbringing was filled with many hardships. His family was very poor, and just like many poor black families of the '30s and '40s when he was growing up, the emphasis on education often took a backseat when it came time to finding work to keep the family surviving. So, as a young boy, and even as a young man, he had to struggle and work hard for what he got. Because he had a very strong, tough-loving mother, her courageous spirit gave him the strength and character to persevere against the odds and against the hard times that life would oftentimes bring him. His hard times were not only related to his condition of being poor, but they were also a result of the persecution and discrimination that he experienced as a black man in white America.

He became deeply bitter over the issue of having to fight so hard and so fiercely to earn respect and dignity for himself and his namesake. His bitterness was manifested most notably through his drinking. His drinking created an escape for many of the pressures that he dealt with, and unfortunately for my family, his drinking oftentimes created major problems and serious drama within our household. To put it mildly, there were days that I wished my mom would have never married this man, and I often wished that she would have left him. But, my mom is a woman of faith and commitment and she chose to stick it out. And due to the grace of God they are still together today. And as life would have it, my stepfather changed with time and so did our feelings about him. We grew to love him for who he was and we came to understand that he tried to do the very best that he could in raising us, caring for us, and trying to love us the best way he knew how. With time, we grew to understand him, accept him, and lovingly appreciate him.

As life so often does, my mom and stepdad experienced their share of difficulties and everything that goes along with the challenge of raising four kids and supporting three of us through college. Taking out a second mortgage on our new house to help pay the tuitions for each of my sisters' college educations plus dealing with other financial hardships made staying in our home too difficult for them to manage, and it was no longer an option. We eventually had to move out of our home in Shiloh and moved into a newly developed low-income housing complex. This housing complex was intended to be an upgrade from other project housing, but in a few short years the living conditions of this housing community was no different than all the rest. Drugs and its associated lifestyle became the norm.

During the time we lived in Shiloh and up until the time we had to move, my brother was experiencing some challenges of his own. Like so many young African American males in the early '70s, as well as today, he experimented with drugs in his teenage years.

And like many young African American males, his experimentation eventually caused him to get caught up in the criminal justice system. He ended up serving a few years in prison for selling drugs to an undercover narcotics agent. Being the supportive and loving mother that my mom was, she visited him every chance she could. My mom never learned how to drive a car, so she was always dependent upon others to help her get around. She would have my stepdad, other family members, or friends drive her to visit him. I remember visiting my brother on a couple of occasions with my mom, but it was my sense from him that he didn't want me to be there. He never said it to me directly, but in a strange kind of way, I sensed that he did not want me to be there. It seemed to me as though he thought that if I did not physically see him in prison this would somehow protect me from being associated with the stigma of his misfortunes. And maybe deep down inside I really didn't want to visit him in there either. But the reality for most black families then, as well as now, is that the criminal justice system touches us all, and this is a reality of our place in America.

Visiting my brother in prison was one of my earliest and most direct experiences with our criminal justice system. Needless to say, at that time in my life, being 13 or 14 years old, I had no inclinations whatsoever to want to work in a prison, and I certainly had no clue that I would one day become a warden of one of the largest prisons in this country. That's like President Obama when he was 13 or 14 years old not having any aspiration or inclination of becoming the first African American President of the United States. But the circumstances of life tend to bring about unimagined stories and the ironies of life are oftentimes quite different from what we imagine them to be.

The positive thing for my brother, at least as far as I am convinced, was that his experience did exactly what the system is intended to do. It made him not want to go back. Most people (approximately 98 percent) who go to prison get out of prison at some point. They may go back, but they do get out in most cases. The issue becomes how functional they are academically, mentally, emotionally, spiritually, and socially when they do get out. And also, what resources are available to help them successfully transition back into society? As far as my brother is concerned, it seemed that the negative experience of having his freedom stripped away and experiencing first-hand the dehumanizing treatment of prison life was enough of a deterrent to radically change his life for the better. He never went back to prison, and therefore he never became one of the common statistics that we so often hear about and associate with young black men who get out of prison only to find themselves returning to prison time and time and time again. He is one of the fortunate few whose success is measured by his ability to have remained out of prison and in free society, but his story, and other stories like his, are far too few and certainly too seldom achieved.

The Transition of My Youth

Growing up in Asheville in the late '50s through the late '70s were very interesting times. I grew up in a predominantly black neighborhood where we had our own businesses and professional people. Black grocery stores, black doctors and dentists, black schools, and other black-owned businesses were all a part of my community. For much of my upbringing, it was a very segregated way of life, but it was also a very rich and vibrant way of life. Mr. Green's barbershop on Southside Avenue and Mr. Haynes's grocery store on the corner of Phifer and Blatant Street were just two of the many gathering places and learning grounds that were fixtures in my community where people would socialize and conduct their daily affairs. These were places that served to bond the community together. From these gathering places and the many other gathering places in the neighborhood, the young boys would watch, listen, and learn from the varied representations of black men in our community. From these varied forms of black manhood, I witnessed all manners of manifestation of the black male experience.

I saw the gifted musician who sang soul music but lived the blues. I saw the socially and mentally outcast persecuted because of our own ignorance and self-hatred. I saw the dope pushers, the players, and the pimps committing their lives to the pursuit of living in a false world by chasing the American dream through earning fast money. I saw the hustler and the gambler trying to make a dollar by whatever con game they could get over on. I saw the numbers runner and the numbers buyer exchanging their hopes and life dreams in the form of a piece of paper with a few numbers written on it, while other folks hoped to get lucky and hit the winning number just to earn a few hundred dollars to help make ends meet.

I saw the aspiring athlete who only became a local legend because his dreams were deferred by a wine bottle. I saw many black businessmen try to pass down the teachings of W. E. B. Dubois and George Washington Carver to inspire the freedom and courage of charting our own destiny. I saw well-respected black men who were doctors, lawyers, and teachers. I saw the pistol whipping of one man by another man simply because he claimed to have disrespected the virtues of his manhood. I saw elder statesmen play checkers in the barbershop and talk about the pride and challenges of being black men in white America. I saw a lot of "cool" brothers hanging out on the street corners teaching the young jitterbugs how to survive in the streets. I saw good, strong, proud fathers working hard every day and struggling to raise their kids the right way while trying to protect them from the pitfalls of an unforgiving white world.

I saw a black coach of an all-black little league baseball team win a championship game, and the whole community celebrated! I saw many black men go in and out of prison as though they were taking vacations from the challenges of life. I saw an all-black men's choir sing old Negro spirituals so powerfully that it caused the whole congregation to shout "Halleluiah!" and made the church mothers break down and cry. I saw the power of a black preacher's sermon make an old wino give his life to Christ, and I saw a whole lot more. But within all that I saw, the most striking thing that stood out to me was the undying commitment of love within each of these varied expressions of black manhood. It was through their unique way of expressing their indomitable collective pride that gave strength to each other, which held the community together and compelled our community to remain inspired to achieve a better way of life for all of us. These experiences have helped shape who I am today.

As much as there was a sense of pride and love in my neighborhood, there was always a reminder of the segregated life that existed between our community and that of the white community. I remember quite vividly seeing signs on public drinking fountains that read "For Whites Only" and when sitting in the front of the bus was still a sensitive issue. During the summer months, the local movie theaters would sponsor matinee movies for kids if we collected six or more Coca-Cola bottle tops. The good part about that was that we got to enjoy the fun of going to the movies for free, but the downside was the degrading feeling that we experienced when we were made to go into the theater through the back door and forced to sit in the balcony. Needless to say, sitting in the balcony didn't last too long after the white kids who sat in the floor seats kept getting soda pop, popcorn, and other not-so-nice things thrown on them. We just simply wanted to be treated equally.

My first six years of formal education were conducted in an all-black school. Hill Street Elementary School was the name of it. It was administered by a strong but kind-spirited black female principal named Ms. Rita Lee, and all my formative grades were taught by wonderfully caring black teachers. In August of 1969, integration was introduced into the city's school system, and for the next ten years tension, school riots, and student protests plagued the city. I participated in many of these events trying to assert my black identity and express my anger against "the system" of white versus black. I was vehemently shouting the black national anthem "I'm Black and I'm Proud!" that was soulfully expressed by the Godfather of Soul, James Brown. And I was caught up in the exploding consciousness of being a free black man that had been so eloquently articulated by Malcolm X and Dr. King and the Black Panther Party. I was trying to become a mixture of both men as well as display the courage of the Black Panthers—fearless and defiant without being apologetic, but resolute in not being ashamed of being black. The foundation of my zest for equal justice was birthed during this time period. During my seventh and eighth grade school years, from 1969 through 1971, I was bused to a middle school in a predominantly white community. In both years I played on the basketball team and would have to walk home in the late evening when practice was over. Many times my friends and I would be chased by white men and young white boys in their cars, and sometimes we were even shot at! These and other encounters of blatant racial hatred were extremely unsettling and will forever be imprinted upon my mind. These events have only served to deepen my resolve to always stand up against racial discrimination and injustice.

In the fall of 1972, during my ninth grade school year, I attended what was once an all-black high school. It was named South French Broad High School and was located in my old neighborhood, right up the street from my grandfather's house. The school was now integrated. I tried out for the basketball team again, but this time I didn't make the cut. I was not tall enough for the coach's height requirements. He required all of his players to be at least six feet tall and I was a few inches too short. Not playing basketball was a hard pill to swallow, so I just drifted through the school year not really focused on much of anything other than just getting by.

I entered high school in the fall of 1973 and, like many high school boys, participating in sports was a highly anticipated moment. I tried out for our junior varsity basketball team that year and this time I made the cut. I became the starting point guard for the team and played okay. We had a respectful season that year and I looked forward to playing on the varsity team the upcoming school season. In between the end of my sophomore year and the beginning of my junior year, I spent the summer with my oldest sister in Charlotte, North Carolina. She had graduated from Johnson C. Smith University and had made Charlotte her home. Visiting her that summer was the first time that I had ever been out of Asheville for more than a week at one time. I was thrilled to death to have the chance to be away from home for almost three months, and I was not about to miss that opportunity.

When school started back in the fall of 1974, I was more than excited about playing on the varsity basketball team. I just knew I would be on the varsity team since it was the customary tradition for starting players from the J.V. team to be placed on the varsity team. Well, I would quickly have the most shocking experience of my young athletic life. A few days before the basketball season began, I was called to the coach's office and he proceeded to tell me that I would not automatically be placed on the varsity team and that I would have to try out like everyone else. To my surprise, he told me that because I had chosen to go out of town for the summer and did not stay to participate in his two-week basketball camp, I displayed a negative attitude toward being a team player. I thought he had lost his foolish mind when told me that nonsense. I was already leery about his attitude toward me anyway, and this foolish decision reinforced for me that he was singling me out. I thought he was using this as an excuse not to let me play on the team because other players didn't want me on the team. I will admit that I had a pretty independent mouth as a youth and would freely speak my mind, but never did I display the attitude of not being a team player as he claimed. That was straight-up BS! But what could I do? My only choice at that point was to try out, but I knew in my heart that he was not going to let me play on his team and, as it turned out, I never got to play basketball during my junior or senior year in high school.

A Turning Point

As fate would have it, for the two years in which I did not get to play basketball in high school I got the chance to play basketball for the Boys Club of Asheville. It was there where a significant influence upon my life took place. I met two coaches at the Boys Club, Larry Grant and Anthony Ellerbee. These two men nurtured my desire to play basketball in such a way that not playing high school ball became insignificant. Their positive encouragement and support helped elevate my confidence in my skills and abilities as a young basketball player, but more importantly they helped me understand how to deal with the adversities of life—lessons that would prove to be useful for the rest of my life.

During those two years that I played for the Boys Club, I was chosen to be the captain of the team, and we won our city tournament both years. Our team also went to Johnson City, Tennessee, both years to play in a regional tournament against other Boys Clubs in the region. We won the championship in one tournament and we came in second place in the other tournament. I felt good about how our team played, but the experience of playing with my teammates and what Coach Grant and Coach Ellerbee taught us were the most rewarding experiences of all.

I graduated from high school in May 1976, but I was not really prepared mentally, academically, or financially to attend a four-year university. But, because I wanted to continue playing basketball, thinking that this would be my ticket out of Asheville, I enrolled in a local junior college in August of that same year. The college was Asheville Buncombe Technical Institute, which was commonly referred to as AB-Tech. I enrolled in their trade program Air-Conditioning and Refrigeration, but truthfully I only enrolled so I could have the opportunity to try out for their basketball team. I didn't have any real intentions of becoming a refrigerator repairman. I just wanted to play basketball, hoping that this opportunity would give me a chance to later play for a four-year university. I was confident that I could play well for AB-Tech and any other school, and as fate would have it again, I tried out and made the team. I was again appointed as the captain of the team and I had a very successful two-year career there. I averaged almost 20 points per game and led the team in almost every category such as steals, assists, points per game, etc. Because of my overall good play, I was selected to the Western Tarheel Conference All-Tournament Team both seasons from 1976 thru 1978. We had a winning record during both seasons, but fell short each year of winning our conference tournament. I received a lot of notoriety in our local newspaper for my performances on the court, which served to some degree as vindication for me against my high school coach for not allowing me to play.

When my two years at AB-Tech were over, I knew I wanted to continue playing basketball, so I applied to a four-year university. I had matured a little bit during those two years and felt I was now prepared to undertake the challenges of a four-year university. I chose to attend Winston-Salem State University. Winston-Salem State is a historically black college located in Winston-Salem, North Carolina. I chose Winston-Salem State because of the legendary coach Clarence "Big House" Gaines. Coach Gaines was most noted for coaching Earl "The Pearl" Monroe, who later became an NBA Hall of Fame point guard for the New York Knicks. Coach Gaines was also recognized for winning the most games ever in Division II basketball. His program featured a fast pace, up-tempo style of basketball, which suited my style of play perfectly. I knew I was skilled enough to play at that level.

Knowing that Coach Gaines had not heard of my basketball talents and therefore had not recruited me as a scholarship player, I sent him several newspaper clippings that featured some of the games that I had played in. In my letter to him, I asked if I could visit his summer camp for a weekend so he could check out my style of play. He gave me that opportunity and my Boys Club coach Larry Grant accompanied me to Winston-Salem. Coach Grant was my biggest supporter and I am forever indebted to him for his personal commitment toward my success as a basketball player and also to my success as a person. He was an excellent basketball coach, but he was an even better mentor. When we arrived at WSSU, we met with Coach Gaines and talked to him about my options for playing on his team. He didn't offer me a scholarship, but did commit to giving me a chance to prove myself. Later that day I got the opportunity to play with some very talented ball players, and I played well enough for Coach Gaines to consider giving me a tryout when the season started that upcoming fall.

I enrolled in Winston-Salem State University in August 1978 majoring in Psychology with a minor in Sociology. I was able to enroll in college with the assistance of financial aid through the Pell Grant. My folks could not afford to pay for my schooling because they had sacrificed everything they had earned to put my two sisters through college and there wasn't anything more that they could afford. However, with the Lord's blessing, I was favored to receive grant-funded assistance.

When basketball season came around, I tried out with many other high school and junior college players competing for a spot on the team. When the tryouts were over, a smooth-shooting brother named Jake "The Snake" Davis and I were the only two tryout players that were selected. Believe me when I say that this was the crowning highlight of my basketball life up to that point. To play for a legendary coach as a walk-on player was truly a sensational moment. Although Coach Gaines kept me on the team for two years, I only got to play for his J.V. squad. I put in a lot of practice days with the varsity team and even had the opportunity to scrimmage with Earl "The Pearl" Monroe himself one summer. But my hay day came to an end when Coach Gaines informed me that he could no longer keep me on the team because my two-year eligibility had expired. Although this was a tremendous disappointment, I also felt that I had been extremely fortunate to have achieved the level of play that I had garnered. When that chapter of my life came to an end, I turned my concentration toward graduating. In May of 1982, I graduated with honors from Winston-Salem State University. The four years that I spent at that university gave me a solid foundation for developing the confidence to achieve whatever I put my mind to, and it helped prepare me for the life that was yet to come.

4

MY ROAD TO PRISON

AFTER GRADUATING FROM college, I was unsure as to what exactly I would do with the rest of my life. However, I was sure that whatever I did, it was going to be representative of my family and all the people from my hometown who were a part of my upbringing, and it would certainly be representative of the stride for excellence that was instilled in me by my alma mater, Winston-Salem State University. When I left Winston-Salem, I returned to my hometown in Asheville for a couple of months. I then moved to Decatur, Georgia, to stay with a high school friend. He offered me the chance to stay with him until I could find a job and move out on my own, and I took him up on his offer. I will forever be grateful and indebted to my homeboy and lifelong friend Anthony Giles for giving me a place to stay to help start me out on my journey of life.

When I moved to Decatur, I wasn't able to initially find the kind of job that I had hoped my degree would afford me. I took whatever was available just to make ends meet until I could find something better. My first job out of college was as a cook at a Pizza Hut restaurant on Chandler Road. While working there, I continued to apply for jobs in the counseling and mental health fields. I went to various mental health and counseling agencies and tried to get hired as a counselor, hoping that my degree in Psychology would be my selling ticket. Well, everywhere that I went I kept being turned down because they wanted to hire someone with a master's degree or higher and someone with experience. Well, since I didn't have either of those, I started weighing my options, and I decided to apply for graduate school.

I eventually applied to the graduate psychology program at Southern Illinois University in Carbondale, Illinois. I chose to apply there for three reasons. The first was because SIU had a long-standing history with Winston-Salem State for accepting students into their graduate school programs. Second, SIU's psychology program at that time was ranked in the top ten for best psychology programs in the country. And third, I had never been to the Midwest and I thought that this would be a great opportunity for me to experience a part of the country that I had never experienced before. So I applied, but as bad luck would have it, my application missed their deadline date by one day and my application was not accepted. Because of their high rankings for their graduate school program, getting accepted into their program was very competitive and missing the deadline date cost me the chance to get in. Consequently, my pursuit to become a psychologist eluded me.

However, unbeknownst to me at the time, my application was sent to another graduate school department at SIU. My application was sent to the Special Education Department chaired by Dr. Norma Jean Ewing, and I received a telephone call one day while at work at the Pizza Hut. A person representing Dr. Ewing's program contacted me and inquired if I would be interested in being admitted into their graduate program. When they initially called me, I had no interest in special education whatsoever, and, to be quite frank about it, I didn't know much about it either. Their graduate department was combining the academic discipline of two fields of study into one graduate course—the field of Special Education and the field of Correctional Education. Although I wasn't interested in either field of study, I knew that this could be an opportunity for me to get into a graduate school program. After much contemplation, I decided that I would make this opportunity work for me. It would allow me to get into graduate school, which is what I wanted to do, and I could earn a master's degree that could be used as negotiating leverage to obtain a higher paying job down the road. This all happened in December of 1982, and a few short weeks later, I found myself on a plane to Carbondale, Illinois. And on Monday, January 17, 1983, I arrived at the Air Illinois Airport at approximately 2:30 p.m. central standard time prepared to embark on a journey unknown.

An Unexpected Lesson

Initially, I found Carbondale to be uninteresting, boring, and lacking the cultural stimulation that I was accustomed to experiencing back in the Carolinas and Georgia. But, I was now here and I had to make the best of it. Much to my surprise and delight, I discovered that there were several students attending graduate school at SIU who were from North Carolina also. Two of them, Michael Sutton and Myra Mitchell, happened to be from my graduating class at Winston-Salem State. Another student, Regina McMorris, was from my hometown in Asheville. Meeting them helped eased the feeling of being homesick and isolated. Eventually, I became accustomed to my new surroundings and made acquaintances with other graduate students and several of the local people from the black community.

As I became more familiar with Carbondale and its customs, I learned that the black community was much like most small town college communities. They were very guarded and apprehensive about outsiders and they did not have very good relations with the local police, which I had the misfortune of learning about through my own personal experience.

On Monday, December 10, 1984, around 9:00 a.m., I had an unfortunate encounter with the Carbondale Police. It was an unseasonably warm winter day when I stopped at a local grocery store to buy a few breakfast items after returning from an early morning bike ride. I had gotten up early that morning to check my girlfriend's mailbox because she had gone away for the weekend and was anticipating receiving some important mail. School was out for the Christmas break and while she was away she wanted me to collect her mail. So, I rode my bike to her apartment that morning because the weather was pleasantly warm and I enjoyed the exercise. On my way back to my apartment, I decided to stop at the store to buy a few breakfast items. I had worked up a good appetite from riding over to her apartment and was now pretty hungry. After going inside and making my purchase, I strolled out of the store preparing to get back on my bike. As I reached for my bike, I heard a voice say, "Move away from your bike, put the bag down, and get face down on the ground." I turned in the direction where I thought the voice was coming from and to my utter surprise there was a police officer standing in a crouched positioned with his gun pointing directly at me.

In total bewilderment, I proceeded to ask the officer what was the problem and he abruptly interrupted me and shouted, "Shut the fuck up and do what I said." He then repeated his commands. So I did exactly what he said. I let my bike fall to the ground, I dropped my bag, and I got on the ground with my arms and legs spread out to the sides. As he walked toward me, still pointing his gun at me, I became very angry and pissed off at being threatened for no legitimate reason, so I stated to him that he was making a mistake because I had not done anything wrong. He then responded, "If you move, this will be the biggest mistake you'll ever make." I instantly knew then that I had a Clint Eastwood wannabe cop on my hands. About the same time that this was occurring, another police officer suddenly drove up in his car and hurriedly jumped out to assist the first officer. The second officer made a V-line directly to where I was, straddled over me, placed my arms behind my back and handcuffed me while the first officer was kneeling beside me pointing his gun directly at my head. I was lifted up on my feet by the second officer and then taken back into the store by the first officer. Once inside the store, the officer proceeded to question one of the store clerks about my activity in the store. The second officer had gotten back into his car and sped off.

Because I lived right across the street from the store and was a regular customer, the store clerk recognized me and attempted to explain to the officer that I had not done anything wrong. At that point, the officer told the clerk that he didn't want to hear anything he had to say and then escorted me outside and placed me in the back seat of his car. He then took me to the police station where I was detained for approximately 25 to 30 minutes before I was released with no charges being filed. During the time I was being detained, the arresting officer left the room and left me under the supervision of another officer. I am convinced that while he was gone, he was trying to get his story together because he knew he had royally messed up. He eventually came back into the room and simply said I was free to go. He gave no explanation for his actions.

The police station was approximately three to four miles from where I had been arrested, so I insisted that he drive me back to the store. While we were en route back to the store, we got stopped by a train at a railroad crossing. While waiting for the train to pass, I asked the officer what I had done to cause him to form the idea that he needed to arrest me. He responded, "You were just in the wrong place at the wrong time." My suspicions were immediately confirmed by his response, which told me that this chump was a racist asshole and he used his badge to harass black folks at his discretion. I had just experienced what many of the local black residents of Carbondale had been experiencing for years—unchecked police harassment. I got his name and badge number and was determined to take legal actions against him. The remainder of the ride back to the store was filled with complete silence. Experiencing racism up close and personal at the behest of a police officer with a gun pointed directly at your head is a feeling that you will never forget, and it will impact your life forever. Many young black men have experienced and will continue to experience this same kind of threat. I personally now knew the level of harassment that the local black community had been dealing with for years and I was determined not to let this incident go unchallenged.

In hindsight, I can tell you that the officer fabricated a story that claimed that I was an accomplice to a robbery in progress. He claimed that he had seen another black guy sitting outside the store in a black Lincoln Continental with out-of-state license plates and with the engine running. This was racial profiling before it became a nationally identified problem. He further claimed that as he approached the car to question the guy about what he was up to, he observed the guy reach down below the dashboard as though he was reaching for a gun. He claimed that he then decided to let the guy drive off and wait for me to come out of the store to arrest me. That's when he confronted me outside the store. Well, that story was completely BS and he knew it. There had been no report of a robbery in progress from the store and the store clerk told him as much. Additionally, I didn't even know the guy who was in the car and hadn't paid any attention to any of the cars that were parked outside. I also learned while I was being falsely detained, that several other police vehicles responded to a dispatched radio report to search and locate the driver of the supposed getaway car. They found the car in a trailer park less than one mile from the store. The car wasn't stolen, but the driver of the car was on parole from Missouri. He had come to visit his girlfriend over the weekend and had gone to the store to buy a toothbrush because he had forgotten to bring one with him. He had committed no crime.

I filed a lawsuit against the officer's actions and it was eventually settled out of court. However, the point of this story illustrates that my experience with the criminal justice system goes beyond the mere fact of having worked in the system. The color of my skin and the community from which I am from has always and will always make me vulnerable to the inherent biases of our criminal justice system. And because of that fact, I too could one day be faced with the harsh reality of being incarcerated. Innocent black men have always been locked up because of unjust racist acts, and this reality does not elude me. I just try very hard not to give the system a reason to exploit their bias. It was this experience along with countless other experiences with racism that gave me an ability to relate to the black inmates in ways that were not always understood or accepted by many of my white co-workers.

ENTERING THE ILLINOIS PRISON SYSTEM

DURING THE COURSE of my graduate school studies, I had to participate in several practicum courses. This required that I go into prison facilities located in the surrounding areas to perform 20 hours a week of hands-on practical experience. This practicum experience was my initial introduction to the Illinois prison system. My first practicum assignment consisted of learning how educational programs and counseling services were provided to inmates. Ironically, this initial practicum occurred at the Menard Maximum Security Correctional Center in February 1983, the same facility where I would years later become their first African American warden.

The educational services that were provided at the time included classes such as Adult Basic Education and the General Education Diploma (GED). There were also a few vocational training programs as well as some college correspondence courses. Counseling services consisted primarily of case management and some limited support counseling. The support counseling consisted of teaching basic coping techniques, interpersonal communication skills, decision-making strategies, and anger management sessions conducted by the correctional counselors. More specialized mental health services were provided by psychiatrists, psychologists, and clinical social workers. They were charged with the task of routinely seeing inmates on an individual basis to ensure their mental health needs were being met. All of these services are still offered today in varying degrees in our nation's prisons.

My initial experience working in a prison as a graduate student was quite interesting to say the least. On many of my visits there, I would routinely hear warning shots being fired throughout the day and witness many confrontational situations between staff and inmates as well as between inmates and inmates. It was truly a test of one's inner fortitude to go there every day. And to consider the idea of regularly working in such a hostile and negative environment was not on my radar. As a graduate student, it didn't really dawn on me that I would actually make this line of work my career, nor did I have any inclination at the time that I would one day be directly involved in managing this very same facility. Because I had hoped to be a psychologist, or at least work in human services in some counseling capacity, I never saw myself working in a correctional prison. It simply did not compute. However, that fortuitous and unforeseen moment would one day become an awakening revelation.

My next practicum assignment involved working at the drug rehab program that I mentioned earlier, Hill House. Hill House was located in a residential area adjacent to the university I was attending. The house blended in very well with the community, and if you did not know that it was a drug treatment program, you would have thought it to be just a regular home. My assignment there entailed learning the treatment modalities and social dynamics of providing individual and group counseling to the substance-dependent person. I was also tasked with the role of being a mentor and sponsor for clients in the program. This practicum experience offered me a more holistic perspective on how to apply different counseling techniques with a very hard-to-treat population. The substance-dependent person typically has a host of other issues impacting their lives that are masked by their substance abuse problem. This experience would prove extremely valuable to me later on in my correctional career.

My last practicum assignment was in a juvenile correctional facility located in Harrisburg, Illinois. It was from this experience that I learned that I would not be very effective working with the incarcerated juvenile population. Juvenile inmates are very immature and extremely challenging of authority. I did not have the mental fortitude at that time to control myself from snapping and going off on one of those young jitterbugs when they became totally out of control. Since it was my responsibility to provide them with a more socially accepted way of dealing with their anger and frustrations, I knew that I wouldn't last too long and wouldn't be the best role model for them because you can't give tough love—an old-fashion grandma butt whooping—to a juvenile inmate. You would lose your job and possibly go to jail yourself. However, I did manage to get through the practicum without having any significantly negative incident happen. I am convinced, though, that it was because the practicum was limited in its duration and I was not working there every day. If I had to make working with incarcerated juveniles my career work, I would not have lasted very long.

This leads me back to the beginning of my story, where I completed all of my graduate school coursework but still needed to write my thesis paper in order to graduate. And as mentioned before, I needed to find a job so that I could stay in Carbondale to finish my degree. It was during this ambivalent period of trying to decide whether to stay and complete my degree or take my chances and return to Georgia without it that became another turning point in my life. I had to make a very crucial, life-defining decision. Up until that point, I had been in school all of my life: 12 years of formal education, two years of junior college (although I don't really count those years as academic advancement because I was only there to play basketball and I didn't earn a degree), four years of undergraduate college at Winston-Salem State, and now two years of graduate school. I was burned out on school and ready to begin my life, whatever that was going to be.

I came to the conclusion that if I were to leave Carbondale without my degree, I would probably never finish it because of my restlessness to begin living my life. I also reasoned that I had come too far and had worked too hard not to achieve this goal. So, I settled with the decision to stay in Carbondale and finish my degree. That is when I applied for a position as a counselor at the Shawnee Correctional Center. I put all my eggs in one basket with the hope of getting hired at Shawnee. Getting hired at Shawnee would allow me to earn the money I needed in order to finish paying my way through college and earn my degree. On August 9, 1985, I was hired as a correctional counselor with the Shawnee Correctional Center, and it was this fateful day that marked the official beginning of my professional career with the Illinois Department of Corrections.

Learning the Game of Prison Life

Shawnee was designated as a high-medium security facility designed to house 1,800 inmates. I was assigned to the housing unit that managed the most aggressive inmates in the facility. There were four housing units in the facility. Three of them were designated for the general population and the fourth unit was designated as an honor unit. The honor unit primarily housed an older population and inmates who were considered trustees. As a counselor, my duties were to assist the inmates in my unit with placement into various programs and activities and to process various paperwork related to their custody and eventual release back to society. My caseload consisted of approximately 250 inmates on average. The housing unit that I was assigned to was commonly referred to as the Thunder

Dome. Fights would regularly occur between inmates, and some incidents involved correctional officers being assaulted as well. Staff assaults occurred more frequently in this unit than in any of the other housing units.

Dealing with these guys required that you assert yourself in a way that let them know you were not afraid of them per se, but that you also were not naive of the trouble that they could create for you. You had to let them know that you had a job to do and that you were going to do your job fairly. Doing your job fairly meant that you tried to ensure that each inmate received what he was entitled to and you did so without bias. Many of the black inmates would often test me to see just how "black" I really was, or, in other words, just how much of an "Uncle Tom Negro" I was going to be. Many of them had already made the assumption that I was an Uncle Tom anyway.

In general, most black inmates reserved an attitude of suspicion about black employees. It is a developed sense of guarded protection for them because they had learned from other negative experiences that some black employees didn't always have their best interest at heart, and they looked at me no differently. If I wanted them to perceive me differently, I knew I had to earn their trust and respect; there wasn't an automatic acceptance of me just because I was black. Their perception of me was that I was a young college boy who thought he knew it all and believed he was better than them. That of course was not an accurate interpretation of what I believed or who I was, but one's perception is usually one's reality most of the time and it is certainly that way in prison until proven otherwise.

The games they used in testing me played themselves out in several different ways over, and over, and over again throughout my career. One game was to see if they could get me to bring contraband into the institution. Contraband is anything that is unauthorized for them to possess. Contraband could be something as simple as a piece of chewing gum or something as serious as drugs. Other games would be disguised in the form of receiving certain inmate privileges. On occasions, some of the black inmates would send white inmates into my office requesting a certain job assignment and then send black inmates into my office a few minutes later requesting the same job assignment. This was simply designed to see who I would recommend for the assignment, a white inmate or a black inmate. The black inmates were trying to justify or rule out their assumption about the Uncle Tomism that they perceived of me.

These and other games were purposefully played just to test how I would treat them and to see how vulnerable I would be to their manipulations. Manipulation games are played out against staff all the time in some form or fashion. That's part of prison life, and if you didn't learn this aspect of prison life quickly, you would certainly be taken advantage of. Over time, I eventually gained the respect of many of the inmates. This became evident to me through an interesting dynamic that helped me realize just how narrow and intricately connected the margin is between being accepted by inmates—a respectful, but guarded trust—versus being declared as their enemy—being considered untrustworthy and representing the status quo.

This came to light when I learned that I had been given the prison nickname Mr. Motherfucker. That's right, they called me Mr. Motherfucker! This had become an unofficial badge of honor bestowed upon me by many of the inmates in my unit, and a couple of them confided in me that this was so. One day while having a conversation with some inmates on my caseload, I took the liberty to ask them what they meant when they called me this. They told that the "Mr." was their way of giving me respect for treating them with respect and the "MF" represented their dislike of me because I played too much by the rules and wouldn't give in to their manipulations or give them more than what they had coming.

Some of the black inmates wanted me to be more of a "brother," as it were, who was willing to bend the rules for them, or at least give them breaks when they knew they didn't deserve a break. I did that within reasonable limits where I could and was very judicious in doing so. But their testing of me was part of the games they played, and it was also a way for them to connect with me as a black man who still faced many of the same issues associated with racism as they did. But I faced them from a different context. I had not been branded with an X on my back; they had!

For some of them, I represented the good, the not-so-good, the hopes, and the fears that they saw in themselves as black men. Strangely enough, it was this subtle, mostly unspoken rapport that existed between us that allowed us to relate to one another in ways that were not mutually exclusive of our different roles. It was a fact that they were inmates and I was a representative of the system, but we were connected to one another by the social condition of our blackness. It was a rapport that I tried to maintain with the black inmates throughout my career and at each level of my career. My experiences with issues of overt and systematic prejudices gave me the ability to relate to black inmates in a way that allowed them to relate to me, despite the educational differences that separated us. Most of them eventually came to understand why I would not necessarily give them any special treatment just for being black. I always tried to make it clear to them that there is a certain accountability that comes with the choices that we all make in life, even when the playing field of life is unequal. And the playing field of the criminal justice system and prison life is definitely unequal for black folks.

They eventually came to understand that I would not mistreat them simply because I had a higher education than the great majority of them, nor because of my position of authority over them. I didn't choose not to mistreat them because I was afraid of what they might do to me if I were to mistreat them. They could cause problems for me whether I mistreated them or not; that was a given. I chose not to mistreat them simply because they were deserving of being treated respectfully, and I felt it was my inherent spiritual obligation to do so. It was just that simple!

It was also important for me to try and make it clear to them that I truly hoped that they would attempt to elevate themselves beyond their current mental and physical confinement. I knew exactly what my responsibilities were as they related to my job duties as an employee of the Department of Corrections, and I tried to fulfill those duties to their fullest. But, I also understood the set of conditions by which many of the black inmates had to deal with. They were faced with the unrelenting challenges of being looked at as inferior and undeserving in every aspect of their existence. Because of that, I tried to instill within the consciousness of many of them a self-empowering mentality to counterbalance the degrading, negative, and self-destructive conditions of a prison environment. My ability to present myself in a non-judgmental way against them and in a way that communicated that I respected them as human beings served to aid me well throughout my career.

My First Career Challenge

I worked at Shawnee as a counselor for five years before my first promotional opportunity was presented to me. The promotion entailed becoming a casework supervisor responsible for managing the program services aspect of Illinois' *first* prison boot camp program. This opportunity occurred in October 1990 when I was appointed to assist in the initial opening of the Dixon Springs Impact Incarceration Program. When presented with the promotion, I saw this as a great opportunity to become involved with a new and innovative program for our agency, and I accepted the challenge.

During the mid '80s and early '90s, prison boot camp programs were highly promoted alternatives to conventional prison incarceration. Many correctional agencies across the country began implementing this form of prison management as a way to reduce the increase in prison populations. Illinois chose to incorporate this alternative sentencing method in its system of prison management for their adjudicated adult male population. Judges now had the choice to either sentence a person to a boot camp program or to a conventional prison. The intent behind these programs was to reduce the recidivism rate of inmates returning to prison. The individuals that were targeted for these programs were first-offenders with nonviolent felonies. The war on drugs was at its peak during this time and hundreds of drug-related offenders were being sent to prison in droves. These programs were used to offset that trend, and boot camp programs became very popular.

Prison boot camps were structured based on a military-style training strategy that was designed to break down the negative, anti-social attitudes of the inmates. This strategy was intended to replace an inmate's negative attitude with a more positive and self-directed attitude. This restructuring of an inmate's attitude was to be accomplished by building up their self-esteem through a regiment of physical exercise, hard labor, education development, substance abuse education, and structured discipline. This management alternative was highly embraced by many correctional agencies at the time. It was viewed as another means by which the overcrowded conditions facing many of our prisons nationwide could be reduced.

Early research regarding the outcomes of these programs reflected that they did have a statistically greater impact in the reduction of recidivism within the first year of an inmate's release from prison. However, over time—three years or more—there was no significant difference demonstrated in the recidivism rates between prison boot camp programs and conventional prison. The recidivism rates remained about the same after three years, ranging in the vicinity of 50 to 70 percent for both groups. It is my opinion, and I am confident that the research will support me, that the failure of both conventional prison and prison boot camp programs to sustain low rates of recidivism for more than one year is directly attributable to inadequate aftercare services. The continuity of systematic support services such as housing, treatment services, job training, and employment opportunities, which are critical to an inmate's successful transition back into society, is greatly deficient. Until this gap in transitional support services is filled, we will not see any substantive decline in our nation's recidivism rates.

As with any innovative prison program or initiative such as prison boot camps, their effectiveness is only achieved when financial support, political support, and special interest groups agree on a common purpose. The financial aspect of this trilateral relationship is driven by the cost-effectiveness of implementing the program. The political aspect is driven by the public support that is received from local and national officials taking a tough position on crime. The special interest group is driven by the humanitarian aspect of ensuring fair and equitable justice is applied. Trying to merge these differing perspectives into one common purpose can be and oftentimes is a lofty task. However, notwithstanding the challenge, it is my opinion that the common purpose is quite simple. It should always be driven by what is in the best interest of public safety first and what will be the quality of the inmate's state of being upon his or her return to society second. Ultimately, the inmate is going to return to society and his or her family and the community that he or she will reside in will be directly affected by his or her return. How well these different competing entities work together for the common good of public safety and the well-being of the individuals being released from prison will determine whether the transition of re-entry into society will be successful or continue to be a repeated theme of society being victimized and parolees reoffending. If these entities remain disconnected from one another, the talk of lowering the recidivism rates will continue to be nothing more than grandiose chatter and empty rhetoric.

After the novelty of boot camp programs wore off, many judges stopped utilizing these programs as an alternative method for reducing recidivism. Judges began to drastically reduce the number of adjudicated persons being sentenced to these programs. Although these programs are still being utilized today, they serve more as a function to lessen the overcrowded conditions of our prison system than a method by which to reduce recidivism. The boot camp program that I was involved in started out as an adult male program, but was later converted into a co-ed facility. I found it quite interesting to observe the tenacity of many female inmates who demonstrated the mental and physical toughness to endure the program. They oftentimes exhibited a greater desire to succeed than many of their male counterparts. The average length of most programs ranged from 90 to 120 days. Within that time, a very rigorous and intense regimentation of physical and mental challenges is required of them. If an inmate chose to quit the program or became a disciplinary problem, they were transferred to a conventional prison to complete the remainder of their sentence. I witnessed many inmates drop out and an equal number transferred for disciplinary reasons.

I was assigned to the Dixon Springs boot camp program for slightly more than two years before I was offered my second promotional opportunity. This opportunity came at a time when our maximum security prisons were experiencing a significant level of disruption and violence due to gang activity. A personal friend and colleague of mine had been promoted to the position of assistant warden and was assigned to manage a lower security facility. When his position as unit superintendent became vacant, I was offered the opportunity to fill his position. Prior to that offer being made, I had never given any consideration to working in a maximum security facility, much less working in the largest and most challenging prison in our agency. Nonetheless, I decided to capitalize on this opportunity by accepting the offer with the underlying motive to strengthen my managerial skills and to learn more about the complex dynamics of managing a correctional facility. It was with this promotion that I received my first assignment at the Menard Maximum Security Correctional Center, and it was at Menard where I began my administrative career as a mid-level manager and eventually became a senior level warden.

6

THROWN INTO THE
LION'S DEN

I WAS FIRST assigned to Menard in January 1993, ten years after I had completed my graduate school practicum there. Not much had changed in that time, with the exception of an increase in the population. However, this time I was not just a graduate student dealing with the inmates in a very limited capacity. I was now a mid-level administrator with the responsibility of being directly involved and on the front line of the war zone. The gang influence was in full swing and was reaching an all-time high with respect to their continual disruption of the day-to-day operation of the prison.

During my first year at Menard, we were on lockdown for approximately 236 days of that calendar year. All of that time, with the exception of about 19 days, was related to inmate violence or the threat of inmate violence. The unrelated 19 days were due to the Great Flood of 1993 when the Mississippi River reached an all-time crest level due to an overflow from excessive days of rain in the northern part of the state. Most of the violence that was perpetrated during this time was directed against other inmates because of gang rivalries and internal power struggles. However, staff and inmate confrontations were also factors that created ongoing tensions and conflicts that oftentimes resulted in assaults against staff. Earlier I mentioned some of my experiences managing the South Uppers Cell House, where one inmate was stabbed several times and another group of inmates refused to lock up. These types of incidents were daily occurrences at Menard. I knew that my learning curve for understanding how to manage this population had to be short, but little did I know at the time that my ability to learn quickly would soon be tested in a much greater capacity.

After I had been at Menard for a couple of months, Warden Welborn decided to reassign me from the South Uppers Cell House to the Segregation and Protective Custody Unit. Although I was far from being a seasoned unit superintendent in the two short months that I had been there, Warden Welborn felt that I would provide a different approach to managing this unit. I learned over time through my development as an administrator that when good administrators are faced with a problem they will take some measure of corrective action to address that problem. I didn't realize it then, but I came to learn later that I was being used as Warden Welborn's corrective action. In other words, he assigned me to this unit to bring a different approach and a different response to managing the issues that were occurring within that unit. But at the time, it simply felt to me as though I was being sent into the lion's den to tame the lions without a whip or chair because the Segregation Unit was our toughest unit to manage.

Although I considered myself to be a quick study, I certainly had not learned all of the subtle dynamics of managing prison life in a maximum security facility in the short two months that I had been there. It also crossed my mind that this was in some way a test by Warden Welborn to see if I had the character and fortitude to manage one of the most problematic units in our agency and to see if I had what it took to become an effective administrator. But whatever his true purpose was, I had committed myself to the principled conviction that I would be diligent in doing what I thought was in the best interest of the safety of staff first and that I would be respectful in my supervision of the inmates second. Simplistic as this might sound, it was certainly by far not without its challenges to achieve.

I concluded that Warden Welborn assigned me to this unit because he was operating off of two assumptions. The first was the fact that I did not have any allegiances to anyone in the unit and, therefore, I could bring a fresh, unbiased approach to an unstable situation. And second, he knew that my desire to learn and do well would be motivating factors that would prompt me to take a vested interest in trying to provide a more effective form of management to this unit than had been previously made. His assumptions were right; I did want to demonstrate that I could be an effective manager. This assignment would serve to be my first major test at learning how to manage chronically disruptive inmates. He indicated to me that there had been a lot of problems within this unit and that the current unit superintendent had not been as attentive or responsive to some of the concerns presented by staff and inmates. Staff assaults were frequent, inmate grievances were regularly being filed, and staff collusion was suspected. Warden Welborn expressed to me that he expected me to bring a more involved commitment to the management of this unit and I accepted his challenge, although I didn't have much of a choice. I had to sink or swim, but I knew I was a pretty good swimmer.

The Segregation Unit is the hellhole of most prisons, and it was no different at Menard. It is the place where the most disruptive and problematic inmates in a prison are housed. Generally, inmates are placed there for rule violations involving aggression and violent behavior, but many are housed there for nonviolent infractions such as escape attempts, verbally threatening staff, possession of drugs, etc. For the most part, these are the more problematic guys in a prison population. What was interesting about this unit was that it also housed our Protective Custody inmates. These were the inmates who had expressed concerns about living in general population because of real or perceived threats of violence against them from the gangs. These inmates are the ones who would typically become victims of the more aggressive predatory inmates in general population.

This particular cell house was divided into two halves, the Segregation Unit which faced the interior grounds of the facility and the Protective Custody Unit which faced the exterior grounds of the facility. Both units were contained within a larger unit called the North Cell House. The units were positioned back-to-back against one another but separated by a narrow passageway. This passageway was designed for staff to walk between the two units, allowing them to have access to the back of each inmate's cell in order to provide maintenance repairs and to conduct routine checks for potential breaches in security.

The majority of our cell assignments required that two inmates share an 8 x 10 foot cell. Our more aggressive and dangerous inmates would be housed in a single cell whenever possible. Assigning an inmate to a single cell was intended to reduce the chances of them acting out aggressively against another inmate. Many of the cells were enclosed by a steel-plated door with a small narrow window centered about eye level so staff could view inside the cell. Oftentimes the window would be disfigured with scratch marks or blackened with residue from attempts by inmates to start fires in their cell. Consequently, the visibility inside many cells was oftentimes extremely poor, which made it much more difficult for staff to provide proper security and to take appropriate actions when responding to a cell. There was also a food port opening located about two-thirds of the way down on the door that allowed staff to deliver and retrieve the inmate's food tray and eating utensils, but also served as a passageway to deliver and retrieve other items such as mail or clothing.

There were other types of cells that were used in this unit that were called open-face cells. They were called this because they were built with cell-bars and not with a solid steel door. The open-face cells presented a major security problem within the segregation unit because inmates could easily, and oftentimes did, throw objects and human waste on staff as staff walked by the cells or when staff attempted to interact with inmates at their cell door. Throwing human waste was a frequently used form of assaulting staff by inmates. During the early '90s, there was a heightened concern about the transmission of the AIDS virus through body fluids. Legislation was eventually adopted into law making it a felony in the State of Illinois for an inmate to assault staff with human waste. As a result of this legislation, we experienced a dramatic decrease in human waste being thrown on staff. Although this legislation did not cause inmates to completely stop throwing human waste on staff, it did have a significant deterrent effect.

Inside each cell, two steel beds were arranged in a bunk-bed style manner. The beds would be positioned against either the left side or the right side of the cell, leaving a very narrow area for movement inside the cell. A wash basin and toilet were affixed to the wall in the back of the cell, providing them hygiene accessibility. A small light was secured to the middle of the wall above the wash basin. The light provided visibility for staff to conduct security checks as well as light for the inmate to read material and not be subjected to sensory deprivation because there was no natural light able to filter into the cell.

The segregation portion of this unit had a recreational area directly adjacent to it. It was designed this way to provide more control of the movement within the unit for escorting inmates to and from their cells. The recreational area was a fenced in location divided into three sections that were separated by mesh fencing and enclosed by a 15-foot concrete wall topped with barbed wire fencing. In addition to this, there were officers assigned to gun towers that overlooked the yard area and provided armed coverage while the inmates engaged in their recreational activities. It was almost a daily occurrence to hear warning shots fired when segregation inmates were recreating. A fight, an assault attempt, or an actual assault would invariably take place when they recreated. I would estimate that 99 percent of the altercations that took place during segregation yard time were related to gang affiliations and their associated activities.

There were many challenging moments in the day-to-day management of this unit, and much of it dealt with inmate-to-inmate confrontations, but there were many inmate-to-staff confrontations that caused moments of concern as well. Staff were always being accused by inmates of deliberately destroying their personal property when conducting shakedowns of their cells. This and other issues invariably caused friction between inmates and staff, and inmates would invariably attempt to get even by assaulting staff. There were other concerns as well, such as inmates being physically and/or sexually assaulted by each other and inmates frequently engaged in other forms of behavior that jeopardized the safety of everyone, which added to the complex task of managing this unit.

The concern about staff being assaulted was of primary importance to me, and I attempted to stay on top of this issue for a number of reasons. Inmates commonly perceive the actions of staff as being unjustified, oppressive, and deliberately indifferent. And because of this perception, staff is always susceptible to inmates lashing out against them. However, it was just as important to know whether or not staff was abusing their authority, which was very critical to my ability to ensure a safe unit. Some staff brought on the attacks against themselves due to their provoking and agitating conduct. It didn't justify the assault by the inmate, but the abuse of authority in prison usually does not go unchecked. There is definitely a code of retaliation against staff for continued abuse of their authority. However, in fairness to staff, the great majority attempt to do their job professionally and some inmates just simply do not always respect that.

They harbor the *them versus us* mentality. So it was very important that I had information about the way staff conducted themselves as well as knowing the temperament of the inmates.

Having this information helped me determine what actions were necessary to take when a potentially threatening issue needed to be addressed. Some actions included removing a staff person from their assignment to prevent him or her from being assaulted or reassigning an inmate to a different housing unit or transferring him to another facility to prevent his continued threat. Most of the time, the inmate exaggerated the allegations of mistreatment to justify his act of assaulting the staff person. However, not all allegations were without merit, but it still did not justify the assault. If we were able to determine that an inmate's allegations were true or contained some partial legitimacy, we would take whatever actions deemed appropriate, and sometimes those actions involved imposing disciplinary measures against staff. Such actions demonstrated to staff and inmates that we did not condone staff misconduct and that we would take actions to correct a situation once we learned of the concern. And likewise, when a staff assault occurred, we took equal measures to discipline the inmate accordingly, and in many cases the entire facility suffered the consequences.

Our responsiveness to such issues paid off in other ways as well. If an inmate were to file a lawsuit against us for allegations of staff mistreatment or violations of his constitutional rights, having investigated the matter and taken corrective actions to resolve the issue would prove valuable in our defense in court. An inmate's legal claim of *deliberate indifference* would not have the precedence to receive a favorable ruling by the court if we could demonstrate our due diligence in attempting to address the issue in good faith. However, what was equally as important to me, irrespective of the legal concerns that we were always faced with, was the fact that it was our charged duty and responsibility as public service administrators to reasonably ensure the well-being of inmates. That included protecting them from the misuse of authority by staff as well as from the harm they frequently inflicted against one another. If these matters were addressed properly, the legal issues would usually resolve themselves.

One of the things that frustrated me the most and challenged my ethical principles to their limit was having a gut-level feeling about a staff person misusing his or her authority but being unable to prove it. I know in my heart-of-hearts that many inmates were and still are mistreated by staff daily, but these incidents will never ever be proven. This is another unfortunate collateral consequence of prison life: unproven acts of victimization endured by inmates perpetrated by staff. This is why, in my opinion, it is harder to protect someone in prison from being victimized than it is to protect someone in free society. Prison life has many ill side effects.

In every cell house at Menard, including the Segregation/Protective Custody Unit, we had inmate workers assigned to do the janitorial maintenance of the unit. These workers were called Cell House Help. They were required to clean the cell houses and perform various janitorial tasks such as sweeping, mopping, dusting, throwing out trash, etc. They were not allowed to clean other inmates' cells, but they did clean the galleries, the shower areas, and other common areas in the unit. The problem that this created was that the dominant gang organizations had members of their organizations assigned to these jobs. Having gang members working in the Segregation Unit contributed greatly to the trafficking of drugs and other contraband into the unit and created an ongoing pattern of disruptive communication between the inmates in segregation and the inmates in general population. The workers were the avenue by which information and contraband were passed between segregation and the general population. This created an enormous level of tension for staff trying to prevent breaches in security from occurring, and it added to the already heightened tensions between rival gangs and staff.

Every organization wanted to protect their members who were locked up in segregation. This led to a concerted effort on their part to try and have as much influence on what happened in segregation as they did in general population. The gangs were always trying to ensure that they had at least one representative member assigned as a worker in the segregation unit. This opened the avenue for all sorts of security breaches to occur as well as competition amongst the gangs. Hits, planned assaults against staff or other inmates, could be and were orchestrated as a result of cell house help workers having the latitude of moving between segregation and general population. Disturbances were sometimes staged in segregation because of what the cell house help workers told or didn't tell their gang leaders about what was going on inside the unit. Information about other conspiracies that threatened the safe operation of the unit could be and oftentimes were communicated back and forth from segregation to general population by these workers.

The presence of gang-affiliated inmates working in segregation was a particularly challenging problem for this unit, but was also an equally problematic situation for the general population. Although these inmates were patted down and strip searched before entering and before leaving the unit, they were frequently able to sneak contraband in and out of the unit quite cleverly. The trafficking of homemade weapons into this unit by the inmate workers contributed greatly to the number of assaults that occurred during yard time. Virtually a week did not go by during the summer months without gunshots being fired to stop an assault between segregation inmates. When fights and other assaultive incidents occurred in general population, it was almost inevitable that retaliation would be attempted when the inmate or inmates were placed in segregation. There was simply no place you could hide from being assaulted, and our segregation unit lived up to its reputation as being the hellhole of prison life.

PROBLEMS IN SEGREGATION

I RECALL ONE day when the inmates in segregation became extremely upset over an ill-advised decision by staff not to allow them their recreational yard time. However, before I became aware of the problem, the inmates had already begun throwing objects at staff from their cells and creating a disruptive situation. They set fires on one of our galleries, which created an immediate security crisis. They started the fires by throwing trash and pieces of bedsheets and pillowcases onto the gallery and lighting them with matches they had gotten from the inmate workers. The situation quickly escalated into a major safety and security problem and was rapidly growing in intensity.

When staff tried to get onto the gallery to gain control of the situation, the inmates repeatedly threw objects at them preventing them from accessing the gallery. We ended up positioning officers at each end of the gallery with fire hoses to douse out the fires. As the inmates' misconduct escalated, we activated our emergency response tactical unit in preparation to use force to restore order. If this situation continued, there was a great likelihood that we would need to evacuate inmates from the unit. They could begin experiencing smoke-related complications, or worse, a cell could unintentionally catch fire and the inmates inside would become trapped. This scenario heightened our concern regarding a potentially fatal outcome.

Instructions were given to activate the overhead exhaust fans to help remove the smoke from the gallery and to prevent the smoke from spreading to other areas of the cell house. But because the inmates had an endless supply of materials in their cells, they kept small fires going. As soon as the officers would put out one fire, another fire would be started. It became a game of cat and mouse. The inmates knew they had nothing but time on their side, and they weren't concerned about the consequences of their actions. They were extremely pissed off about their yard privileges being canceled and they believed they had every right to protest. The ill-advised moment of discretion by staff gave them a reason to flex their anger.

When we, management, learned of the incident, we responded immediately to the unit to deal with the situation. Upon our arrival, we spoke with my unit captain to find out what triggered the situation. We learned that the problem stemmed from an inmate refusing to let staff search his cell. Because of the inmate's refusal to have his cell searched, a decision was made to take away yard time from the entire gallery. The amount of time that was spent attempting to get the inmate to cooperate with the cell search caused a delay in other scheduled movement within the unit. This delay prompted one of my unit lieutenants to make the decision to cancel yard for that particular gallery. The lieutenant let his aggravation of dealing with this one inmate's uncooperative behavior cause him to make a hasty and reactionary decision. The lieutenant did not discuss his decision with my unit captain before he made his decision. As a result, we ended up with a major disturbance on our hands. Had the lieutenant discussed his idea to cancel their yard with the captain first, the captain probably would have suggested an alternative solution and this incident probably would have been avoided.

Prisons are managed by precise, scheduled activities, and when one activity gets off schedule it will invariably affect other scheduled activities. Prison management is predicated on a delicate balance of using discretion within the purview of one's position of authority. The effectiveness of a well-managed prison is greatly dependent upon good, sound decision-making at all levels of personnel. When the discretionary decision-making of staff becomes governed by a sense of rank and/or authority, this attitude will invariably lead to an exploitation of power. In this case, the decision made by the lieutenant to penalize all the inmates on the gallery for one inmate's non-compliance was viewed by the inmates as an exploitation of his authority, and this ignited the disturbance.

We attempted to establish communication with some of the ringleaders, hoping to prevent the incident from escalating in the unit and potentially spreading into the general population. Our attempts were to no avail. They were determined to be disruptive. They felt as though staff were making up rules as they saw fit and they, the inmates, decided not to resolve this issue peacefully. They didn't give my captain or me the chance to try and work the situation out before they reacted. Instead, they reacted with what they knew would get our attention. They used this situation as an opportunity to protest this and other problems they wanted to complain about. This is a good example of how inmates flex their intimidation and power against management in order to get what they want. This is also a good example of how the slightest indiscretions by staff and the short-sightedness of good judgment can ignite a major problem inside a prison within seconds.

When potentially major incidents or actual disturbances like this one would occur, ranking administrative staff from our executive headquarters would always respond to the facility. In this incident, the deputy director of our agency responded to assess first-hand what was happening and to offer his guidance. Upon his arrival, he was debriefed by Warden Welborn before we proceeded to the segregation unit. As a precautionary measure, we put on rain coats to protect us from urine and feces or other liquids that might be thrown at us as we walked the gallery and attempted to talk with the inmates. We also used a portable protective shield that enabled a person to walk past a cell without being struck by an object.

As a result of the deputy director's involvement, the inmates eventually calmed down and were willing to talk. The inmates had learned through years of confrontations with management that if they created enough of a disturbance that someone with executive authority within our agency would eventually come and investigate the problem. This had become a conditioned response that had developed over time as a result of the agency's unwritten policy to negotiate with gang leaders to keep the peace. These power play moves by the gangs were played out on some level by gang organizations every day, and this game had become the order of the day for how we managed our high security prisons.

Notwithstanding the unorthodox method of our management style, there were some positive advantages that resulted from this conciliatory style of management, although they were very tenuous at best. Many potentially serious incidents were averted because of our willingness to dialogue with the gangs. These dialogues contributed significantly to the prevention of many staff and inmates from being hurt. But it was still like playing Russian roulette because we, management, never truly knew when their word would be good and we never had a viable option other than long-term lockdown that could counter their threats. Sure, we had all the guns, but you do not effectively manage a prison solely by force, except in extreme circumstances. There has to be a counterbalance of forceful management and control, with a level of administrative diplomacy that creates the atmosphere of mutual cooperation and expected compliance.

It seemed to me at the time that our agency was reluctant to draw the line in the sand and enforce the control that was so desperately needed to better manage our facilities. I think, in part, it was because we didn't have the resources or political backing to support what needed to be done. But more concerning than that, it seemed to me that there was great apprehension by executive management regarding the anticipated resistance that the gangs would put up against our efforts to take control of our prisons, and this resistance was believed to be bloody and violent. The Illinois Department of Corrections was not ready to enter into an all-out war with the gangs for control. Our conciliatory style of management served as a diversionary approach to buy time until the agency formulated a more strategic plan of gaining control.

I can vividly recall another incident in the Segregation Unit that involved the murder of an inmate. Most of our cell assignments required that two inmates live together, and only a few inmates had the benefit of living by themselves in a single cell. Prior to assigning an inmate to live in a cell, a screening process is done to determine if an inmate is reasonably compatible to have a cellmate. The inmate's aggression level, the nature of his case, his mental health history, and other criteria are all evaluated to determine what an inmate's cell assignment status would be. Once the review was done, the inmate would be assigned to live in a two-man cell or a single cell. Having two inmates cell together is always a crapshoot because you have no real way of ensuring that they will get along. And it is no different for assigning inmates to live together today than it was when I was in the system. Even when two inmates are considered reasonably compatible to live together, it does not mean that they will automatically get along, nor does it mean that they will not develop problems with one another over time. Assigning inmates to a single cell would be the ideal housing arrangement for any prison population, but due to the rate of incarceration in this country—1 out of every 100 adults—we could never afford the price tag of having this kind of equitable living arrangement in our prisons.

In this particular incident, an inmate with a serious mental illness was inadvertently assigned to cell with another inmate. He reported experiencing hallucinations and hearing voices. As he became more and more out of touch with reality, and obviously more prone to acting out his hallucinations, he violently attacked and killed his cellmate. He strangled his cellmate to death with his bare hands and skinned portions of the inmate's face off with a crude homemade knife. He then plastered the skin of his cellmate on the wall of their cell as though it was a ritualized ceremony. This incident is a grave example of the inherent potentiality of an inmate's life being senselessly snuffed out as a result of the collateral consequences of being confined in an overcrowded prison system. Because most segregation units have inmates with mild to acute forms of mental illnesses, this type of incident will no doubt repeat itself again, somewhere, someday, in one of our nation's prisons. This again, is the harsh, but factual reality of prison life.

Being on Lockdown

As I became more cognizant of the realities of managing a highsecurity prison, it also became very evident to me that the gang presence in Menard specifically, but in Illinois' prison system in general, was the prevailing challenge that permeated throughout the tense and volatile existence of prison life. Not a day went by where there wasn't some kind of incident or confrontation that was not influenced by gang-related motivation. As I mentioned earlier, during the first year of my assignment at Menard, we were on lockdown for approximately 236 days of that calendar year. All but 19 of those days were related to inmate violence or the threat of inmate violence. The focus of the violence that transpired during the other 217 days would constantly shift from gang rivalries to retaliating against staff. But no matter which way the threat shifted, the safety and security of the entire facility for both staff and inmates was always the primary concern.

When a facility is placed on lockdown, all inmate movement, except for select authorized situations, is discontinued and inmates are confined to their cells for at least 23 hours a day. In the minds of the public, this may seem like it would be the easiest way to operate any prison, the thinking being that with no inmates out of their cells you don't have as many problems. To some degree that is correct, but lockdowns are actually more of an administrative challenge for prison officials, and it is much more labor intensive for the staff to manage. When a facility operates normally, which is referred to as running an *open facility*, inmates have the ability to move about the prison compound somewhat freely. They are permitted to go to the chow hall, to the yard, to school, to the commissary, to the library, to the health care unit, and to other places in the facility to receive services provided by each of these areas. Movement to these places is conducted either in mass groups consisting of 50 inmates or more, in smaller groups, or by individual escort. Mass movement is always supervised by unarmed staff escorting the group to their destination and overseen by armed staff positioned in a gun tower or a catwalk.

In high-security prisons, armed coverage is always provided in the highly trafficked areas where large numbers of inmates are allowed to congregate, such as cell houses, dining rooms, recreational areas, and chapel areas. Because of the freedom of movement in an open facility, it makes the delivery of these services more efficient. However, when a facility is placed on lockdown, it requires that all of these services be delivered to the inmates at their cell.

When you consider the manpower and effort that it takes for staff to prepare and deliver hundreds of meals three times a day—breakfast, lunch, and dinner—to an inmate's cell over an extended period of time such as weeks or even months, then you can began to get an idea just how labor-intensive and counterproductive being on extended lockdowns can be. And when you consider combining all of the other services that must be provided such as education, medical, legal, and religious services, just to name a few, you may then begin to understand more clearly the demands involved with regard to time, energy, and dollars spent in operating a facility in this manner. It is much more cost-effective and less labor intensive to operate an open facility versus a facility that is on extended periods of lockdown. Only super maximum security prisons and segregation units operate this way as a routine method of operating because they have a specific and defined mission of operation. If you were to compare the two styles of operation, you would learn that the operating budget per inmate in a super maximum security prison is considerably higher than it is for an inmate in a reduced-security setting.

Although the initial few days of a lockdown offers temporary relief from the stress of ongoing conflicts for staff and inmates, it is not the preferred method of operation by management, and it is certainly not the preferred method of operation by inmates. When administrators make the decision to lock down a facility, it should be for legitimate safety and security concerns. A prison official should never lock down a facility to gain the popularity of his staff or to exert superficial control. If an administrator attempted to gain the support of his staff or demonstrate his control at the expense of penalizing inmates by placing them on lockdown for every incident that involved an assault on staff, this would create an even greater rift of animosity and resentment against the administration by the inmates. In my opinion, this would be a very dangerous management approach to take, and the prison would be set up for serious conflicts.

Not every staff assault is a planned attack, and each assault has its own dynamics that require consideration before a decision is made to lock down the facility. Given that fact, when a lockdown occurs that is perceived by inmates to be unjustified, inmates typically will give the administration a *real* reason to lock down the facility. They will either assault a staff person or create a disturbance of some kind to serve as retaliation against their perceived injustice. Inmates are very sophisticated at doing time, and they are quite astute at discerning when they are being punished for illegitimate reasons versus being managed firmly for the legitimate penological interests of security. Inmates don't like being locked down, but they will normally respond more cooperatively and compliantly when they believe that the reason for the lockdown is legitimate.

During the last seven months of my career, which was from June 1, 2004, through December 31, 2004, I was assigned to Menard to serve as the warden. During that period, there was an assault incident that involved a correctional officer, which called into question whether or not I should place the facility on lockdown. Because I made the decision not to lock down the facility, some of the staff became extremely upset with my decision. They went as far as to accuse me of being too lenient with the inmates and not being concerned about their safety and well-being. This, of course, was far from the truth. However, because several staff did not like my style of management and harbored racial animosity against me, they tried to use this incident to cast a negative perception about my leadership as warden.

Here is what happened. An inmate attempted to leave his housing unit without his identification card, which was against institutional rules. An officer confronted the inmate about not having his identification card as he, the inmate, is required to have every time he leaves the housing unit. When the officer instructed the inmate to return to his cell to get his I.D., a brief verbal exchange took place between them. The inmate took exception to the officer's instructions and passively resisted the instructions by slowly walking back to his cell. The inmate's defiant reaction to the officer's instructions agitated the officer and the officer touched the inmate's shoulder to nudge him along. When the officer touched the inmate, this triggered the inmate to react defensively, and the inmate spun around and struck the officer in the face with his fist. At that point, the fight was on and other officers who were in the area quickly responded to the aid of the assaulted officer. There was a brief struggle before they gained control over the inmate, and both the officer and the inmate suffered minor injuries. They both were taken to our Health Care Unit and received treatment for their injuries. The inmate was later placed in segregation. The officer suffered a fractured finger and was permitted to leave the facility to see his personal physician for a more thorough examination of his injury.

After personally talking with both the officer and the inmate about what happened and having personally gone to the housing unit where the incident took place to assess the tone and the mood of staff and inmates, I concluded that this was an isolated and spontaneous incident that was not part of a larger conspiracy by any gang organization to retaliate against staff. For those reasons and other confidential information that I learned about the inmate's mental health, I decided that it would not be in the best interest to lock down the facility in this particular instance. I believed that it would have been merely a punitive response against the entire population to lock down the facility for this inmate's ill-warranted and spontaneous reaction. Had the officer not nudged the inmate, the incident probably would not have occurred. This didn't justify the inmate's assault, but his assault of the officer did not merit the entire facility being placed on lockdown. I also learned from talking with staff and other inmates that this officer had a history of writing disciplinary reports against inmates, as well as being known for provoking and instigating confrontations with inmates. The situation wasn't as one-sided as some staff wanted to make it out to be.

Locking down the facility in this situation would have given the larger inmate population a perceived reason—not a legitimate reason—to create a retaliatory situation against staff. Although some inmates may have wanted and were even glad that the officer got assaulted for his provoking conduct, they would have known that this was an unplanned spontaneous assault and not a conspired situation to retaliate against him. Inmates only need a perceived wrong to justify their actions to strike out against staff. They play the odds that the issue will get figured out later, and they don't usually concern themselves with the long-term consequences of their actions. They usually want and attempt to get immediate retribution for the perceived injustice that they have suffered.

Had I wanted to gain the popularity of staff or exercise a level of authoritative control, I could have easily decided to place the facility on lockdown. I would have then been perceived by some staff as being on their side and would have been given their superficial seal of acceptance. I say *superficial* because as soon as I would have made a decision that they didn't like, I would have been quickly castigated as being against them. Within minutes of learning of my decision not to lock down the facility, a select group of staff began to villainize me by insinuating that I did not regard their safety as being a priority. That of course was also untrue. And as it turned out, the decision that I made was proven to be the more prudent choice. When the inmates were allowed to resume normal movement, they cooperated in going to the dining hall and other activities without further problems. There were no other assaults against staff related to this incident, as some staff tried to create the perception that there would be, and we experienced a reasonable time without other incidents.

It's not uncommon for staff assaults to occur in prison. It's an inherent condition of the job. And because of that fact, a good administrator will always factor in all of the information available to him or her before he or she makes the decision to lock down or not lock down a facility. This can be a split-moment decision based upon knowing the pulse of your institution and the seriousness of the incident, or this could be a delayed decision as you gather more information. Either way, it should be based on the premise of ensuring safety and maintaining control of your facility and not on the premise of gaining popularity with your staff just to be punitive or to exert your authority and control. Trying to be popular for your staff will only lead to someone getting hurt and possibly killed. I wasn't trying to gain the popularity of staff; I was simply administering sound, experienced judgment that was aimed to prevent staff from getting hurt in the interim. A select few staff didn't seem to understand that, nor did they wish to understand it.

As a result of the frequent assaults and disturbances that were occurring at Menard and in our other maximum security facilities, our prisons were frequently on lockdown. The safety and security of a facility is paramount, and lockdowns are the only sure way to maintain absolute control. During periods of lockdowns, programmatic services are interrupted and, consequently, the opportunities for inmates to gain any substantive preparation for rehabilitation or self-improvement are nullified. It's difficult enough to keep inmates engaged in positive programming when a facility is operating normally; it's virtually impossible to keep them from losing interest when you are constantly locked down. When a facility is on an extended lockdown, limited services are occasionally provided to inmates at their cells, but this becomes very taxing on the staff who must provide these services and it is very limiting in its overall effectiveness.

It is widely accepted within the prison community that roughly 10 percent of the inmate population disproportionately creates 90 percent of the problems in prison. It is also a shared belief that most inmates, about 99 percent, would truly like to do their time and go home, but it's the 10 percent that makes it difficult for most of them to live out that goal. They are constantly being pressured and influenced by the intimidations and threats of gang leaders and other rogue inmates, which gives them little choice but to go along or face some form of retribution. This element of prison life was very prevalent when I was in the system, and I have no misgivings that this is still very true today.

Because we were experiencing a significant amount of disruption in our prisons, the agency began to explore options as to how we could best bring more order and control to our facilities. This became even more critical when a videotape of Richard Speck, an infamous serial killer, was released to the public in 1994. A Chicago television station aired footage showing Speck and other inmates getting high and engaging in various sexual escapades in the basement of one of our maximum security facilities. This embarrassing incident exposed how the management of our prison system had become severely compromised and how our high security prisons were teetering on the verge of being out of control.

As a result of this incident, the general assembly ignited a major investigation to thoroughly review the security practices of our agency. A task force was commissioned by Governor Ryan to examine our agency's security practices and to provide recommendations as to how we should correct our errant deficiencies. This spearheaded a major effort by many frontline correctional staff in concert with several prison administrators to ratchet up our lobby efforts for the construction of a super maximum security prison. The purpose of this prison was to help the agency gain better control in managing our maximum security prisons and to serve as a management tool that could be used as a deterrent against the ongoing violence and disruptions in our prisons. At the conclusion of the task force's inquest, they agreed that a super maximum security facility should be built to provide the agency an additional tool to more effectively manage our wayward population. They recognized that our gang problem had reached a critical point of insurrection and their violent behavior could no longer be overlooked. The stage was now set for a test of wills: the lawmakers versus the lawbreakers!

THE GANG INFLUENCE

THERE WERE APPROXIMATELY nine major gangs in Illinois' prison system during the time I worked in the system, but there were several more splinter groups that comprised multiple affiliated organizations from these nine groups. Approximately 97 percent of all inmates in Illinois' prison system are validated gang members, whether they are an active or inactive member. This is a startling statistic when you consider that Illinois has a prison population of over 45,000 inmates. Illinois has a long history of gang-related problems within its prison system, with most of their gangs originating from the Chicago area. Because of this large gang presence, the agency structured much of its operating strategies around the aspect of how to minimize their influence. The gangs' influence has always presented the greatest challenge in managing Illinois' prisons and particularly Illinois' high aggressive maximum security prisons.

The largest gang organization, or Security Threat Group (STG) as they are now referred, operates under the umbrella called the Gangster Disciples, or GDs. Because of their long history of operating inside our prisons, they are a well-structured and sophisticated organization, and they pride themselves on being progressively cunning. Their major enterprise is money-making through selling drugs, offering protection, and gambling. The leader of the organization is referred to as the King, and there is an established protocol for addressing other ranking members through a chain of command. Their symbol of affiliation is the six-point star of King David, and all members are expected to honor this symbolism. In an effort to disguise their involvement with illegal activity within our prisons, they promoted the concept of "Growth and Development" as the mantra for their abbreviation GD. This was intended to project the image that their organizational activities were geared toward personal improvement and oriented toward positive social efforts. In truth, this was just a clever way that they tried to mask the real purpose of their organization's criminal activity, both in and outside the prison walls. They operate from a position of strength in numbers, and they use the threat of violence and/or the force of violence to gain what they desire. They thrive on the fact that they command the attention of the administration, and they use this status to promote their image as being the elite gang organization within Illinois' prison system.

The Latin Kings are the largest and most violent of the Latino gangs in Illinois' system. Members of their organization are usually hardcore members who are extremely loyal. They frequently are involved in assaults, intimidating and threatening incidents, and the manufacturing of contraband weapons that they sell to other gangs. Drug trafficking is a lucrative activity for them as well. With a few exceptions, the high ranking members of the Latin Kings are all schooled in the art of dealing with the administration. They rarely engage in dialogue with prison officials, but when they do, they have a certain style unique to their culture. It is a mixture of machismo, street wit, aloofness, and sophistication that reinforces their reputation as being hardcore and dangerous. If you crossed them, they would surely hold a grudge for a long time and you could count on them to retaliate. Whether it was a rival gang, a correctional staff person, or even one of their own who had violated their code, they would not let a disrespectful incident go without some form of consequence being imposed. This let everyone know that they had better think long and hard before they disrespected a Latin King.

The Vice Lords street gang is comprised of several factions, and they are the second largest gang in Illinois' system. They allied themselves with the Latin Kings under the five-pointed star and are opportunistic in making their presence known among the gang culture. They would attempt to co-opt their influence with other gangs to earn money through selling drugs, trafficking weapons, and engaging in gambling enterprises. They especially do not like being considered second class to their arch rival, the GDs, and would often have conflicts with them to establish respectability among the gang hierarchy. Their leadership was made up of reputable long-term members who had varying degrees of sophistication and long-term experience in gang life. They competed with rival gangs for having their fare share of every form of money-making enterprise in the prison. They use schemes of extortion, bribery and intimidation of staff, and other small time hustles to wedge their way into the lucrative business of gangbanging.

The Northsiders were a white organization that came into existence at Menard primarily because of the need to protect the interest of white inmates from the ever-increasing black gangs that had formed at Menard. As mentioned earlier, Menard is situated in the rural Southern part of Illinois and in its earlier years housed a predominantly white inmate population. This began to change in the late '60s and early '70s when more and more black inmates from the Northern part of the state—Chicago—were sent there to do their time. The Northsiders were a small organization compared to most gangs in terms of their membership, and they allied themselves with other white gangs such as the Aryan Brotherhood and the Bikers. They mainly engaged in activities dealing with drugs, prostitution, assaults, and gambling, not unlike all the other gangs. Their symbolism and gang subculture was heavily influenced by Nazi propaganda, and they advocated white supremacy. Although small in numbers, they were a very hardcore and ruthless organization. They were not afraid to fight or go to war with any gang. They were motivated by their hate of all non-white inmates and sought to gain as much of an intimidating reputation as they could through their violent behavior. They would be just as likely to inflict violence against one of their own for violating their code as they would against a rival gang member. They had no tolerance for members who were not committed to their beliefs.

I recall an incident at Menard when two ranking members of the Northsiders were stabbed to death in separate incidents. One incident occurred in a communal shower area, and the other incident happened in a cell in the West Cell House. Both were killed by members of their own gang. The victims had created problems related to the leadership of the organization—an internal power struggle—and this created enormous tension among their rank and file. A power struggle was not good for the organization and the situation had to be dealt with in a way that left no questions about the message being sent. The Northsiders also had a reputation for being disorderly and routinely provoking incidents due to their regular indulgence of hooch. They weren't considered to be as sophisticated in their methods of operating as some of the larger gangs; however, they were a group that had earned a level of prison respect because of their ruthless behavior.

One of the shared characteristics of all the gangs is that they operate from a paramilitary style structure. There is a clear hierarchy of leadership and a chain of command that ensures all affairs and gang business are handled according to the leadership's directions. By-laws and specific rules have been created to give order and structure to their organizations. Each member has to learn these rules and take a solemn pledge of allegiance to uphold them. Disciplining members to enforce the rules is routinely done through acts of violence and/or monetary penalties. The act of enforcing physical discipline is called a *violation*. This is when a member is beaten about the head and face to instill fear and to induce blind loyalty. The results of these beatings often caused the face and head to swell to unbelievable sizes, which led to the prison slang *pumpkin heads*.

I have witnessed the aftermath of many pumpkin head violations of inmates who allegedly did not honor the rules of the organization, and these scenes were not very pretty. I used the term *allegedly* because many times gang members will set each other up because of power struggles or personal dislikes within their own membership. They will frequently lie on one another about things that were allegedly said or done in an attempt to gain a personal benefit, rank within the gang, or prison recognition. Being in a prison gang is extremely stressful because of the mistrusting and controlling way of life endured by most of its members. Only a few members at the top of the chain actually receive the majority of the monetary benefits of their activities. The foot soldiers receive only cursory benefits based upon what the leader or leaders allow them to have, and that's usually very little.

All of the gangs required their members to pay dues to what they call the *poor box*. This was a collection process designed to buy various items pertinent to the survival and well-being of members who had no resources of their own. Cigarettes, food, gym shoes, clothing, and other items of this type were purchased and given to members who couldn't afford it. However, this was not without its consequences. There was an interest penalty attached to paying back to the box, and if this interest was not paid, other sanctions or forms of discipline would be imposed. In many instances, members would be forced to engage in sexual favors as a way to satisfy their debt. The poor box was often the source of many conflicts that resulted in someone getting violated because members would inevitably misuse the collection of the dues for their own personal benefit and not for the benefit of the organization.

All in all, it was the competition for controlling the drug profits and exercising power through intimidation and violence that caused these organizations to clash with one another. Racial overtones played some role in the clashes between the white gangs and the non-white gangs, but primarily it was the motives of each gang to control the criminal enterprises of the prison that created the greatest source of conflict between them. Internal power struggles among each gang would also periodically occur, and this too would create tension and related problems among their own, which often resulted in violent incidents that prison officials had to deal with.

Even problems that occurred on the streets between rival gangs would create disruptive situations within our prisons, and many times these disruptions had violent outcomes. Due to the pervasive gang influence in and outside of our prisons, our maximum security prisons were always in a heightened state of uneasiness and simmered with the potential to erupt at any moment. The hierarchy of power that was created by the need for each gang to control a piece of the prison landscape added an element of increased tension that permeated the hostile environment of prison life. All it took was a small gesture of disrespect and the entire facility could explode instantly!

Gang Violence Against Staff

As I think about the many incidents that I have witnessed or the ones that I have heard about involving gang violence, there are a few that immediately come to mind. I will share a couple of them with the hope of providing a greater understanding as to the kind of environment that prison officials and their staff have to contend with every day, 24/7 when dealing with gangs.

On September 3, 1987, Superintendent Robert Taylor was killed in the Pontiac Correctional Center. Pontiac was the third largest prison in Illinois at the time and was one of four maximum security prisons in the state. I did not know Superintendent Taylor personally and have never worked at Pontiac. However, by virtue of having worked many years in Illinois' prison system, I had the occasion to visit Pontiac several times and learn of its operation and much of its history. I had been working in the system for two years at the time Superintendent Taylor was killed, so I have a very vivid memory of the state of affairs that our prisons were in when this incident happened.

Superintendent Taylor was stabbed and beaten to death by four inmates of the Gangster Disciples street gang. He was stabbed with a ten-inch shank two times in the chest and four times in the back and sustained several blows to the head with a pipe. He was attacked in his office, which was located in the housing unit that he managed, and it was reported that he put up a reasonable struggle before he was overpowered.

The institutional leader of the Gangster Disciples had called a hit on Pontiac's administrative staff because the GDs were upset about an incident that had occurred a few weeks earlier. One of their members had died as a result of swallowing a balloon filled with cocaine. He swallowed the balloon to prevent it from being detected during a strip search after a visit. Members of his gang believed that staff let him die or in some way were culpable in his death, and they wanted revenge. It was believed at the time that they actually wanted to kill one of the wardens, but Superintendent Taylor was more accessible and he ended up being their victim.

The assault of Superintendent Taylor was their way of communicating to the administration that the gangs were a real threat and that the administration was not immune from becoming victims of their street justice. An assault on administrative staff makes the already high tensions between staff and inmates that much more intense. It takes many, many years for a prison to overcome this level of trauma (if they ever do), and it's a stark reminder that prison life is a very serious matter for everyone. The inmates involved in the murder of Superintendent Taylor were identified and eventually prosecuted. Two were given death sentences and two were given life. In my opinion, this kind of incident underscores exactly why a facility such as Tamms, a super maximum security prison in Illinois, needs to exist, not to mention why the death penalty should as well.

I recall a less traumatic, but nonetheless still very telling, incident of how the gangs would use violence to try and exert control over prison staff. This incident involved another superintendent and occurred at the Menard Correctional Center in 1992, a few months prior to me being assigned there. The superintendent was a personal friend as well as a colleague, and his assault was perpetrated by gang members. He suffered several bruises and several minor injuries that caused him to be hospitalized for several days. In this particular incident, the gang members simply didn't like the way the superintendent was managing the cell house and interfering with their gang activity. So, as a way to intimidate him into backing off, they assaulted him. He was not of the mindset to let them intimidate him, and upon his recovery he stayed vigilant and did not allow their gang activity to run rampant in his unit.

Their motivation for assaulting the superintendent—the signature symbol of a gang's power and viciousness—was partially spurred by their need to save face and uphold their reputation as being a notorious gang. They couldn't just sit back and do nothing while the superintendent continued to disrupt their gang activity of drug distribution. This would make them look very timid in the eyes of the other gangs and their reputation would be tarnished. So, to save face, they assaulted him.

A similar assault was conspired to happen against me and two of my senior unit security staff on our Death Row Unit. However, through the help of an informant, we learned of their conspiracy and were able to intercede before the assault on us was carried out. These are a few examples of the day-to-day concerns that are a constant challenge in trying to safely and effectively manage our maximum security prisons. This is another example as to why it was necessary for our agency to build a super maximum security prison.

An assault of an assistant warden also occurred at Menard. Keep in mind that Menard is the largest correctional facility in Illinois, and the gang activity there was extremely prevalent. In this particular incident, the assistant warden was touring the prison grounds with other VIP staff when he was unprovokingly confronted by an inmate. The inmate came out of nowhere, catching him totally by surprise, and punched the assistant warden violently in the face. The assistant warden fell backward onto the walkway and, being unable to break his fall, struck his head on the concrete, causing him to be knocked unconscious. He was hospitalized for several days afterward and he never returned to work. He suffered emotional and physical side effects from the assault and subsequent head injury.

Neither the administration nor the assistant warden had done anything against this inmate. The assistant warden regrettably became the victim of a prison gang's hardcore violent lifestyle. His assault occurred as a result of an initiation ritual that some inmates are required to go through in order to prove their loyalty when joining a gang and being considered a hardcore member. The inmate who assaulted the assistant warden was a young inmate who was serving a life sentence. He didn't have anything to lose, as far as being convicted for another assault, because he knew that he was never going to get out of prison anyway. It is this type of inmate—young, scared, easily intimidated, seeking protection, and doing a lot of time—that is used to carry out these kinds of assaults against staff.

Within a few hours of this incident, the inmate was transferred to our super maximum security prison, Tamms, where I was assigned as an assistant warden at the time. Tamms proved to be the right level of custody for this inmate. Due to the high profile nature of the incident, it was decided that an administrative level person should conduct the disciplinary hearing. Disciplinary hearings are a mandatory procedure for all rule infractions designed to ensure that each inmate is properly afforded their legal due process. Normally, a lesser ranked security personnel would conduct this hearing, but because of the magnitude of this incident involving a senior administrative person, it was deemed more prudent for a higher-ranking person to conduct the hearing. I was the higher-ranking administrative person selected to perform this duty.

The hearing did not immediately take place when the inmate initially arrived. A thorough investigation of the incident had to be completed before this could happen. However, a preliminary hearing was conducted to formally cite the alleged rule violations and to continue the proceedings until the investigation was finalized. The investigative period would afford the inmate the opportunity to prepare for his defense and to be ready to offer a written and/or verbal account of his version of the incident. Disciplinary hearings are not criminal proceedings; they are only an administrative procedure that is routinely performed for all rule infractions. A criminal proceeding would only occur if an official charge of "Assaulting an Employee" was filed with the local District Attorney's office. In this incident, charges were filed for prosecution. An inmate could actually end up receiving administrative sanctions as well as criminal sanctions for violating an institutional rule.

Once the investigation was completed, it proved to be a pretty straightforward hearing. Although the inmate offered a defense for why he assaulted the assistant warden, his justification did not merit any leniency. The fact that he acknowledged being the perpetrator of this planned assault warranted a decision of guilt, and his actions justified his placement in a more secure and restrictive confinement. He was recommended to receive the maximum administrative sanction that could be applied for an assault charge—one year revocation of good conduct credits, one year demotion in C grade status, and an indefinite term of segregation placement resulting in his confinement at Tamms. His home would now be in our super maximum security prison for a very, very long time.

The examples that I have shared all dealt with administrative personnel, and although assaults against administrative personnel do occur, they are the exception rather than the rule. The majority of the assaults that occur against staff are perpetrated against frontline correctional officers who are duty-bound to be in the trenches every day. They are the folks who endure the constant onslaught of being threatened, punched, and spit on. They have hot liquids and human feces thrown at them. They are stabbed and, even worse, killed. They are the true heroes when it comes down to literally fighting with the inmates who persist on being problematic. There are countless incidents of assaults on frontline staff that I could have easily mentioned rather than the assaults that I did mention. However, my purpose for selecting administrative staff was to highlight the reality that everyone who works in a prison, whether they are an administrative person, a non-security person, a civilian volunteer, or a security officer, is subjected to the violence and dangerousness of inmates. I will offer other examples to add credence to this point.

On December 14, 2009, at the Pinckneyville Correctional Center, a medium security facility located in Southern Illinois, an inmate took a female librarian hostage in the prison library. To put this incident in context, Pinckneyville houses an average of 2,200 inmates, which is more than it was designed to hold, and it too is dangerously overcrowded. After several hours of failed negotiations, the agency authorized a tactical team unit to execute an assault plan. The team executed an assault plan that resulted in the inmate being shot and killed. The librarian was rescued unharmed and taken to a local hospital for appropriate medical attention. As I state throughout this book, prison life is oftentimes a very unforgiving experience. For this particular inmate, he experienced the harsh reality of losing his life by way of deadly force, and his surviving family members have been left to mourn the tragedy of his death. For the librarian, her life will forever be impacted by the recurring thoughts and anxiety associated with being victimized by an inmate, and her family members will have the lifelong challenge of helping her overcome that traumatic experience.

I was very fortunate not to have been assaulted in any serious way during my years in the system. However, I was assaulted once, although it was extremely minor in comparison to many of the assaults I witnessed inflicted upon other staff. I was an assistant warden assigned to our super maximum security prison when my assault occurred. One day while conducting rounds in the housing units, I stopped to talk to an inmate at his cell door. He wanted me to address his dissatisfaction about being at Tamms. In hindsight, I now know that his complaint was only a lure to get me to stop at his cell, but he was an inmate who frequently complained about many things so it was not unusual for him to start complaining when I walked in his unit.

This inmate was a member of a white prison gang, and he had made it very clear to me on several occasions prior to that day that he did not like me simply because I was black. He also had made it known that he resented the fact that I had authority and control over him. Despite his overt dislike of me, I dealt with him as I did with every other inmate. If he presented a legitimate issue, I would attempt to ensure it was addressed properly. However, my interactions with him were a little more guarded than usual since I was armed with the knowledge of knowing his dislike up front. My cautionary approach with him was not entirely due to his expressed racist attitude toward me, but stemmed primarily from the approach that I took to try and always be aware of an inmate's state of mind and the context for which we interacted.

Understand that there were many black inmates who disliked me as well and probably would have loved to do harm to me too. I attributed much of their dislike of me to a learned self-hatred mentality, much like the black-on-black crime syndrome that causes many young black males to inflict harm upon one another. And to illustrate this point, the two assaulted superintendents that I mentioned earlier, the one who was killed and the other who was hospitalized, were black and were assaulted by black inmates. So the color of my skin was not necessarily a protective shield of immunity from being assaulted by black inmates. As mentioned earlier, black-on-black crime is just as prevalent in prison as it is in many black neighborhoods. This made the odds for me being assaulted by a black inmate versus a non-black inmate very high. I could have easily become a victim of this misguided way of thinking on any given day of my career. I was not naive to that possibility.

When I approached this inmate's cell, I noticed he was acting a little peculiar, somewhat agitated and fidgety. He was normally calm and collected. The way our cell doors were designed, you could see directly inside the cell through small dime-sized holes that were cut into the physical structure of the door. Try to imagine a solid steel door with lots of small holes from top to bottom. That's what the door looked liked. Our cell doors were designed with this perforated pattern so that staff would have the advantage of being able to see what was taking place inside the cell at all times.

As I began to talk with this inmate, keeping my eye on his every movement, a lieutenant entered the unit to ask me a question about another situation. In responding to the lieutenant, I took a few steps backward away from the door and turned my head slightly toward the direction of the lieutenant to respond to his question. In that brief moment of stepping away from the cell door and turning my attention away from the inmate, the inmate grabbed a cup of water from his sink and threw it on me striking me in the face and chest area. That was the extent of my assault and, as I said, that was the only assault that I experienced throughout my career. I have been threatened thousands of times, but those threats were never acted out until that moment.

I reacted to this by simply instructing the lieutenant to write the inmate a disciplinary report, and I activated our tactical team to come and perform a cell extraction of the inmate. When the tactical team arrived, the inmate complied without putting up a fight. He was handcuffed and removed from his cell. I placed the inmate on what is called *property reduction status*. Property reduction is an administrative sanction that authorizes the removal of an inmate's personal belongings from his cell for a specified period of time. As an administrator, I had the authority to take any of his personal items, such as his mail and reading material or everything in his cell, including his clothing, bed linens, and mattress. Placing an inmate on property reduction sometimes resulted in all of his property being removed and the inmate sleeping on a cold concrete slab without a mattress, pillow, or bedsheet. In this incident, I authorized all of his belongings to be removed with the exception of his clothing.

A lot of times inmates do things that they think will get them favor among their fellow inmates, and this was one of those moments. The inmate had gotten his frustrations out and he was feeling pretty good about his assault on me. However, I know that because of the level of security that he was subjected to at Tamms, his ability to inflict more harm to me was greatly restricted. Had I been in another security setting where the level of control of inmates is not as restrictive, such as Pinckneyville or even in our maximum security facilities, the outcome of my assault would have probably been a lot different.

After his fun-in-the-sun moment was over, it was back to business as usual. I dried myself off and continued making rounds in the cell houses, talking to staff and other inmates. The other inmates in the unit had been watching to see what my reaction would be so they could learn how they might push my buttons too. The games inmates play are very subtle and they absorb every bit of information they can about you so they can find a way to use it against you. That is why I always took the approach to be consistent with how I interacted with each inmate so they would have less of a chance to exploit me.

9

MAXIMUM SECURITY

THE MAJORITY OF my correctional career was spent working in maximum security and/or super maximum security settings. Each of those settings offers different memories and experiences for me. Some I will never talk about, and others I will replay over and over again in my mind for as long as I have the ability to remember. One such moment happened during my first tour of duty at Menard when I was an assistant warden.

We had received information from our Gang Intelligence Unit that issues between the Latin Kings and the Gangster Disciples were beginning to stir up again. There are many moments in prison when rivalries and bad blood between prison gangs turns into violent encounters, and these situations can be, and oftentimes are, bloody incidents. Gangs typically try to cohabitate with one another, but it's usually done with a very guarded sense of suspicion and extreme caution.

Our Intelligence Unit had provided us with information that indicated there was an explosive situation brewing between the Latin Kings and the GDs, and we needed to diffuse the situation if possible. This meant that we needed to talk to the leaders of both gangs very quickly to see if we could sort out what the problem was and bring some level of understanding to the issue before it got ugly. Well, before we could act on the information, the situation erupted!

In our East Cell House, which is the largest cell house at Menard, members of these rival gangs clashed into a hellish fight. Their skirmish prompted an officer who was assigned to our catwalk area to fire several warning shots in an attempt to get them to stop fighting. In most instances, officers use a 12-gauge shotgun to get the inmates' attention. The shotgun is used first because it makes a tremendously loud booming sound when shot inside our concrete cell houses, and this would normally get the inmates' attention right away. Secondly, the shotgun is used as the first option in the use of lethal force because it is less likely to cause a fatal injury when shot from a long distance. Officers are trained to shoot their warning shots into shoot boards that are positioned in the upper corners of each cell house. Inmates understand clearly what this sound means and usually comply immediately when they hear the first shot fired. Collateral injuries are always a high probability when a shotgun is fired because an inmate could receive non-fatal wounds from the ricocheting of the gun pellets, which has happened on occasions. Officers are also armed with a mini-14 rifle that they will use as a secondary option in the use of lethal force, when it is determined that an imminent threat of bodily harm is about to be inflicted against a staff person or another inmate.

In this particular incident, the warning shots from the shotgun did get the inmates to break up the fight, but it did not force them to go into their cells and lock up as they were instructed to do. The inmates knew that as long as they did not display any further aggressive or violent behavior toward each other, the officer was not authorized to use lethal force against them. So instead of locking up in their cells as they were instructed to do, they stood their ground and engaged in a verbal standoff!

Both groups were shouting threats and insults back and forth at each other and trying to incite the whole cell house to become involved. The officers who had been assigned to supervise that gallery were able to get off the gallery safely and keep the inmates contained on the gallery. The officers' ability to contain the incident to this one gallery prevented the incident from spreading to other parts of the cell house. The two groups had taken up positions at opposite ends of the gallery facing one another and daring the other to make the next move. Although they were yelling at and taunting each other and creating a very dangerous situation for that particular cell house, it was a greater concern to us that this situation could become an even larger disturbance for the rest of the facility. Once the word got out that the Latin Kings and the Gangster Disciples were at odds with each other, it was inevitable that the conflict would spread. These situations can easily escalate and get out of control very quickly.

Upon receiving radio communication about what was occurring, Warden Page, Assistant Warden Cowan, several of our unit superintendents, and other security personnel immediately rushed to the East Cell House. When a major incident happens, protocol requires that at least one of the top three administrators remain in a neutral location or a command post area so we can communicate with our executive commanders, such as the assistant deputy director, deputy director, or director, if the situation warranted the director's involvement. This protocol is also established to safeguard administrators from becoming victims of a hostage situation and/or becoming incapacitated during an incident and thereby putting the leadership of the facility in jeopardy.

If the warden or the highest ranking administrator is overtaken in an incident, they automatically forfeit their authority to give commands, and this could render the facility leaderless. The protocol of having someone remain in a neutral location serves to ensure that there will always be someone in an administrative position of authority to direct the management of a facility's operation in an emergency situation. In this incident, I remained in the warden's office to direct the management of other logistical operations of the facility. I maintained radio communications with Warden Page as he responded to the cell house to investigate what was actually occurring and what would be the best response to bring this situation under control.

While Warden Page and the other security staff responded to the incident, I contacted our deputy director to advise him of the situation. While I was contacting the deputy director, Assistant Warden Cowan was instructing other security personnel to ensure that the facility was secured and that all movement was immediately stopped. The safety and well-being of everyone, staff and inmates alike, immediately becomes the focus when disruptive incidents occur, and swift, decisive actions must be taken to ensure that this is accomplished. In situations like this, the overall safety of a prison rests in large part on having multiple contingency plans and how quickly we respond.

Just as important as having these plans, the execution of these plans hinges on the administrator's ability to quickly discern which contingency will be the most effective plan in any given situation. Not only that, being prepared to adapt your plans to fit the circumstances is equally critical to the success of bringing a situation like this to order. In this incident, Warden Page's savvyness was aptly demonstrated and the incident ended without anyone getting hurt. I frequently updated the deputy director of our ordeal until the situation was resolved.

When Warden Page arrived at the cell house, he was given a quick debriefing by the captain of that unit as to what had taken place up until that point. After Warden Page assessed the situation, he gave explicit orders to the two groups to stand down and prepare to exit the gallery. The inmates were so hyped up and agitated with hostilities toward one another that they defiantly ignored Warden

Page's commands and continued to shout threats and insults at each other. The standoff was on!

Having met resistance in getting them to comply with his orders, Warden Page gave instructions to our tactical team commander to assemble his unit and prepare for a use-of-force confrontation. If the inmates continued to refuse all orders to comply, our tactical team would be authorized to use whatever measure of force necessary to gain total control of the situation. Chemical agents and the use of explosive disorientation devices would be their first measure of force. This would be done to subdue the inmates and make them less resistive when the tactical unit entered the gallery. If they continued to resist after that, the use of force would escalate in its severity.

Every prison has a special unit of officers who are trained to respond and handle inmate protests. Because Menard was the largest facility in our agency, we had over 100 officers trained to respond to these kinds of situations. While the tactical unit was being assembled and getting into position, Warden Page's next plan of action was to give one last set of commands to the inmates to come off the gallery before force would be used. If they continued not to adhere to his orders, he planned to instruct our commanding officer, the major, to shoot a warning shot directly above their heads.

If this level of intent did not render their compliance, he would then order the tactical team to execute their assault plan and use whatever level of force necessary to gain control of the situation and remove all the inmates from the gallery. When Warden Page gave his final commands to the inmates, they realized that the deployment of the tactical unit was in position and ready to engage them head on. Realizing they were at a disadvantage, the inmates begrudgingly complied with Warden Page's last order and they came off the gallery one inmate at a time without incident. As the inmates exited the gallery, they were immediately placed in handcuffs and escorted to segregation.

In a situation like this, the facility is normally placed on lock-down until a thorough investigation is completed. The investigation would attempt to determine the issue or issues that caused the confrontation and to reasonably assure us that once we resumed normal operations there would not be any retaliatory response by either group. A lockdown could last for one day, one week, or indefinitely. It just depends upon the seriousness of the situation that led up to the lockdown and the lingering effects that could surface once we come off of the lockdown. In this case, we were locked down for several weeks.

Over the course of the next few days, we talked to the leading players who we knew were responsible for giving the approval for this incident to happen. From those conversations, we ended up transferring two ranking members of the GDs to other facilities within the state, and we transferred one member of the Latin Kings. This was the standard operating procedure for how we managed our ongoing gang problems. The need for a super maximum security prison was long overdue and, without question, desperately needed.

THE WAR ON GANGS

BEFORE I TALK about the implementation of Illinois' first super maximum security prison, I will share some historical background as to how we operated prior to its inception. From the early '80s to the late '90s, several Illinois prisons, and particularly our maximum security prisons, were managed with a unique style of inmate conciliation. Administrators routinely acquiesced to the demands of gang leaders in an effort to avoid acts of violence and disruptions in order to balance the thin line between safety and chaos. As much as this was the reality of how we operated, I was often conflicted with the belief that inmates should be made to comply with the rules without regard to their say in the matter. But I knew that there was a certain reality that existed—inmates outnumbered staff and were willing to use violence at almost any cost to get what they wanted. I felt that there had to be a better way to manage our prisons, and it seemed so foreign to me that we had to bargain and negotiate with inmates in order to manage our prisons. But the truthful reality was, we did.

Negotiations between administrators and gang leaders were daily occurrences. They were done with the intention to keep staff from getting hurt and, sometimes, to prevent inmates from getting hurt as well. These conciliatory agreements would sometimes involve allowing rule infractions to go unpunished or minimally punished at best. For example, if an inmate was caught with hooch, homemade alcohol, in his cell, instead of requiring him to remain in segregation for the maximum length required, he would be released after spending a marginal portion of his time in segregation. In some instances, an inmate might not even be placed in segregation. For their return concession, gang leaders would offer their commitment not to assault staff or create other conflicts between rival gangs, with the expected return of receiving certain privileges. These privileges would be things such as allowing gang leaders to select which inmate was given a particular job assignment or to have an inmate's visitation restriction reinstated. These were common scenarios that involved administrators and gangs co-opting our prison existence in order to survive.

Our conciliatory method of management was spurred more from a lack of resources and political intervention than from a deliberately chosen operational style. I often wrestled with why persons in positions of political leadership and influence would not be diligent in their commitment to address our agency's limited resources to effectively combat our gang problem. Not supporting our need to increase the inadequate ratio that existed between staff and inmates was completely baffling to me. I never understood this and I never agreed with the arguments that were put forth to defend their position. This was one of the few issues that I wholeheartedly agreed with the union on—the need to increase frontline correctional staff.

Prison officials with limited staffing cannot provide the proper level of supervision necessary to enforce good security practices. It's unrealistic and impractical to think otherwise. Inadequate staffing creates very dangerous conditions for breaches in security to occur. Something will inevitably go wrong, and then the powers that be will be looking for a scapegoat to blame for the breach. Inadequate staffing also contributes to increased burnout of staff and, consequently, other security problems tend to manifest from this one area of deficiency. I could never come to terms with understanding the politics of why some things were the way they were. However, as I came to learn more about prison management, I discovered just how influential politics was with regard to the way prisons are managed.

Some of the conciliation that took place between administrators and gang leaders was fostered by laws that resulted from lawsuits filed by inmates. These court rulings gave more latitude to inmates to exercise their rights and to be entitled to receive certain privileges. The more sophisticated gangs took advantage of these legal loopholes to advance their own influence and reputation among the inmate population.

Inmates oftentimes try to turn privileges that have been granted to them through court rulings into actual rights for them. An example of this is job assignments. Job assignments are privileges in prison, not a legal right. However, inmates oftentimes argue the position that if they are not given a job assignment, prison administrators are violating their constitutional rights. They file grievances and frivolous lawsuits on issues such as this. On the other hand, religious beliefs and the customs associated with those beliefs are constitutionally established as an inmate's legal right. However, this legal precedent was and still is a major area of manipulation by inmates. Inmates frequently attempt to misuse this legal authority to exercise certain liberties of their religious rights to obtain special privileges. Inmates have argued for the right to smoke marijuana or drink wine as a part of their religious rights. Obviously, these types of religious practices are not consistent with the safety and security of prison management and are prohibited.

Gangs cleverly use religious symbols to represent their gang affiliation and declare the constitutionality of their religious freedom as the precedent for them to do so. An example of this would be the six-point star of King David. This religious symbol was adopted by the Gangster Disciples street gang to represent their allegiance with their organization, and their members were required to wear it at all times. Because the Star of David is a recognized and accepted religious symbol and is a permissible item to possess in prison, members of this gang would purchase this medallion and wear it openly to signify their gang affiliation. The wearing of the medallion for them had nothing to do with their religious faith. It was exploited as a means to promote their gang affiliation. This is but one example of how inmates attempted to use their constitutional right to express their freedom of religion while simultaneously, and ingeniously I might add, promoting their affiliation and loyalty to their gang culture. The level of their sophistication is quite refined.

Inmates in the Black Mafia street gang would use the Moorish Science Temple of America's half-crescent moon enclosed within a circle as their symbol. Other gangs had their chosen symbols as well. Once we realized how these symbols were being incorporated into their gang culture, the agency instituted a policy requiring that all religious medallions had to be concealed underneath the inmate's clothing, except when worn inside their cells or when participating in an authorized religious event. This did not violate their constitutional right to express their religious faith because they were still permitted to possess any religious medallions of their choice. However, due to the penological interests of safety and security that prohibited the overt representation of gang symbolism, we could and we did restrict the manner by which religious items were displayed. Their attempt to use religion as a front to perpetrate and promote their gang activity was just one of many strategies they used to manipulate constitutional rights to their advantage. Gang leaders are very good at creating a perception of legitimacy using constitutional law to support their illegitimate intentions. They constantly seek ways to exert influence and control over their members, and misrepresenting legitimate rulings of law is a frequently used tactic. They will attempt to use any legal loophole that they can in an effort to infuse it into their gang lifestyle so they can be perceived as legitimate.

To offer another example of how gangs attempted to take advantage of privileges afforded to them, I'll share the following case in point. In an effort to be more responsive to the issue of strengthening inmate/family relationships, our agency instituted a practice called Inmate Family Picnics. Inmates were permitted to receive visits from family members in a more social context. Inmates could visit with their family members on the inside grounds of our prisons and not be restricted to the normal visiting room arrangement. These visits would take place in the recreational yard of the facility and would occur during the summer months to help minimize summer tensions in our maximum security facilities. Food would be catered from our Dietary Department and various outdoor activities such as softball, basketball, and football would be allowed. This gave the inmates an opportunity to interact with their families in a more sociable atmosphere. All of this was supervised by correctional staff to ensure that no breaches in security occurred. This event was intended to give the inmates an incentive to maintain positive behavior during the hot summer months and to encourage family contact.

However, as with most situations in prison, when gang members wedge themselves in between opportunistic situations, they usually try to influence and control who among them will ultimately benefit the most from the privileged opportunity. In this case, gang leaders began to use their leverage of intimidation to coerce administrators into letting them select which inmates they wanted to participate in the event versus those inmates who truly deserved to participate. They even began demanding that family members who were restricted from visiting be allowed to visit. Over time, the inmates developed the attitude that they were entitled to have this special event and that they, not the administration, should be responsible for who selected which inmates could attend.

This arrangement eventually became a pawn used by the inmates to negotiate for other forms of privileges, and the agency was not about to give them this kind of power. In addition to the concern over who controlled the event, several security issues also developed. Drug trafficking became a major problem. Sexual encounters between inmates and their visitors frequently occurred, and inmates were frequently being caught high on drugs or intoxicated from drinking homemade alcohol. This privileged opportunity had turned into more than just a family-oriented event. The agency eventually recognized that the decision to allow this event to occur proved to be an unwise decision and wisely discontinued this privilege altogether.

As I alluded to earlier, two key factors that contributed to the conditions in which prison officials engaged in conciliatory negotiations with inmates were our overcrowded conditions and the lack of resources to effectively deal with our most problematic inmates. When there are more inmates in your custody than you have room to effectively manage, inmates will quickly learn of their advantage and use it to their benefit. Intimidation tactics are their primary method of choice. If inmates can intimidate prison officials into letting them get away with certain situations, take my word for it, they will. They are masters at it! Although this conciliatory style of management didn't happen by choice and it developed subtly and gradually over many years, it nonetheless became an accepted way of life within Illinois' prison culture. It was an extremely complicated dilemma compounded by layers of outdated prison practices competing against an ever-changing prison culture.

Shifting the balance of control back into the hands of prison officials would require that we take a drastically different approach in the way we operated our prisons, and it would also require a major shift in the agency's way of thinking about how we would deal with our gangs. Overcrowded conditions severely limit an administrator's ability to effectively maintain order. When those limitations are stretched to the breaking point, the situation then becomes conducive for areas of weakness in your operation to be exploited. That is exactly what happened in Illinois' system. Inmates seized their opportunities to take advantage of our administrative weaknesses and they exploited the limitations and deficient practices of our system.

Our system had become ineffective in several areas of our security practices, and the consequences of this ineffectiveness manifested themselves through our conciliatory style of management. One of our shortcomings was the fact that we did not have enough segregation beds to house the number of inmates that needed to be put in segregation. Consequently, in order for us to put an inmate in segregation, we would oftentimes have to release other inmates from segregation without them completing all of their segregation time. That's like the police letting someone out of jail who shouldn't be out of jail just so they can put someone else in jail who needs to be in jail. This was a very crippling position for our management.

The limitation of not having adequate segregation housing for our problematic inmates gave impetus for the gangs to freely engage in inappropriate activities with a sense of immunity. There were just not enough teeth in our authority to impose the deterrent effect that our disciplinary sanctions were intended to have. Administrators would often negotiate with gang leaders in an effort to persuade them from creating problems. This was done primarily for the overall safety of the facility, but also for the logistical concern of not having enough cells to put inmates in when they did create problems. It was this recurring cycle of having to deal with limited management resources combined with the reality of being outnumbered by very aggressive and violent inmates that gave reason for administrators to do what we thought was in the best interest of keeping the facility from erupting. We were simply trying to survive and keep staff and inmates from getting hurt and, even worse, from being killed. Sometimes our conciliations paid off and other times they did not!

Because of the tacit power that was given to the gangs through our conciliations, they frequently used their leverage of intimidation against us. The fear and threat of a staff person being assaulted was a real fear, and because of that reality, many staff persons would find themselves aiding and abetting gang members. Some staff would choose not to write an inmate a disciplinary infraction for fear of being retaliated against, even though the inmate had clearly violated the rule. In some instances, staff would even aid inmates in their illegal activities of trafficking drugs and other contraband into our facilities in an effort to try and earn the inmates' protection. It was a very complex game of survival and control for everybody involved, administrators, staff, and the gangs.

It is well-known in the prison world that anything that happens involving a gang-affiliated inmate only happens with the approval and sanction of the ranking leader or leaders of that gang. There are a few exceptions when a renegade member acts of his own accord and causes problems, but notwithstanding that exception, only gang leaders give orders to create problems. With that knowledge being universally understood as to how gangs operate, it only made sense that our approach for reclaiming control of our prisons would focus on the gang leaders. This is where the concept of our super maximum security prison gained its most notable popularity. It was also the impetus for giving us an additional management option to enforce greater leverage of control in our prisons. We were positioning ourselves to take our prisons back!

As I mentioned earlier, 10 percent of the prison population creates 90 percent of the problems in prisons. In Illinois' system, that 10 percent can be attributed directly to the gang leaders who control the behavior of 90 percent of all the other inmates. When the conduct and/or presence of a gang leader became too threatening or too disruptive, one of our security methods in dealing with that inmate was to transfer him to another maximum security prison within the state. This served to remove that particular inmate from being an immediate threat to the facility that he was in, but it did not serve to resolve the problem entirely because the threat that he created was most often associated with himself rather than with the facility that he was being removed from.

The issue of him being a threat at one facility was now simply shifted to another facility, and the warden of the new facility now had to deal with the same potential threat. This was a short-term, stall-for-time method of managing that was only effective for the immediate situation of a particular facility. It prevented the initial facility from having further problems associated with that inmate, and it usually caused the current problem to subside. That facility was then able to regain some sense of normalcy because the threat had been alleviated, but the issue of the inmate's *threat factor* never went away. It just relocated with him to another facility.

Another procedure that we used to deal with gang leaders and problematic inmates was transferring them from one facility to another facility every 30 days. We called this putting an inmate on the *circuit* and the inmate was referred to as a *circuit rider*. This procedure was designed to be punitive. It reduced the inmate's ability to use his influence against staff and other inmates and prevented him from becoming too familiar with his surroundings. This practice also served to disrupt his adjustment to settling down into a routine, which kept him off balance. His ability to communicate by mail and/or visitation was also significantly disrupted by this practice. A circuit rider would be kept on the circuit for as long as he kept creating problems or for as long as we felt it benefited the safety of the agency as a whole. However, there was no long-term deterrent effect associated with this method of imposing discipline to gain their compliance with the rules. When this method proved to be ineffective, our last resort was to send them out-of-state to another prison agency.

Most prison agencies participate in an arrangement called an Interstate Compact Agreement. This agreement allows prison agencies to exchange difficult to manage inmates from one prison agency to another. Illinois utilizes this agreement as a last resort method of deterrence for problematic and high-profile inmates that persist on being non-compliant. This method of punishment is intended to send a clear message that the gang leaders and other problematic inmates will be sent as far away as possible in order to lessen their negative influence within our prisons. In other words, we wanted to take away the power base of gang leaders by significantly minimizing their influential status, and transferring them out of state gave us that option.

The act of singling out gang leaders who were a threat to our system oftentimes heightened the glamorization of their hardcore status and, in turn, emboldened their reputation within prison folklore. Nevertheless, when we weighed the consequences of their heightened reputation within prison folklore versus their menacing presence in our prisons, we always sided on the side of safety and security of our prisons. Once a gang leader or problematic inmate was identified as a continual threat, we would transfer them as quickly as the ink could dry on the signed agreement and as fast as we could put them in a van. Not only did this buy us relief from their threatening presence and influence, but this created a condition of extreme hardship for the inmate.

Once transferred out-of-state, the inmate would not be able to receive routine visits from their family and friends, as they were accustomed to receiving. This also served to significantly alter their ability to communicate and continue their subversive gang activity. Gang leaders do not want to be in a prison system outside of their own state because it lessens their influence among their power base and it makes their leadership vulnerable to an overthrow. The great likelihood of an out-of-state transfer was usually enough of a deterrent to force gang leaders to lay low and be more compliant for longer periods of time. However, because the pressure is so great for them to continue demonstrating their leadership, they inevitably find themselves in situations that challenge their leadership role, and these challenges usually lead to confrontational or disruptive situations. Whether the problem was due to an internal power struggle, a gang rivalry, or retaliatory actions against the administration (meaning any correctional staff person), the gang leader felt compelled to take some kind of action to keep his leadership from being viewed as weak. This awkward predicament placed him in a situation where he would defend his reputation by reacting in ways that would bring unwanted attention to his role as leader. When that happened, we held him responsible for any problematic situation that occurred and targeted him to be transferred out-of-state immediately. They usually did not want this kind of high profile attention, so they tried very discretely to keep the peace and avoid making any trouble for as long as they could. This method of disciplinary control had a slightly longer deterrent effect associated with its enforcement.

However, one of the limitations in using the Interstate Compact Agreement was that it was a costly arrangement. Each state bears the expense for the custody of the inmate they exchange. For that and other reasons, our agency was very selective in deciding how many inmates we would have out-of-state at any one time. This kept our numbers very low. In my opinion, the long-term impact of using the Interstate Compact Agreement was marginal. This method of disciplinary management did not have the overall impact of reducing problems in our day-to-day operations that we would have liked to experience. Removing one gang leader from power did nothing more than make room for another gang leader to step up and take his place. We were still faced with the same problems in dealing with gang-related issues—internal power struggles, gang rivalries, staff assaults, drug trafficking, etc. This method of security management only served to punish the gang leader by cutting him off from his base of operation and influence. It did nothing to actually curtail or stop the prevalence of gang activity. And another shortcoming of the Interstate Compact Agreement was the fact that we usually ended up receiving an equally problematic inmate from the reciprocating state. And more often than not, they created more problems for us than the inmate we transferred. So in essence, the exchange of inmates normally ended up being a trade-off.

What the agency needed was a facility specifically designed to manage our aggressive and problematic inmates. We needed a facility that was geographically isolated from the general public for enhancing public safety; a facility with heightened methods of security, custody, and control; and a facility conducive for long-term housing of non-compliant, dangerous, and disruptive inmates. These elements would give our agency a much-needed management tool for which we could impose immediate and/or long-term disciplinary actions against inmates who persisted in being problematic and non-compliant. The agency operated from the perspective that if the 10 percent of our problematic inmates were removed from our general populations, the remaining 90 percent would comply more readily with the rules and be less disruptive, consequently making the operation of our facilities safer and more conducive to a better prison environment. This philosophy was the genesis for why the Illinois Department of Corrections sought to build a super maximum security facility.

THE RISE OF ILLINOIS' SUPERMAX SYSTEM

BECAUSE OF THE agency's increasing concerns for how to regain control over our prisons and better manage our highly aggressive inmate populations, the idea to build a super maximum security prison received much interest and support. In January 1994, George Welborn was appointed as warden of Tamms, Illinois' first and only super maximum security prison. I had worked for Warden Welborn as a unit superintendent the previous year at Menard and was very confident in his ability to manage a super maximum security prison. Warden Welborn had previously worked in other responsible positions within the agency and had several years of experience as a senior administrator in maximum security.

When Warden Welborn was appointed to be the warden of Tamms, his position as warden of Menard became vacant. His position was filled by Thomas Page, who at the time was the Assistant Warden of Operations and second in command. Warden Page's position as the Assistant Warden of Operations was then filled by

Roger Cowan, who was one of our unit superintendents. The Assistant Warden of Programs at that time was reassigned to another facility, and I was appointed as his replacement. That is how I became the *first* African American to be appointed to a senior level administrative position in the 116-year history of Menard. The fleeting moment that I had experienced just a year earlier in the foyer of the warden's office—imagining my picture displayed on the wall with all of the previous wardens of Menard—was now closer to becoming a reality.

This was the first time in the history of Illinois' correctional system that all three top administrative positions of a maximum security prison were filled at the same time. I had only been assigned to Menard the year prior to receiving this promotion, and this, in effect, was the beginning of my career as a senior level administrator in prison management.

My appointment to Menard's administration was also historic in another way. The Director of the Illinois Department of Corrections at that time was the first African American to have been appointed to the position of director. His name is Howard A. Peters III, and he was an exceptionally dynamic administrator who had risen to leadership as an astute correctional professional. It was ultimately his decision that gave me the opportunity to make history at Menard. His confidence in me to take on this responsibility set a precedent that would open the door for other African Americans in later years to be appointed to positions of senior management at Menard.

Director Peters's appointment of me as an administrative warden gave me the chance to have an impact on how our agency would operate and, more specifically, how Menard would operate. He stated to me at the time of my appointment that if I could survive managing Menard, which he referred to as the Super Bowl of prisons for our agency, I would be able to manage any correctional facility in the country. His football analogy was used to highlight the tremendous challenges that lie ahead of me in order for me to be successful at helping manage this facility and become a good administrator. Similar to the physical, mental, and emotional challenges that are required of coaches, assistant coaches, and their players to win a Super Bowl, there are parallel challenges for wardens, assistant wardens, and their staff in effectively managing a maximum security facility.

Director Peters gave the analogy of the entrenched gang presence that was so disruptive to our everyday operations and how we would be challenged with keeping this under control. He spoke about the overcrowded housing conditions of Menard that presented many systemic problems as well as litigation challenges that were an outgrowth of these problems. He referenced the antiquated physical design and structural integrity of the facility, which presented ongoing challenges with maintenance up-keep that directly impacted how we would ensure that good security practices were implemented. He also spoke very candidly about the intense scrutiny that I would receive based upon the cultural opposition of some staff who would be resistive to my role of authority because of their inherent prejudices against me as a man of color.

And lastly, he referenced the constantly changing dynamics of corrections itself due to politics, legal mandates, national prison crises, and other peripheral situations that would have a direct influence on prison life and inevitably affect how we would operate our prison. He knew that all of this would require a tremendous effort of teamwork and cooperation between our newly appointed administrative staff in order for me personally, and for the facility in general, to be successful. These challenges only served to fuel my determination not to fail, and I am forever indebted to Director Peters for giving me the opportunity to have had a respected influence upon Illinois' prison agency.

Upon his appointment as warden of Illinois' first super maximum security prison, Warden Welborn spent the next three-and-a-half years planning the operation and construction of the facility. He visited several states throughout the country to study the physical designs of their supermax prisons, their staffing patterns, their security procedures, their programmatic services, and their litigation issues to ensure that our practices would meet and/or exceed prison confinement standards. Because super maximum security prisons were extremely controversial then (and are still today), the implementation of intense security procedures and highly restrictive programmatic services required well thought out and carefully written policies.

Every aspect of how this prison would be managed would be contested through litigation as well as from human rights groups. Warden Welborn understood this very clearly and structured the operation of our supermax prison with that element being the central foundation of our management philosophy. How would our security procedures and custodial practices stand up against litigation? This would be our toughest challenge to overcome and it would become the litmus test for the agency's ability to properly use our super maximum security prison as the tool we needed it to be. And we needed it desperately to help us more effectively manage our highly aggressive inmate populations, both from the physical violence that they perpetrated against staff and other inmates and from the increasing number of lockdown days that their threats of violence and disruptions were causing. The agency knew of the immense challenges that lie ahead, and we were positioning ourselves to take them on without apology or fear of the criticism that was sure to come.

Being Schooled in Prison Management

During the three-and-a-half years that Warden Welborn was preparing for the opening of our super maximum prison, I was at Menard being schooled in the skills of managing a highly aggressive prison population. This education not only included learning how to manage inmates and the physical plant operation, but also included learning how to manage a culturally biased staff. Being the first African American warden at Menard—albeit, an assistant warden at the time—placed an extraordinary level of expectations and responsibilities on me. Director Peters made it very clear to me that I would be thoroughly scrutinized and tested for how I would handle my new role. As much as he was speaking about the challenges of dealing with a very aggressive and violent inmate population, he was speaking equally about the challenges I would face from the predominantly white staff, and his words were never so true.

However, three years and nine months later, after surviving many harrowing challenges at Menard, Warden Welborn extended an offer to me to become his Assistant Warden of Operations and to help him operate Illinois' first super maximum security prison. I apparently had passed the capability test at Menard and had demonstrated the ability required to help successfully manage a Super Bowl-caliber prison. I accepted his offer and would now be responsible for managing the security operations of Tamms. I was officially appointed as the Assistant Warden of Operations, second-in-command, on October 1, 1997.

Warden Welborn's selection of me represented his level of confidence in my ability to assist him in managing the highest security prison in the Illinois Department of Corrections. My appointment to Tamms was certainly a major highlight of my advancing career and the beginning of a very special relationship between Warden Welborn and me that remains to this very day. However, as much as I respected and greatly appreciated Warden Welborn's selection of me to be his second-in-command, I would be remiss if I did not mention that my ultimate appointment to Tamms was due to the decision of another African American director, Odie Washington. Director Washington succeeded Director Peters in becoming the second African American to be appointed as Director of the Illinois Department of Corrections. And just like Director Peters, Director Washington was also a seasoned correctional professional who was extremely talented in his abilities to manage our agency. His support of me also contributed greatly to my professional success as a correctional administrator.

Our super maximum security prison was an innovative but reactionary response to the ever-increasing problems that our prisons were facing due to ongoing inmate violence and constant disruptions. The operation of a super maximum security prison would be a new challenge for our agency and one that would require a lot of oversight and intimate involvement from our legal department. The prevailing sentiment of many individuals and human rights groups is that super maximum security prisons constitute cruel and unusual punishment. Well, without the proper checks and balances built into the philosophy of how a closed facility is operated, then yes, the potential for it to be mismanaged and consequently have an adverse affect on the inmates confined to this level of custody could occur. The term *closed facility* simply means a prison that is managed with tighter and more secure procedures than conventional prison custody, and the inmates confined there are separated from the general population.

Contrary to popular belief, super maximum security facilities *do not* drive people insane as the advocates against super maximum prisons would have you believe. This is the primary argument that advocates against super maximum prisons use to advocate shutting down these types of prisons. It is, however, logical and reasonable for any sensible person to believe that long-term "isolation" would contribute to the debilitation of one's mental health and therefore cause someone to go crazy. However, the term *isolation* is often misrepresented when talking about super maximum security prisons. This term is usually intended to imply that the inmate is undernourished, given poor clothing, has no means for proper exercise, has limited medical care and is confined to a cell that has no windows, no lights, and no adequate bedding. Have such conditions existed in prison settings before? Regrettably, yes they have. And if a prison were to operate in this manner today, I would be the first to agree with the advocates' position that such confinement constitutes cruel and unusual punishment. However, the more accurate use of the term *isolation* for my purpose simply means separating non-compliant and problematic inmates from the conventional confinement of a general population setting.

The design of Tamms, as with most contemporary super maximum prisons, is atypical to what most people visualize when they think of a super maximum security prison. People generally imagine a place such as the Alcatraz prison and the horrific stories associated with prisons like Alcatraz or the exaggerated and distorted Hollywood versions of prison life. Tamms is not the stereotypical version of isolated confinement as depicted in sensationalized movies. However, is Tamms highly restrictive in its regimentation of security and custodial practices? The answer is a resounding *yes*! It was designed for that purpose. But does this constitute cruel and unusual punishment? The answer is a candid *no*!

Two of the major questions that had to be answered before we could place any inmate in Tamms were "Which inmates would be placed in Tamms?" and "How long would they remain in Tamms?" Because Tamms was designed to be a small facility consisting of only 520 beds, the "right" inmates had to be placed there in order for the deterrent effect and stabilizing condition of our facilities to be actualized within the day-to-day operation of our prisons. There were over 45,000 inmates in Illinois' prison system during the time I worked in the Department, and 520 beds were an extremely minimal option in comparison to our overall prison population. However, we were confident that if we placed the right inmates in Tamms, the rest of the inmate population in our agency would get the message and fall in line.

From the research that Warden Welborn had done, our agency decided that we would have two types of inmates confined to Tamms and that their minimum stay would be 12 months, pending their behavioral adjustment and/or their security threat as a high-profile gang leader or problematic inmate. The two types of inmates were a *segregation inmate* and an *administrative detention inmate*. A segregation inmate was one who was already confined to a segregation unit in another facility but continued to exhibit disruptive and non-compliant behavior within that unit. An administrative detention inmate was an inmate who was in a general population setting who had not technically committed a rule infraction per se but had a documented history of gang affiliation and/or leadership influence. Housing inmates in segregation status would be a much easier position to defend against any legal challenges, whereas housing inmates in administrative detention status would require a more detailed and documented justification.

The mere fact that segregation inmates were already confined separately from the general population because of their non-compliant behavior and the fact that they continued to demonstrate non-compliant behavior in segregation gave us a sound penological rationale to justify their placement in Tamms. On the other hand, for the administrative detention inmates, our rationale would be held to a much higher standard and would require a more sound justification against the inmate's claim of loss of liberty. Their loss of liberty argument would be based on the premise that because they had been living in a general population setting and had not been found administratively guilty of any rule violation, their placement in a more restrictive and controlling environment was purely punitive, retaliatory, and without penological justification. We had to doubly ensure that the documented evidence we relied upon to place this classification of inmate in Tamms would be substantially credible, be reflective of a preponderance of gang activity, gang involvement, and/or influence, but more importantly, be corroborated by good solid investigative information.

The litigation test regarding their claim of loss of liberty was an inevitability that could not be avoided. Knowing that this would be the case, we knew that we had to be very prudent in how we developed our operating procedures because these procedures would be extremely critical in determining how we justified our penological interest of safety and security. The agency knew that a super maximum security prison was our last option for trying to restore control in our prison system, and it was essential that we do our due diligence to prepare for all criticism, both legally and otherwise.

Identifying the Bad Guys

While our administrative policies and the actual physical construction of Tamms were being completed, the wardens of our four maximum security facilities were commissioned by Director Peters to begin reviewing their populations to identify which inmates would be recommended for placement in Tamms. This undertaking transpired over the three-and-a-half year period that it took for Tamms to become operational, and this involved several meetings of the minds between the wardens, our legal advisors, and our executive directors. These meetings were very tedious, time consuming, and thorough, but were an absolutely necessary process for developing the *right* criteria for identifying the *right* inmates and for establishing the *right* level of control that would be needed to stabilize our prisons.

This process required the collaborative efforts of all of the Inmate Intelligence Units in each facility. They collected thousands of pieces of information that were used as supportive documentation for recommending high-ranking gang leaders to Tamms. This was a very critical undertaking and required a shared effort of cooperation and knowledge between the wardens of each of our maximum security facilities. Each warden had to systematically review each gang organization in their respective facility and identify the members who they considered appropriate candidates to be sent to Tamms. At the end of this arduous three-and-a-half year ordeal, there were 100 inmates identified as major, high profile candidates who would initially be placed in Tamms. Several hundred more were identified and would also be transferred to Tamms over time.

On a bright, warm, unceremonious day, Tamms opened its doors on March 12, 1998, with the arrival of eight inmates. We received a total of 40 inmates during that initial week and continued receiving inmates over the next several weeks until we reached a placement level of 240 inmates.

Tamms consists of eight primary housing units each constructed in a quadrant-style design and one specialized unit constructed in a half-quadrant-style design. The eight primary units are designed with six wings in each unit and consist of ten cells per wing, five cells on the lower gallery and five cells on the upper gallery. Each unit has the capacity of housing 60 inmates. Our Specialized Unit was designed to house 40 inmates. It was never the agency's intention to fill all 520 beds at any one time. The agency wanted to have a contingency of available beds in the event that an emergency or major disturbance occurred in one of our facilities. The additional cells at Tamms gave the agency the ability to immediately transfer inmates to a secure location in case of such an emergency.

The first inmate that we received at Tamms was the most notorious inmate in our prison system. His name is Henry Brisbon, also known as Omar. Prior to his placement at Tamms, Brisbon was housed on our Death Row Unit, and he was already separated from having contact with other inmates. He had been placed in a specially designed cell located in a quarantined section of our Death Row Unit at Menard. The interior of his cell had been modified with stainless steel paneling to prevent any possibility of him destroying his cell and making a weapon from broken pieces of concrete or metal. His cell door was made of solid steel and secured with a three-foot long, 2 x 4 metal plank. His quarantined living arrangement was designed to restrict his ability to have access to any conventional prison living. These security precautions were a result of the continuous threat that he exhibited toward staff and the extraordinary influence he had over other inmates. He was extremely manipulative and influential in getting other inmates to assist him in carrying out acts of protest, disruptions, and assaults.

One of the incidents that contributed to Brisbon's special condition of confinement prior to his placement at Tamms was a conspiracy that we uncovered involving him and another death row inmate. They were conspiring to assault two of my ranking security staff as well as myself. One of my responsibilities as an assistant warden at Menard was to provide administrative oversight for our Death Row Unit. Any changes in security procedures would be reviewed by me first and then submitted to the warden for his review and ultimate approval or disapproval.

As part of the supervision of this unit, I had a superintendent and a captain assigned to handle the day-to-day management. One day while acting on a tip, we searched Brisbon's and his accomplice's cells and discovered several musical cassette tapes that had been converted into conversational tapes. He and the other inmate had figured out a way to record messages to one another using their music cassette tapes as a clandestine way to conceal their conspiracy. After listening to the tapes, we learned of their scheme to assault me and my staff. They were planning to assault us in protest of a new security procedure that we had implemented, which involved strip searching the inmates going to and from their visits. This procedure was one among several things that Brisbon disliked about how we managed our Death Row Unit. The discovery of this conspiracy led to his restricted confinement at Menard about a year or so prior to his placement at Tamms. And the only reason why he wasn't immediately transferred to Tamms at the time of this conspiracy is because Tamms had not yet been built.

Brisbon was initially sentenced to prison for two consecutive life terms of 1,000 to 3,000 years for the brutal slaying of three people in 1973. His crime is commonly known in the Chicago area as the I-57 murders. According to news reports and court records, he and three other men would ram their car into the back of other cars on the interstate causing the motorists to pull over. When the occupant(s) of the vehicle would get out, Brisbon and his accomplices would take them captive and murder them. In the case that he was convicted for, it is reported that after he forced a car to pull off the road, he made the occupants, a young couple, get out of the car and lay face down on the ground. The couple was reported to be engaged. Allegedly, Brisbon forced the fiancé to watch as he, Brisbon, shot and killed the intended bride with a shotgun blast to her back. He then shot and killed the fiancé. The case was highly sensationalized by the media reporting that the couple had pleaded mercifully for their lives before being killed. It was even rumored that Brisbon made a chilling comment to the couple before he shot them. The comment was allegedly something to the effect of "Kiss your last kiss," and then he shot them.

At the time of his sentencing in March 1977, the death penalty in Illinois was not validated and could not be imposed. His life was spared due to the controversial debate over the constitutionality of the death penalty. Because the death penalty was invalid, the judge had no choice but to spare his life. As an alternative to the death penalty, the judge sentenced him to a term that reflected the gross contempt that the court had for Brisbon's heinous act. He sentenced Brisbon to a term of 1,000 to 3,000 years. Had the death penalty been validated at the time of his conviction, there is no doubt in my mind that he would have been sentenced to the death penalty. In part because he was black and the victims were white, but more so because of the senseless and heinous disregard that he demonstrated for human life.

Because Brisbon was not put to death, his violent and predatory nature had the opportunity to kill again, and he did, but this time the death penalty had been reinstated. Brisbon killed an inmate while serving his life sentence, and that is when he received the death penalty and was placed on death row. I highlighted Brisbon's case only to serve as an illustration of one type of inmate that Tamms was designed to house—a dangerously violent and manipulative inmate, a continuously problematic inmate, and a major security threat to the agency. However, Brisbon was just one of many.

Another type of inmate that Tamms was designed to house was the high-ranking gang leader. The reckless violence and subversive criminal activities that gangs repeatedly engaged in inside our prisons as well as outside in the community led to their reclassification from being called gangs to being labeled Security Threat Groups, or STGs. Their continuously threatening and disruptive behavior had developed into a serious problem and had become a major threat to law and order for our communities and for our prisons. Their predatory and violent activities had become a disruptive menace within our maximum security prisons. Our agency focused its attention on the high-ranking leaders of these organizations, and they became the targets of our efforts to bring order and control to the day-to-day management of our prisons.

We knew that the leaders of these organizations were the ones who organized their activities, made all the decisions for their activities, and had earned their status through ruthless and/or cunning means. They typically had a more sophisticated style of operating than their members, and, as a rule, they would not be the person who would actually carry out any of the gang activities such as assaults, protests, or smuggling of drugs. However, they were the ones who orchestrated the activity, gave the approval for the activity, and directly benefited from the activity. We wanted to remove their presence from our facilities to help reduce the level of gang activity within our prisons, and Tamms provided us the option to do that.

Tamms was also designed to house inmates who were identified as being extremely high escape risks. These are inmates that have either escaped from a prison or some other level of law enforcement custody or have demonstrated a consistent pattern of possessing escape materials such as homemade handcuff keys, drawings of escape plans, and letters discussing plots to escape. Inmates who attempted to escape from prison would obviously become a threat to the public if they were to escape. Because of the increased level of security at Tamms, it provided a higher level of protection for the general public against potential escapes. There have been no escapes from Tamms since its inception in 1998, and I think it would be fair to say that Tamms has certainly served its purpose in that regard.

When Tamms was built, our strategic management for curtailing the gang problem in our maximum-security facilities took on a more aggressive approach. In December 1999, slightly less than two years after Tamms had been in operation, the agency implemented a Gang Renunciation Policy. This policy was intended to allow gang members who wanted to get out of the gangs a legitimate avenue by which to do so. The customary and unofficial way of getting out of a gang was known as dropping your flag or retiring. When a gang member dropped his flag or retired, got out of a gang, or became inactive, prison officials could only verify this by word of mouth from sources within the gang. Although this form of verification proved to be fairly reliable, there was no official record that we could rely upon to document this for administrative or legal purposes.

The renunciation policy was intended to provide the agency with a quantifiable way to document an inmate's renounced inactive status. Although, in principle, the concept of our renunciation policy was based upon sound logical reasoning, in practicality it had its shortcomings. Every inmate in the agency who considered himself to be a gang member, whether they were validated as such or not, would now have the option to willingly and officially renounce their affiliation if they wanted to get out of their gang. This could be done through a systematic and confidential process that involved the Internal Affairs Division of each facility. It required the review of the warden to authorize the final decision to approve or deny an inmate's request to renounce. However, the implementation of this policy had a very specific condition associated with it for inmates who were assigned to Tamms. This condition stipulated that any inmate who was assigned to Tamms *had* to renounce their gang affiliation before consideration would be given to them for their release back to a reduced security setting. This was not a condition for inmates in other security settings. It only applied to inmates housed at Tamms.

This condition, however, created a very dubious dilemma for how we would transition inmates back into our general populations. For the most part, the inmates assigned to Tamms were the hardcore, diehard leaders of the gang hierarchy. They would rather die first (or at least that was the superficial impression that they wanted us to believe) rather than renounce their affiliation. And herein lies our dilemma. If these hardcore inmates were to choose not to renounce their affiliation, they, in effect, sealed their own fates to remain at Tamms for the remainder of their prison terms because no other consideration would be given to them for being transferred out of Tamms. And therefore, for all practical purposes, they would never leave Tamms.

However, if they elected to renounce their affiliation, they felt that they would be betraying their loyalty to their gang family. This, they claimed, would seal their fate for their own death or that of a family member because of retaliation by their own gang. They believed that they were being put between a rock and a hard place in having to choose to renounce their affiliation or remain in Tamms. If they didn't renounce their affiliation, they would be in Tamms forever, and if they did renounce their affiliation they would be looked upon by members of their gang as a snitch, and their life or a family member's life would be in jeopardy. The reality was it was their choice to be in a gang that put them there, not the Illinois Department of Corrections who they were now trying to blame for their current misfortune of being housed at Tamms.

The renunciation process involved gang members being interviewed by members of Internal Affairs and an administrative official. In the case of the renunciation process at Tamms, I was the administrative official. A series of questions would be asked of the inmate to determine his level of sincerity to renounce his affiliation. Our questions were based upon factual information that had been obtained through many, many hours of research. We had documented evidence corroborated by court records, police reports, institutional records, tape recordings of telephone conversations, confiscated gang documents, and other credible sources. We did not ask an inmate to snitch on his gang members, as was the common belief about this process. To the contrary, we simply wanted them to acknowledge their involvement and/or knowledge of certain activities that we already knew were factual. If an inmate did that, that gave us reason to believe that he was sincere in his effort to get out of the gang and attempt to finish the remainder of his time without continuing to be a threat to our agency.

Upon answering truthfully about his knowledge of the questions we asked, his appeal to renounce would be approved. At that point, he would be given consideration for a transfer out of Tamms. However, if he chose to minimize, disassociate with, be less than forthright about what he knew or straight-up lied to us about his role in his gang's activity, this gave us reason to believe that he was being less than sincere in his actions to renounce his affiliations and was only trying to manipulate his way out of Tamms so he could resume his gang influence. Our renunciation process prevented high-ranking gang members who had no intentions of changing their behavior once back amongst their power base from returning to our general populations. The renunciation process was used as a check and balance review process for transfers out of Tamms.

On the other hand, a shortcoming of this process was that many inmates could potentially vegetate in Tamms and not ever be given the chance to conform to the rules of a reduced security setting. However, for a select few, their long-term confinement to Tamms was the best option for the overall safety of the agency. But for the majority, preventing them from returning to a conventional prison setting would prove counter-productive over time. The effectiveness of Tamms was contingent upon its ability to transition inmates back into a conventional prison setting after a prolonged period of isolated confinement so that these inmates could spread the word that Tamms is not the place you want to be.

The carrot and stick concept of the behavior modification strategy that Tamms was designed to be could potentially lose its effectiveness as a management tool if inmates were not given the chance to demonstrate compliant behavior in a conventional prison setting after spending considerable time in Tamms. This would be counter-productive to the overall purpose of how Tamms was intended to be used, and the renunciation process added another layer of controversy for our critics.

I participated in 100 renunciation interviews at Tamms and very few of them involved the major players. Most of the hardcore leaders chose to take their chances on riding it out and playing the odds that time would work in their favor. They wanted to be known for standing on the principle of not being broken by the system. Some of them are still there because of this diehard belief. I never learned of any gangs retaliating against those inmates who did earn their return back by renouncing their affiliation. So, the notion that their lives would be in jeopardy was not ever actualized by any accounts that were ever reported to us. The stipulation that required inmates at Tamms to renounce their affiliation before being returned to a reduced security setting was met with mixed feelings.

However, the prevailing school of thought was that the majority of inmates who were confined to Tamms would at some point be given the chance to return to a general population setting. This would either be through a direct transfer or through a step down process. Either way, if they later demonstrated that they were still a threat, the agency always had the option of returning them to Tamms, and this time their placement would be for a very long and indefinite period of time.

I have attempted to provide you with some insights as to the intimidating and life-threatening behaviors perpetrated daily by inmates confined in maximum security facilities nationwide, but more specifically confined in Illinois' prison facilities. I felt that this aspect of prison life was important for you to know in order for you to develop a better understanding and appreciation for why Tamms and other super maximum security prisons are built. They are not built with the intent of inflicting cruel and unusual punishment. To the contrary, their primary purpose is to aid in the control of the most problematic and dangerous inmates in prison settings while at the same time being a tool by which a prison agency can manage the overall safety of its prison population more effectively. For those who still disagree and oppose this level of prison custody, I offer no apology because prison life is as prison life dictates.

12

DEALING WITH RACISM AND SURVIVING THE PRESSURES OF PRISON LIFE

AT THE ONSET of my assignment at Menard to manage the Segregation Unit, I was met with some resistance from a few staff. My initial gut instincts told me that their resistance was primarily due to me being black and having the authority to give them orders. As I mentioned in the opening chapter, Menard is located in a pre-dominantly white rural community and it had a reputation as being a highly racist prison.

Menard was a very close-knit and closed prison community. It was very guarded against outsiders, and I was definitely an outsider. Although there was a fair representation of black employees working at Menard when I started there, there were only a few black staff assigned to the Segregation Unit.

Some of the resistance against me was due in part from them not knowing exactly what to expect from me. They perceived me as a college-breed boy who had only worked in a medium and minimum security facility up until that point. I wasn't viewed with having any real experience in dealing with gangs in this type of prison setting. I think many of them were apprehensive about how I would handle this kind of inmate population. I remember getting the impression that the staff felt as though I had not earned my position to supervise them because I had not yet experienced the blood, sweat, and tears of prison life that many of them had faced while working in a maximum security prison. I'll admit, maximum security is a different animal.

To some extent they were right; I had not experienced what they had. But what they didn't factor into their premature judgment of me was my ability to use my interpersonal communication skills and apply my common sense exceptionally well. My training in psychology along with my mother's wit and street sense would prove to be a great asset in this environment. Nonetheless, with those oppositional perspectives at play, I strategically tailored my approach for how I would establish my leadership within this unit.

The opposition against me because I was black became evident very quickly. There was one sergeant in particular who was looked upon by many of the officers in this unit as the leader for how the unit was managed. Although I had a captain and a few lieutenants assigned to help me manage the unit, this sergeant was the one guy that many officers seemed to give their allegiance to. It was a representation of the good ole boy mentality that was entrenched in many of the prison staff. I learned very early that this sergeant harbored deep racial animosity for black people and he didn't mind letting it be known. I quickly sized him up as the likely individual who would become the test case for how I would enforce the management of this unit.

His racist attitude came to a head one day when I confronted him about some racial comments that he had allegedly made about me. He had made racially derogatory comments about me very openly in the presence of inmates and staff, and his comments got back to me. I questioned him about his comments in the presence of my unit captain. I wanted my captain, who was also white, to be a witness to my conversation to neutralize any false reports about how I had addressed the situation. I did not want what I said or how I handled the matter to be misrepresented if it had just been the sergeant and me having the conversation. In short, the sergeant admitted his racial dislike for me and admitted making the comments reported. In response to his acknowledged racial attitude, I immediately had him removed from my unit. I could not nor would not be placed in a position where my authority to manage this unit was going to be openly undermined by one of my staff or any other staff for that matter. The tone of my leadership had to be established quickly or else I would have lost the chance to earn any respect from my staff or the inmates.

My ability to gain the needed trust and confidence in me from staff and inmates would have been lost had I allowed his conduct to go unchallenged. Although this situation was predicated upon a racial element, he being white and me being black, it wasn't so much about his racist attitude toward me that was my major concern. It was more so the dangerousness of his attitude and how his negative influence upon staff could lead to the disruption and unsafe operation of this unit. He was a very dangerous presence within this unit because his prejudiced conduct and racial attitude could cause someone to get seriously hurt. He could have not liked me because I was black for the rest of his life. That didn't bother me nor was it a personal concern. But it instantly became a management concern when he chose to openly display his racism in my unit. His inappropriate conduct put staff and inmates' lives at risk due to his racially motivated behavior.

Racism is a highly sensitive and potentially explosive issue for inmates in prison, and his conduct was completely unacceptable and made this unit very unsafe. Was I to accept his blatant defiance of my authority and passively tolerate his undermining of my leadership or was I going to take some measure of corrective action and confront him? In hindsight, I believe that this was partially why Warden Welborn assigned me to this unit—to bring a more involved level of management and to confront the suspected abuse of authority by some of the staff assigned there. The answer to my question was an easy decision for me to make. I stayed, he left.

The Segregation Unit is a closed unit, which means that the staff who are assigned there are usually handpicked and the camaraderie among them is extremely close. The relationships and attitudes that form between staff assigned to a unit like this is very similar to that of the code of silence that police departments have been known to experience from select officers in their police force. Although I knew that I was not there for them to like me, and it did not matter to me if they did or didn't, I was astute enough to realize that it would be prudent of me to establish a cooperative but guarded alliance with staff in order to have a reasonable chance to safely manage this complex unit.

My approach was to be highly visible and accessible to both staff and inmates. A combination of observing, listening, and talking with staff was the strategy that I used to gain allegiance within this guarded and untrusting world. This approach was officially called *management by walk around,* but I looked at it as *getting to know the pulse of the institution.* This was the only way that I felt would prove dividends in getting to know both the staff and the inmates. As the senior manager of this unit, it was critical for me to develop a good sense of how this unit operated. I needed to be actively engaged in the day-to-day operation of this unit in order to be able to provide trusted and sound guidance. It proved to be a reasonably effective approach.

With time, I gained a respected level of trust and confidence from most of the staff as they learned that I would not automatically take the side of the inmates simply because I was black and had the authority to make decisions in opposition to theirs. Many of my staff believed that this is what I would automatically do simply because I was black. However, I am convinced that they found my approach surprising and somewhat reassuring as well when they learned that I would also seek their input before I would make a decision about how certain matters would be handled. Demonstrating that their opinions and perspectives were important in deciding the safest and most effective way to manage this unit helped them develop the confidence in me to dispel their initial apprehensive attitude. Once they learned that my primary objective was for the overall safety of the unit, they developed a more respected confidence in my leadership.

I also gained a reasonable level of respect among many of the inmates. I demonstrated to them that I would listen to their complaints and would follow up as I said I would even if the end result was not what they wanted, and in most cases it was not. It was important for me to have them understand that I knew that inmates did not always lie about every situation and that staff did not always tell the truth. It was within this context of exaggerated ambiguity by both staff and inmates that made learning the subtle dynamics of this unit essential for my successful management and survival. It was also equally as essential for me to learn this for the successful management of the general prison population and for my overall survival in prison culture.

Fighting the Dark Side

Trying to survive and remain well-balanced in prison culture is an ongoing challenge for staff just as much as it is for inmates. I'll attempt to share some insights into the ways in which we—prison administrators—coped with the pressures of prison life and how that served to strengthen our bond and kept us from adopting a jaded perspective of what our purpose was.

As I mentioned in the opening of the book, Menard sits on the banks of the mighty Mississippi River. There is a bridge about a quarter of a mile east of the facility that crosses the river and connects Illinois to Missouri. On some of the more challenging days that we would face, my assistant warden counterpart Roger Cowan and I would often joke with one another about how it was time to go sit on the bridge. Roger was an old-fashioned, homegrown country guy who had a heart of gold and grew up working in the prison. He had been there 20-plus years at the time we met. By mere proxy, Roger had developed a very good understanding of how to deal with inmates and their gang-related activities. I probably learned more from him about dealing with gangs than from any one person I worked with.

Roger had worked in the prison system about ten years longer than I had. He stood about 6 feet 3 inches tall with broad shoulders, and he had very common facial features. Although he was a tall, fair-sized man, his demeanor was not intimidating or threatening at all. He projected a very even-tempered nature and was a good-hearted guy, but he was certainly capable of being tough when it came time to be tough. There is a story that we often teased Roger about. It happened one day when he responded to an incident where a group of inmates were threatening not to lock up. When Roger learned about the situation and responded to where the inmates were protesting, he firmly told the inmates that if they didn't lock up right now, he would order the officer on the catwalk to blow their motherfucking heads off! Obviously, they locked up, and that's an example of Roger's toughness as well as the kind of mindset it took to manage our prisons. Although Roger had a nice-guy personality, he was definitely no pushover.

Anyway, getting back to my story about Roger and me sitting on the bridge, we would engage in a playful banter with one another about who was going to jump first. We even embellished our story a little bit by adding the exaggeration that we took our state-issued pistol with us to the bridge and placed it between us. We would then dare one another to either jump or shoot ourselves, claiming that it was better for us to end it now than to continue dealing with the shear madness that the gangs were constantly creating for us. This is a very cursory example of the odd but most essential humor that we relied upon to help us cope with the many challenging days of intense life-threatening situations. Obviously, there were many days that our humor was nowhere to found. But likewise, there were many times when our humor was the sanctified anointing that helped us get through the day. And at the end of the day, it was simply divine grace that protected us all!

When I was appointed as an assistant warden of Menard, Tom Page was appointed as the warden. Tom was the opposite of Roger. He was a short 5 feet 8 inches tall, high energy, feisty individual, but like Roger, Tom was also a good-natured homegrown country guy. One of the personal things I learned about Tom was that he is deathly afraid of snakes. So, on many days, Roger, me, and some of our staff cohorts would hide rubber snakes in and around Tom's desk so that when he would open a drawer or move papers around he would get the scare of his life. His reactions were priceless! Because Tom never knew when we were going to pull this prank, it was always hilarious to see his short little body jump ten feet in the air when he got surprised by the rubber snake.

There were several of my prison colleagues from Menard and other facilities that I would classify as straight-up Looney Tune cartoon characters. They made prison life a lot more tolerable with their real, homegrown, down-to-earth humor. There was even an assistant deputy director who worked very closely with us, but who I will keep nameless for his own privacy, who was the looniest of us all. He made it his life's purpose to ensure that we never allowed a day to go by without experiencing a laughing moment. He truly believed in the resiliency of humor's power to conquer the pessimistic syndrome of the harsh negativity of prison life. The humor that we shared with one another was our way of coping with the tremendous pressures that we dealt with every day. We tried to preserve our sanity by extracting as much humor as we could out of the insane reality of what we were charged to do. We could have very easily drifted into the dark side of a jaded mentality that is commonplace in a prison environment had we not made it a priority to pay attention to our own well-being. Humor was one of our outlets.

Our everyday environment thrived in constant negativity that was filled with threats, intimidation, disruptions, manipulation, assaults, violence, and death. Dealing with these adverse situations day-in and day-out for years on end created a level of respect, trust, and loyalty between us that fused our friendships for life. But make no mistake in your assumptions about our playful humor, because when it came time for us to perform our duties, we did so with the utmost degree of professionalism and with an extraordinarily acute sense of diligence. Difficult and challenging situations oftentimes unite people in unanticipated ways, and working with several of my colleagues under these extremely stressful and demanding conditions produced a relationship between us that fostered a genuine regard for one another. This allowed us to work well together for the good of everyone involved, staff, inmates, and the public.

There was a pervasive attitude among a few staff—primarily among the ranks of correctional officers, sergeants, and some lieutenants—who did not like to see inmates treated with respect or any kind of decency. They would oftentimes misuse or abuse their authority whenever they felt they could get away with it. When they would observe another staff person, particularly an administrative staff person, interact with inmates in a respectful manner it would seriously agitate them. Any act of decency that was extended to an inmate went against their mindset of being superior and better than the inmate. They didn't believe that an inmate was worthy of being respected and they often voiced their vile dislike for anyone that showed an inmate respect by labeling that person a "hug-a-thug."

A *hug-a-thug* is a prison term created by correctional staff to project a negative perception about any staff person who treated an inmate with respect. This was an absurd but real attitude that administrators had to constantly deal with from some of our staff to ensure that inmates were treated fairly. It was a constant effort of putting out flames before they became full-blown, out of control wildfires. Some staff would instigate situations with inmates only to have another staff person become the victim of the inmate's retaliation. Some staff didn't seem to have a clue or, worse, didn't seem to care how their mistreatment of an inmate would create an unsafe situation for themselves or their co-workers. They simply relished in the idea of having the authority of being in a position of power to degrade an inmate without experiencing much, if any, consequences for their actions. There is no doubt that I was labeled as a hug-a-thug because I always made it my business to treat inmates with respect whether their behavior warranted it or not.

Some staff would also play games of exploitation with administrators, similar to those the gangs used with administrators. The comical part about this was that they, the staff, didn't seem to realize that we knew that they were playing those games. It didn't matter to most administrators that some staff would talk negatively about us when we weren't around and then pretend that they were supportive of our leadership when we were. Those games were played all the time. They would frequently create false gossip about what we had said or didn't say or what we had done or didn't do. They simply reveled in the idea of creating negative propaganda against us to try to undermine our authority. I simply dealt with those kinds of staff with a no-nonsense approach and kept it by the book.

Let me just say for the record and make it perfectly clear that the few staff that did not like me because of my approach in dealing with the inmates or because I was a black administrator in a position of authority over them were in the minority. There were far more staff who treated me with respect than those who did not. I

141

can confidently say that I formed some of my best lifelong friend-ships with many of my white colleagues and co-workers. They served to counterbalance the narrow-mindedness of those jaded few who harbored racial animosities. And throughout my career, I benefited greatly from a strong support group among many of my black col-leagues and black co-workers, which was extremely essential to my overall survival and success. From the many intense and challenging moments that I underwent with both my black and white colleagues, we formed a camaraderie that produced a bond of mutual respect. And because of our ability to extract a portion of humor from the everyday challenges of our job, we were able to stay grounded to the reality of what we were faced with every day. This helped us see the humanity of life in a much more appreciative way and elevated us with a sense of duty and moral high-ground to rise above it all.

THE DEATH PENALTY
IN ILLINOIS

WHEN THE IMPLEMENTATION of Tamms was being considered, a critical penological component was factored into its physical design. This component dealt with the dubious function for which Tamms would serve. In addition to housing the worst of our worst inmates, Tamms was charged with the responsibility of carrying out the state's most severe level of capital punishment, the death penalty. The act of carrying out a sentence of death is known as *legal homicide*. Legal homicide is the lawful statutory sanction that gives a state the constitutional authority to take a person's life. However, before I continue to talk about the death penalty and the controversial perspectives surrounding its value or lack of value for society, I will provide you with some historical context regarding the death penalty and executions in Illinois.

The very first execution in Illinois happened in 1866, the year after the Civil War had ended. An inmate who had killed a deputy warden while trying to escape from a county prison was hanged.

Since that auspicious beginning, records show that 248 other individuals were hanged in Illinois between 1866 and 1928, but it was the introduction of the electric chair in 1928 that changed how executions would be carried out in Illinois for the next 34 years.

Between 1928 and 1962, 98 people were executed in Illinois by use of the electric chair. However, many advocates and human rights groups who were against the death penalty vehemently argued that the use of the electric chair was a barbaric and uncivilized method of punishment for a society that claimed to be civilized. Because there had been so many reports of botched executions using the electric chair, opponents argued that it was cruel and unusual punishment to take a person's life using this method of retribution. As these groups gained public sentiment and legislative support, the tenor of society's moral compass began to shift regarding how a human life should be taken. This shift in attitude ushered in a strong resentment against the use of the electric chair and ultimately caused the discontinuation of executions by this method in Illinois.

In June 1972, the U.S. Supreme Court voided all state death penalty laws citing that they were *"racially discriminatory and haphazard."* Prior to this decision by the court and during the period of reprieve on executions granted by the Supreme Court's ruling, there was a growing sentiment among many people in the criminal justice field who felt the need to develop a more humane method of performing executions. This sentiment received growing acceptance among many supporters of the death penalty, and a new method for how inmates would be executed was eventually developed. This new method has now become the most widely accepted form of execution used today; it is lethal injection. With the introduction of lethal injection in 1978, a dramatic turn in the way correctional agencies would now carry out executions changed almost overnight.

Upon the reinstatement of the death penalty in June 1977, states across the country welcomed this decision. This decision gave states the legal right to reserve their discretion for the use of capital punishment for the most serious crimes against society. So, in 1978 when the lethal injection process was introduced, advocates for the death penalty touted this as the most humane way to carry out a court's compelling mandate of legal homicide. The pendulum had now swung back in support of executions and the litmus test had now been passed with respect to countering the argument that executions were cruel and unusual forms of punishment. Being able to take the life of a human being without it being a visibly violent act, like that of the electric chair, has served to make the lethal injection process much more palatable for the general public. The only debate left now is whether or not the taking of someone's life by execution is morally justified because the Supreme Court's ruling in 1977 clearly established that it was constitutionally justified.

The first execution by lethal injection in the United States was conducted in the state of Texas in 1982. When Illinois resumed conducting executions in 1990, they were carried out at one of Illinois' oldest correctional facilities, the Statesville Maximum Security Correctional Facility located in Joliet, Illinois. Statesville is located approximately 60 miles south of Chicago and is frequently featured in area newspapers and TV media regarding stories related to ongoing issues with their inmates. Because Statesville is in such close proximity to Chicago, every time an execution was conducted there, there would be an influx of media presence and public fanfare that literally gathered right outside its front door.

Prior to Tamms being built, all of Illinois' lethal injection executions were conducted at Statesville. However, there were many issues related to the architectural layout of the Execution Unit as well as other operational concerns. Statesville was initially designed to carry out executions by way of the electric chair. However, when Illinois changed its practice to lethal injection, Statesville was not physically designed to carry out this method of execution. As a result, modifications were made to one of their existing housing units so this method of execution could be performed. Even after the modifications were made, the original architectural layout of the unit presented challenges that made it a less-than-ideal location for this process to be continued.

Because of the many issues surrounding lethal injection executions at Statesville, the agency decided to construct Tamms with an additional unit specially designed to carry out the lethal injection process. This is how Illinois' Execution Unit came to be located at Tamms.

As a point of interest, Illinois had two death row units, one at the Pontiac Maximum Security Correctional Center located in Joliet, Illinois, and the other unit at the Menard Maximum Security Correctional Center located in Chester, Illinois. Between both units, they housed an average of 150 to 167 inmates on death row. The death penalty in Illinois was reinstated in 1977, but the first execution in Illinois using lethal injection did not occur until 1990, 13 years after the reinstatement of the death penalty. This execution occurred at Statesville on September 12, 1990, and involved inmate Charles Walker.

His execution received a notable amount of attention at that time because his was the first execution to be carried out in Illinois since 1962 (28 years) and the fact that Walker insisted on being put to death. Walker elected to forgo all of his appeal rights to continue fighting for his life, and he adamantly insisted that he wanted to die. He stated that he simply could not accept living in prison for the rest of his life and he wanted to end it all. He got his wish.

The second execution in Illinois using lethal injection occurred on May 10, 1994. This execution involved Illinois', and possibly the nation's, most notorious serial killer, John Wayne Gacy. Gacy was also executed at the Statesville Correctional Center. And because of his notoriety, hundreds of boisterous onlookers were there to cheer his demise. About a year-and-a-half prior to Gacy's execution, I had been assigned to Menard as a superintendent, but at the time of his execution, I had been promoted to assistant warden and was responsible for managing our Death Row Unit. Because of my responsibilities related to the operation of that unit, I had several occasions to interact with Gacy while he was assigned there. His infamous notoriety garnered him a tremendous amount of public interest for which he seemed to thrive upon, but his notoriety was not viewed with the same level of regard by his fellow death row inmates. Gacy's crime involving the sexual murders of several young men was a stigma for which he could never escape from in prison.

Gacy was initially sentenced to death in 1980 for the killing of over 30 young men in the Chicago area over a period of six years. News reports indicate that he was known to have dressed up like a clown and would use his charm to lure young men to his home by befriending them in some way or by simply kidnapping them. Once he got them to his home, it is reported that he would overpower them with drugs and forcibly rape them as well as perform other lewd homosexual acts with them. Once he had his way with each victim, it is reported that he would sadistically murder them and bury them underneath the crawl space of his house. At the time of his crimes, he was considered to be the poster child for executions.

As far as his prison life was concerned, Gacy was a mild-mannered and generally compliant inmate, but he was also a very prideful and arrogant inmate who kept to himself much of the time. He spent a lot of his time drawing and painting pictures of clowns, which were sold for him through a third party. Gacy wasn't very popular with most of the inmates on death row, and on a few occasions he was assaulted by other inmates, including inmate Brisbon, who I had mentioned in an earlier chapter. Inmates have their own code of honor among themselves and Gacy certainly was not known to have been very well respected by any of them.

After Gacy was executed on May 10, 1994, there were ten more death row inmates executed in Illinois over the next five years. Of those ten executions, two were conducted on the same day, November 19, 1997. This was the first double execution in Illinois since

1952. I took part in this particular execution process as part of my preparation for carrying out this responsibility at Tamms. Nine of the ten executions occurred at the Statesville Correctional Center, and the last execution occurred at the Tamms Super Maximum Security Correctional Center. These ten executions occurred on 3/22/95, 4/6/95, 5/17/95, 9/20/95, 11/22/95, 9/18/96, 11/19/97 (two inmates), 1/21/98, and 3/17/99.

Because I was responsible for providing the administrative oversight for the Death Row Unit at Menard during much of this time period, it was necessary for me to learn the protocol for carrying out the state's highest and most controversial mandate. It was also an inherent condition of my responsibility as a senior administrator at Tamms to understand this process because I could be called upon at any time to have a role in this process. It was highly necessary for me to be prepared to assume the responsibility of assisting in an execution if charged with the duty to do so. My peripheral involvement with a couple of our prior executions later proved to be foretelling omens regarding my direct involvement with Illinois' last execution.

The Death Row Unit at Menard was commonly referred to as the Condemned Unit. It was situated on a hillside overlooking the general population prison. The Condemned Unit was a small three-story concrete building consisting of several narrow corridors leading to individual cells where the inmates were housed. The inmates that were assigned to death row had their own individual cells, unlike the inmates in general population who were usually double celled. There were several reasons why our death row inmates were assigned to individual cells, but to keep it simple, I will simply state that it was a matter of security.

Security is the primary rule of law inside the walls of a prison, and for this particular classified group of inmates—those on death row—it was the focal point of their custody. All of the cells were designed with an open-face door, which means that iron bars ran from top to bottom and from side to side forming a steel framed doorway with open gaps between the bars. This was the conventional cell door of its time and it made it very easy for security staff to see inside the cell. The exceptions to this type of door were the doors used for segregation confinement. These doors were made of solid steel and had a very narrow viewing window for staff to observe the inmate's activity inside.

Unlike other correctional agencies that allow their death row inmates to live and intermingle with the general population, Illinois kept their death row inmates segregated from the general population. As a result of this separation, the inmates assigned to the Condemned Unit were considered to be a special population. And by virtue of their special status, a separate set of administrative directives and security procedures were established to manage their custody.

Most of the policies that governed their custody pertained to their level of conviction and sentence of death. Being classified as extremely high escape risks and having special privileges tailored to their visitation, recreation, personal property, and religious practices required policies written with very restrictive security protocols. However, an equally proportionate amount of policies were written to address their legal rights to have access to the courts. Inmates on death row are always engaged in some stage of their appeal process regarding their conviction, and having access to legal resources to exercise this right was mandatory for us to provide. We frequently dealt with issues related to their due process to the courts. These issues often led to confrontational incidents related to the management of their custody.

Prior to the abolishment of the death penalty in Illinois in March 2011, there was a prison watchdog group called the Illinois Coalition Against the Death Penalty. They served as an intermediary organization that dealt with issues related to inmates on death row. They were appointed by the governor and reported their findings and/or concerns to the governor and to officials of the Department of Corrections. Coalition members had blanket permission to visit any inmate housed on death row. They would visit the inmates housed at Pontiac and Menard. These visits were intended to give them first-hand knowledge about the conditions and treatment of the inmates confined on death row.

After each visit, members of the Coalition would have a debriefing with the administrative staff of the facility. Issues that the inmates had concerns about were discussed during this debriefing. We would listen to their concerns and, if warranted, follow up with corrective actions to address the issue or issues. There were many times that we did not agree with issues that the Coalition presented to us. We knew that the inmates would typically misrepresent the actual facts of a situation and the exact truth would be buried in the embellishment of what the issue truly was.

On balance, we established a respectful but tenuous relationship with the Coalition. I choose the term *tenuous* only to highlight the differences in our perspectives. Most coalition members operated from a very liberal perspective regarding how they thought the inmates should be treated. We, on the other hand, had a more security-minded perspective that dictated how inmates were actually treated. Their treatment was based on the security conditions of their confinement status, not on the rehabilitation conditions of social reform.

For example, I recall one request that two members made insisting that we allow the inmates on death row to have yarn and the accompanying needles to do the yarning. Well, I don't think I have to explain why our decision was an emphatic *no*! You can use your own common sense and figure out some of the security concerns that these items would present if we were to allow these items in our prison. We simply operated from two completely different frames of reference. However, in fairness to the Coalition, I will state that we came to a mutual understanding in most instances for resolving issues they brought forth on behalf of the inmates.

Menard's original Condemned Unit was designed to house slightly more than 50 inmates, but because of its aging condition the building was ordered to be torn down. As a result of tearing down the unit, the inmates had to be relocated to another area of confinement. They were moved to an existing unit within our general population. Some structural modifications had to be made to a section of this unit in order for us to comply with required living standards of their confinement. These modifications made it possible for us to increase our cell capacity by a few additional cells, giving us the ability to house more inmates on death row. It also gave us an added advantage of providing more security supervision to them because they were now located inside the confines of our prison walls. This arrangement also allowed us to have more armed security coverage for this high risk population.

Before the Condemned Unit was torn down, it was physically located in the same building as our medium custody unit, but was separated by natural wall barriers. In anticipation of tearing down the Condemned Unit, we built a new 400-bed medium security unit on an adjacent hill overlooking the main prison. Our medium custody inmates were moved into this new unit and our death row inmates were moved to our general population. With the addition of our new medium security unit and the restructuring of our Death Row Unit, our ability to house more inmates was increased and, consequently, so did our population.

·14·

TAKING THE LIFE OF
A HUMAN BEING

AS I MENTIONED in the previous chapter, when Tamms became operational it also became the facility designated to carry out all future executions in Illinois. When Tamms opened, I was serving in the capacity of the Assistant Warden of Operations in charge of the security division of the facility. Statesville had served out its operational purpose for being the facility that conducted the state's executions, and it was administratively relieved of its duty to perform that mandate. Tamms was summarily delegated that responsibility.

It was exactly one year to the month after we had received our first inmates at Tamms in March 1998 that we were charged with the responsibility of carrying out the mandate to perform legal homicide. However, before that infamous day came on March 17, 1999, there were several nondescript events that occurred leading up to our moment with fate.

A few months before our appointed date with what I consider to be the direst consequence of prison life, the execution of an inmate,

Warden Welborn received directions from our executive directors that we needed to begin preparing for our most challenging and institutionally defining moment. Armed with information regarding the anticipated date of our first execution, Warden Welborn and I began the solitary process of preparing ourselves for the task that we must now perform. We spent many days and many, many hours discussing the details that would be involved in carrying out this most important event.

Although Warden Welborn and I knew that we would not be the ones who would actually inject the lethal dose of chemicals into the inmate's veins to cause his death, we knew nonetheless that we would be totally responsible for arranging this final moment to occur. Because of the immense gravity of this responsibility, it forced us, perhaps for the very first time in each of our professional lives, to critically examine our role as administrators relative to the issue of our duty as public servants upholding the law for social order. This issue deeply penetrated the depths of our personal beliefs and challenged us to seriously question our own positions on the death penalty. We had been thrust into the role of being executioners for society's attempt to redeem a violent loss of life of one human being, through the enforcement of corporal punishment at the behest of taking the life of another human being. Would our actions be considered being on the right side of justice in the end? We hoped so!

We spent several private moments critically soul-searching our personal convictions. We were trying to come to terms with a sense of assurance that our role in this complex situation to ensure that justice was served would indeed be served through our appointed duty to conduct this execution. Warden Welborn took a more pragmatic and intellectual approach toward this issue, which seemed to have given him his sense of resolute comfort. I, on the other hand, took a more spiritual and introspective approach.

My contemplation with this quandary led me to have several discussions with my pastor, Reverend Norman S. Greer, who I often sought counsel from. I was confident in his teachings about God's role in establishing society's governing laws, and I believed that his interpretations as a gifted pastor teacher were grounded in sound doctrine based upon solid biblical precepts. I heeded his encouragement to prayerfully meditate over a passage of scripture in Genesis 9:5-6, which states in part, ". . . At the hand of every man's brother will I require the life of man. Whoso sheddeth man's blood, by man shall his blood be shed . . ." It was the enlightening insight of his teachings of this scripture that helped me come to terms with my moment of fate at a time when I was searching to understand the purpose of my role in all of this: "Why me and what did this all mean?"

From this insight, my philosophy regarding the death penalty dramatically shifted. I once held the belief that the death penalty had no real value in our society. I held this belief in part because I knew that African American men suffer at a greatly disproportionate rate of executions than any other group of people. I also believed that the death penalty did not serve as the deterrent to stop people from committing murder, for which society has been conditioned to believe that it is supposed to do. When I came to the understanding that this form of punishment represents an aspect of *divine authority* rather than a self-serving *man-made law* intended to impose a level of superiority over others, my whole perspective changed. It crystallized very succinctly for me why corporal punishment is a necessary part of societal order. At the moment in which I comprehended this concept, I adopted the position that the death penalty *does* have a proper role in the retribution of societal restoration for acts of gross malfeasance.

The belief that I adopted at that time, which is the belief I still hold today, is that most people tend to think of the death penalty as being a self-imposed man-made law rather than a law of divine authority. Because of this distinct difference in perspectives regarding the way people perceive society's role to impose this level of justice, many people have trouble with the concept of the death penalty as being morally justified.

It is my opinion that for many people the biblical commandment "Thou shall not kill" literally means just that. So, in their mind, there is no latitude of acceptance that allows them to believe that man has the right to kill another man in the name of justice, regardless of the circumstance. For that reason, they vehemently reject the notion that executions are a justified form of punishment. However, the true translation of this commandment is "Thou shall not *murder*", and when considered from this perspective, one can begin to discern the significant distinction between killing someone, such as in wartime, versus murdering someone with deliberate intent based upon the motives of greed, jealousy, hatred, or just for the simple pleasure of inflicting harm on someone else.

I will not attempt to elaborate on the biblical principles that give reason to the position that I have taken regarding the issue of the death penalty. However, what I will say is that I grew into the understanding and acceptance that the death penalty *does* serve a defined, but limited, role in protecting our society. This is the ultimate form of punishment and retribution that a society can impose against a person who has grossly violated the tenets of social order through their actions of deliberately taking the life of another human being for no justifiable reason. But, even more profound than that, I came to the understanding that the death penalty *is not* a universal deterrent as it is commonly purported to be, but rather, it is specific in its intent.

If a person harms another person with premeditated malice and forethought, and the harm inflicted results in the death of that person, it is my opinion that the person who inflicted the harm automatically forfeits their right to remain in free society. In addition to that, they forfeit all consideration for any degree of leniency in judgment of their crime, providing there are no mitigating factors that would otherwise suggest differently.

Because of the egregious act of violence that they committed, they placed themselves in the position to be judged absent of partiality, indifference, or preferential treatment. Surmising that the person is judged fairly by society (meaning without cultural or systematic bias) and society's judgment renders the penalty of death as the form of punishment required to make amends to society for this level of victimization, the greater good of society is then preserved by this decision. Furthermore, the fundamental principle for a governing society to protect the rights of its people to safely and peacefully coexist is thus given vindication.

Contrary to opposing views about the morality of the death penalty, it is my opinion that the authority to take a person's life due to the consequence of a murderous crime does have foundation rooted in biblical principles. I believe that God ordained human government and because of this divine authority to govern ourselves, He demands submission to it when the civil authorities have established laws that attempt to justly govern the civil liberties of all its people. Be this as it may, it became my professed belief that the deterrent effect of the death penalty is specific in nature against the individual. It is not universally attributable to society as a whole with respect to the notion of it deterring people from ever killing another human being again, because that's just not reality. In other words, the mere threat of the death penalty as a societal consequence does not deter people from murdering other people; it never has and it never will. It is the *enforcement* of the death penalty specific to the individual who commits the murder that deters that *specific* individual from ever harming anybody else again, because they will no longer have the opportunity to do so.

It is without question that the death penalty has been disproportionately imposed against African American individuals in this country. I am not suggesting that this disparity in our justice system be allowed to continue unchallenged, for I too vehemently oppose the imposition of its use unjustly, whether the person is black or white, and the story of Troy Davis is a prime example.

Troy Davis was executed on September 21, 2011, for allegedly killing a police officer in Savannah, Georgia, on August 19, 1989. However, several witnesses recanted their testimony claiming that he was not the perpetrator. With this compelling new information and other circumstantial evidence introduced, it gave caution for reasonable doubt. A case for clemency was presented to the Georgia Board of Pardons and Parole, but they denied his appeal. A last-minute appeal was made to the United States Supreme Court, who also denied his appeal. The denial of his appeals highlighted the deep and troubling concern that so many African Americans have about the use of the death penalty. Many people viewed Davis's execution as another blatant and gross miscarriage of our justice system perpetrated against a black man by White America, and I viewed it the same way.

However, I am not opposed to using the death penalty *justifiably* when all aspects of the evidence being considered is decisive in its findings of guilt, is decided without cultural or systematic bias, and if the situation meets the conditions I previously stipulated regarding premeditation and malice of forethought. I stand by my conviction that a free society has the inherent obligation to protect its citizens, and I view the legal administration of the death penalty as part of that protection. The issue of the death penalty will no doubt continue to be an area of passionate debate for many people as long as mankind exists. However, my position has been shaped by my direct and indirect experience with individuals who have demonstrated a total disregard for the value of another human being's life, and I waiver not on this position.

The Countdown to Fate

Warden Welborn and I eventually came to terms with our roles to carry out this extraordinarily unique duty of being a public servant and protector of the law. Our challenge now was in selecting the personnel that would best help us carry out this assignment. We certainly did not want staff who would merely accept this assignment for the short-lived fame of being able to tell their family and friends that they took part in an execution. They would be counterproductive to the process and serve a meaningless role in the accomplishment of our objective to conduct a humane and respectful execution.

To the contrary, we selected staff who wanted to be recognized as being good correctional professionals and who looked at this as an opportunity to demonstrate their leadership, their dependability, their trustworthiness, and their willingness to accept tough assignments. After selecting the staff we felt would best serve our mission, we assigned them to the respective roles they each would play in the process. We also utilized other correctional personnel from other facilities within the agency to aid us in preparing for this challenging responsibility. Everyone involved was required to sign a statement agreeing to the confidentiality of the process before they would be allowed to participate. A few weeks after we had selected all of our personnel, we began the arduous task of conducting practice drills to get everyone comfortable with the role that they each would be required to fulfill on the day and night in question. This was a very precise and time-structured process that required hours upon hours of practice to ensure the readiness of everyone involved when that moment was at hand.

During our preparation for this task, our legal counsel for the agency was closely monitoring the actions of the court. They needed to stay abreast of any decisions made by the court and/or the governor's office that could potentially impact whether or not this execution would indeed take place. It is not uncommon for the lawyers representing the inmate to argue for a stay of execution right up until the last possible moment. We actually experienced that situation in a previously scheduled execution where an inmate was exonerated and released from our death row 48 hours prior to his anticipated fate with death.

In total, there were 12 inmates exonerated from Illinois' death row units between 1987 and 1999. This remarkable number gave the presiding governor at the time, George Ryan, enormous leverage to impose a moratorium on all executions in the State of Illinois. In doing so, he commuted the death sentences of 167 inmates who were on death row at the time to a sentence of life in prison. They will still die in prison as ordered, just not by execution. The governor's decision was made nine months after the first and only execution that was carried out at Tamms.

I did not agree at the time with the manner by which Governor Ryan made his decision to impose the moratorium. He did not require an independent review to be conducted for each individual inmate on death row. He simply made a blanket decision to commute all death sentences citing the inherent flaws within the death penalty process as his reason for doing so. It is without question that some of the individuals, if not most of them on death row, were guilty of the crime they were charged with. And I have no doubt that there may have been someone who was *not* guilty of the crime they were charged with committing. However, placing a moratorium on executions at that time did not prevent the courts from continuing to sentence persons to death; they could and did continue to impose that sanction. The moratorium just temporarily inhibited the courts from carrying out their sentence of death until a ruling on the efficacy of its constitutionality was finalized.

In my opinion, the commuting of their death sentences to life sentences without having properly reviewed the facts of each individual case was a blatant disrespect to the victims' families and a blatant disregard for the integrity of the cases that were properly litigated. It is my belief that Governor Ryan made his decision solely for political reasons and not so much because he believed that the death penalty was inherently unjust or inhumane. At one time in his career, Governor Ryan supported the death penalty, which was contrary to the position he was now upholding. Don't get me wrong, I understand perfectly that people have a right to change their views on a given subject; I did so as well. However, his switching of his position at the time only served to reinforce my opinion that he was simply trying to embolden his legacy as a governor hoping to offset the negative impact of a criminal scandal that he was facing at the time. And as the records will show, he was eventually convicted and sentenced to prison as a disgraced governor.

Since Governor Ryan's ungracious political demise, Illinois has served under two governors, Governor Rod Blagojevich, who I will speak more about later, and Governor Pat Quinn. It was Governor Quinn of Illinois who controversially took on the highly charged debate regarding the constitutional efficacy of the death penalty. And on March 9, 2011, 12 years after Governor Ryan imposed a moratorium on executions in Illinois, Governor Quinn signed legislation abolishing the death penalty in Illinois. In signing this legislation, he also commuted the death sentences of the remaining 15 inmates on Illinois' death row to life imprisonment. The pendulum of public opinion and political posturing had shifted back in favor of the moral imperative versus that of an eye for an eye.

As the highly anticipated day approached for us to carry out our mandated duty, we meticulously reviewed every detail and possible scenario that could occur. One of the things we had to do to prepare for this event was to establish a media and protest area. This area was set up several hundred yards away from the prison facility. With most executions, there is some level of media attention given to the event, be it locally or nationally, depending on the notoriety of the inmate. The media will typically highlight the human interest side of the story by profiling the life of the inmate while at the same time reflecting the nation's perspective on executions.

At the event itself, there normally are people gathered outside the prison that are protesting the death penalty and trying to bring awareness to stop such practices. And likewise, there is usually a small group of observers and protesters in support of the execution. The latter group usually is advocating the position of not letting the victim's life be overshadowed by the attention that the person being executed is receiving. In preparing for our event, we developed a contingency plan to account for any confrontation that could potentially occur between the groups. We collaborated with local law enforcement agencies to assist us in establishing our protocol for handling any crowd control issues.

In the early morning hours of March 16, 1999, around 6:00 a.m. the day prior to the scheduled execution, our inmate arrived at Tamms by helicopter. He was dressed in a standard green death row jumpsuit, secured in handcuffs, leg irons, and a waist chain, and was closely guarded by security personnel. Two executive directors also accompanied the inmate on the flight. Upon exiting the helicopter, six of our security officers met the escorting officers and they exchanged the supervision of his custody. He was then led directly to a holding cell in the execution unit, where he remained until his final moments before being taken into the execution room later that night.

His cell was situated approximately 15 feet from the execution room. The location of the cell was strategically designed to be close to the execution room. This allowed the process to be as systematically controlled as possible. One of the things we had learned from our experiences with executions at Statesville was that having a holding cell in close proximity to the execution room improved the logistical management of the process. The two holding cells that we had were directly adjacent to the execution room, which made the handling of the inmate from point A to point B much more controlled.

The execution room itself was a highly sanitized and sterile area. The entire unit was painted white, which gave it a clean hospital-like appearance. Every aspect of the chamber, from the mattress and bed linen in the inmate's cell to the instruments in the lethal injection room, were immaculately arranged and laid out. The lethal injection room itself, which was a smaller room contained inside the larger execution chamber, was equally pristine and sanitized. Every instrument was frequently and thoroughly examined for their functionality to ensure there would be no flaws when it came time to carry out the execution.

During the course of that day, the inmate was allowed to receive visits from his attorney, his family, and any faith representative of his choice. All visitations were discontinued by 6:00 p.m. that evening. He was frequently checked by our medical staff several times throughout the day and evening to make sure that he was okay and that he did not need any kind of sedative to help him remain calm. A security officer was seated at a table directly outside of his cell to provide direct observation of his behavior and to report any unusual development. His behavior was also monitored via a hidden camera that allowed video observation of his activity in the cell. We monitored his actions from the warden's office. And as customary, during the earlier evening hours of that day, he was offered his last meal.

One of the least talked about issues that prison officials concern themselves with when preparing for an execution is the adverse effect that this type of event will have on the other inmates, both those assigned to death row and those assigned to general population. Usually there are one or two inmates who will attempt to use this situation as an excuse to create some form of protest. Because of this possibility, prison officials prepare contingency plans to respond quickly to any instigative behavior so that the inmates do not incite others to join in. Quick, decisive actions must be taken when this happens so as to not end up dealing with a massive protest or major disturbance.

Our Execution Unit was strategically designed to be separated from our general population units, and this separation served as a buffer to prevent inmates from gaining any direct knowledge of what was taking place. They were aware that an execution was being prepared for because of the news reports on TV and from over-hearing staff talk, but they did not have any ability to witness any activity associated with the process. This was one of the collateral concerns we had when conducting executions at Statesville. Their general population units were in such close proximity to the unit where the executions took place the inmates could observe a lot of the preparatory activity going on. As a result, on many occasions, they became unruly and voiced their protest by shouting and yelling at staff as they observed them moving about. As a rule, most inmates treat a day of execution as a moment to show respect to the inmate being executed, so they generally do not cause problems. This rule held true when our execution took place and we did not experience any problems from our inmates.

About 30 minutes prior to the time of the scheduled execution, which was designated to occur at 12:01 a.m., a six-man security team approached the inmate's cell and began to prepare him for his execution. They conducted a strip search to ensure that he had not concealed any item that could be used to interfere with the execution process or to inflict harm to himself or a staff person. After the strip search was conducted, the six-man security team placed him on a gurney and secured him with arm and leg restraints. His arms were pulled slightly away from his body and placed on specially designed arm extensions, and his legs were secured close together. Upon being secured to the gurney, he was wheeled to a designated spot outside the execution room. The team was required to wait there until they were instructed to bring him inside the chamber.

Before I continue describing more of this process, I will take a brief moment and share a little insight about why 12:01 a.m. is des-ignated as the more common start time for an execution versus any other time. The time, 12:01 a.m., establishes the beginning of a new day, and from 12:01 a.m. until 12:00 midnight there is a 24-hour time period. Starting the process at 12:01 a.m. allows prison officials the benefit of the entire 24-hour time period to be used, if necessary, to carry out the execution. When a death row inmate exhausts all of his appeals, the court sets a specific date for the inmate to be executed. This order of death is a legally binding sanction and must be performed on the declared date as so ordered.

The 24-hour timeframe gives prison officials ample time to adjust for any glitches or delays that might happen that could have an impact on the execution being carried out. There are known incidents involving executions where technical problems have occurred with the equipment and/or the apparatuses used to perform the execution. To account for these potential problems, most executions are started at 12:01 a.m. in order for prison officials to have a reasonable amount of time to make adjustments if a problem were to develop. In other words, the state has the entire 24-hour day to make good on its sanction to kill someone on the declared day of the execution. Hypothetically speaking, if I were sentenced to be executed on January 1, 2014, the state has from 12:01 a.m. that morning until midnight of the same day to ensure that I die.

Inmate Andrew Kokoraleis was the first and only inmate to lose his life by way of lethal injection at the Tamms Super Maximum Security Correctional Facility. His execution occurred on March 17, 1999. He was secured to a gurney and wheeled into the execution chamber by six security staff shortly before midnight on March 16, 1999. Upon entering the chamber, the security team positioned him in a slightly upright manner facing a one-way see-thru window. He was covered with a white bedsheet from his feet up to the baseline of his neck. Only his face was visible. His arms were pulled slightly away from his body and secured on arm extensions to make it easier for the nursing staff to insert the IV needles into his veins. Both arms were prepared for receiving an injection of the medications. This was done simply as a precautionary measure. If the primary line used for injecting the medication were to become clogged because the medication coagulated in the IV tubing, the other line would be used as a secondary option for the injections.

Kokoraleis was strategically positioned in the center of the chamber so that the media and official state witnesses could see exactly what was occurring inside the room. The witnesses were seated on the opposite side of a one-way window in a small auditorium-like room. When the execution was ready to begin, the lights in the auditorium were dimmed very low so the witnesses would be able to see clearly inside the execution chamber. There was another one-way window situated behind Kokoraleis that allowed the lethal injection team to observe what was taking place inside the chamber. The lethal injection team was a clandestine group of individuals responsible for injecting the chemicals into the IV units and ultimately into Kokoraleis's veins, causing his death.

There was also a specially designed viewing room connected to the execution chamber for the director of the agency to observe the process. His room was hidden from view of the witnesses. His viewing area was also equipped with the legendary red phone that has been glamorized in several movies. This is the phone that a governor would use to make a last minute call to the director to stop the execution. However, in this real-life execution, that call never came.

Once Kokoraleis was positioned in place, two nursing staff were instructed to enter the room to insert the IV units into his arms. After the IV's were inserted, the nursing staff was instructed to leave the room. Only Warden Welborn and I remained in the room with Kokoraleis. Warden Welborn positioned himself on the left side of the gurney close enough to hear any last words that Kokoraleis may want to say. Because Kokoraleis had provided us with a written statement earlier that evening, he did not make a verbal statement when offered to say any last words to Warden Welborn. At that point, Warden Welborn gave the order to the lethal injection team to proceed with the execution.

I was stationed in the front of the room hidden from view of the witnesses. Part of my role was to open and close the curtains when the process began as well as when it ended. I was also Warden

Welborn's backup should he not be able to continue his role in the process. If that were to happen, I would have been required to step in and carry out the execution proceedings. I also had the responsibility of recording the exact time when each injection was administered. Everything was done with precise detail.

I also monitored a group of phones that were affixed to a wall near where I was stationed. They were there in case that infamous phone call came from the governor directing us to stop the execution. The red phone that was in the director's viewing room was connected to a red phone inside the execution room where I was standing. Had the director received a call from the governor directing him to stop the execution, I was responsible for receiving the call from the director and relaying the message to Warden Welborn to stop the execution. But that call never came. There were other phones that I had to monitor as well in case I needed to communicate with other members of our team who were stationed in different parts of the facility.

And lastly, I was responsible for recording the precise time of death, as pronounced by the medical doctor, and relaying that information to the director. All of our communications were done by way of earphone headsets, which streamlined our coordination of the process. Our Execution Unit also had a viewing room designed for the family members of the victim and, in this case, there were a few family members of the victim present to witness Kokoraleis put to death.

When Warden Welborn gave the instructions to the lethal injection team to proceed, it was literally within seconds after those instructions were given that the execution was over. Almost instantly after the first chemical was administered, I saw Kokoraleis take what appeared to be a deep breath, and it was over. The lethal dose of each chemical is so powerful that they cause death literally within seconds upon entering a person's bloodstream. The first chemical, sodium thiopental, renders the person unconscious. The second chemical, pancuronium bromide, paralyzes the muscles to keep the person from convulsing. And the third chemical, potassium chloride, stops the heart. In my opinion, this process is by far the most humane way of carrying out this sanction.

After the chemicals were injected and it was apparent that Kokoraleis had no more life, Warden Welborn communicated to me to close the curtains and the matter was unceremoniously brought to an end. I closed the curtains and the medical doctor who was sequestered in a private area waiting to officially confirm Kokoraleis's death was brought into the chamber. I recorded the official time of death as pronounced by the doctor and provided that information to the director so he could address the media. From that point, it was simply a matter of bringing the coroner in from his sequestered area and removing Kokoraleis's body from the room to take him to the morgue.

Once the body was removed from the premises and the media protest area was cleared, Warden Welborn and I conducted a debriefing with all of the staff who participated in the process. We wanted to make sure that everyone was handling the enormity of this event okay. Everyone indicated that they were handling the situation well and we expressed our appreciation to them for their high calling of professionalism in response to a most challenging duty. Although that event is now a postscript in the history of Tamms, it will never be just a postscript in the history of my life.

ONGOING CHALLENGES

WHEN I SUPERVISED the Segregation Unit at Menard, there were many incidents in that unit that I remember being quite interesting to witness. One such incident involved an inmate that I will call MG. MG was an inmate who constantly engaged in confrontations with staff every chance he could get. He was so problematic that we ended up assigning him to the very last cell at the end of a gallery on the highest floor that we had in that unit. We wanted to isolate him as much as possible to lessen his continuous disruptive behavior. MG was put in a single cell fortified with a solid steel door to help reduce his chances of assaulting staff.

One day MG decided to tie his cell door shut with his bedsheets and we could not get his door to open. He would not comply with any of our orders to untie the door and, as a consequence, we were unable to remove him from his cell. MG saw this as a way to make our day difficult and provide amusement for himself to pass his time away. This situation bore truth to the old saying, "An idle mind makes for the devil's workshop." He had nothing else better to do while sitting in his cell all day other than to think of ways to create problems. And believe me, he thought of many ways to create his own fun, and he got his kicks out of seeing us react to his antics. He knew that we had to react to his shenanigans and he deliberately set this situation up so that we had no choice but to respond.

For us, it was a matter of safety and security, life and death; it was not a time for fun and games! We didn't know whether or not he was engaging in self-inflicting harm or if he was engaging in some other form of security breach. The situation was a very serious matter to us whether MG saw it that way or not. Initially, we tried talking to him hoping to reason with him and get him to understand why he needed to untie the door and let us search his cell. This approach failed miserably!

It became obvious very quickly that he was determined to drag out his playtime for as long as he could. This incident turned into another situation that required members of our tactical team unit to respond. When the tactical team arrived, the team leader gave MG our standard three direct orders to comply before force would be used. MG simply ignored the orders as though the team leader was not even there. The team leader then administered two canisters of Chemical Mace into his cell through his food port opening in an attempt to get him to comply. MG was so hyped up at that point that the chemical agent didn't have any deterrent effect on him whatsoever. Usually when chemical agents are deployed into an inmate's cell, the inmate becomes very agitated by the effects of the chemical, and he usually complies with the orders to cooperate. But, in MG's case, it had no apparent affect on him whatsoever. He had wrapped his head and face with as many layers of clothing as he could to lessen the irritating effect of the chemical and he seemed to have inhaled the chemical as though it was fresh oxygen. He actually started laughing at us like we were the Keystone cops or F-Troop.

In hindsight, this was a pretty funny incident in many respects, and we did laugh about it once it was all over. This was one of those moments when we relied on extracting the humor out of a very serious event. However, at the time, it wasn't very funny because he had created an extremely unsafe situation and we knew he had the potential to harm himself. We eventually had to call our maintenance staff to come and physically remove the door off its hinges. Because he had tied the door so tightly together, it took well over an hour to get the door off. And when we did get it off, MG put up his typical fight with the tactical team and, as always, the team prevailed. MG was secured in restraints and moved to a different cell.

That's one thing about inmates who resist complying with a cell extraction or any order to comply. They never win in the long run. Performing a cell extraction to remove an inmate from his cell is always a violent encounter; there is just no way to avoid that. Sometimes we would lose an encounter from the standpoint that a staff person would get injured during the altercation. However, we would always win in the end because we would always gain control of the inmate and induce his compliance. Prison life is not pretty, and order and control will be enforced at all costs. MG was eventually transferred to our psychiatric facility for a mental health evaluation and I never heard what happened to him after that. There were many MGs in our prison and there are many more MGs in our nation's prison system.

I recall another incident that required all of our administrative staff to report to the facility on a Saturday morning because several inmates were refusing to lock up. Inmates refusing to lock up were a routine part of our prison life and this did not come to us as a surprise. It happened after the breakfast meal had been served for inmates assigned to our South Lowers Cell House. But before I talk more about this particular incident, I think it would be helpful if I gave you a glimpse as to what a warden and his duty warden staff responsibilities are as it relates to the management of our day-to-day operations.

During my first tour of duty at Menard, we had an administrative staff of 11 people. This included the warden; his two assistant wardens (me being one of them); six unit managers, or superintendents as they were commonly referred; and two chiefs of security, or majors as they were commonly referred. Menard at that time, and still today, is the largest correctional facility in Illinois. It encompasses a large area of land and it is a physically imposing facility. Each superintendent and both majors were assigned the responsibility of being the first responders to an incident or a potential incident. They would be delegated this responsibility for a week at a time and then rotate with one another every week thereafter throughout the calendar year. When it was their turn to assume the responsibility of being the first responder, they were called *duty wardens*. This meant that they were the individual on duty who would be the initial contact person for the shift commander when there was a problem or a potential problem. The duty warden's responsibility would be to assess the situation presented to him and then give directions to security staff and/or non-security staff as to how a given situation should be handled.

The warden and his two assistant wardens would be the superintendents' backup, and were respectively called *backup duty wardens*. If a duty warden felt that he needed further direction or approval to authorize a decision, he would call his backup duty warden to get advice, to seek clarification, and/or get verbal authorization to carry out his decision. This chain of command extended itself to include assistant deputy directors, deputy directors, and ultimately the director if a situation warranted that level of involvement. The responsibility of a backup duty warden was 24/7/365 days a year. Anytime of the day or night, wardens and assistant wardens had to be ready to respond to the facility at a moment's notice. Our responsibilities were that serious and equally as demanding.

Having provided some insight as to the responsibilities associated with the day-to-day management of a facility, I will proceed with telling about the incident that I alluded to a short moment ago. As mentioned, there were several inmates who were refusing to lock up after they had returned to their cell house from eating breakfast. The duty warden was notified of the situation by the 7-to-3 shift commander and, in turn, the duty warden notified his backup duty warden. After they discussed the situation, a decision was made to have all administrative staff immediately report to the facility. All inmate movement was stopped and the facility was placed on temporary lockdown.

During the times that I was assigned to Menard, I lived approximately 30 miles away from the facility. This required that I be able to respond to the facility as quickly as possible whenever I was summoned to report for an emergency. As an assistant warden, I was assigned the use of a state vehicle as a function of my duties as a senior administrator. My car was a refurbished Crown Victory equipped with emergency pursuit lights and other police accessories. In response to reporting to this situation, I activated my pursuit lights and arrived at the facility in less than 20 minutes.

When we all had arrived at the facility, we met in the major's office and were debriefed on what the situation was about. In short, one of the ranking leaders of a major gang had been taken to segregation earlier that morning because he had been found intoxicated from drinking hooch. He had given orders to members of his gang not to lock up until he was released from segregation. This is another example of the power and influence that gang leaders have over their members. Whenever gang leaders give their members orders, the members automatically obey them for fear of retaliation by the leader.

When Warden Page had the leader brought from segregation to the major's office, he also had one of the ranking members from general population brought to the meeting as well. Warden Page explained to both of them in very clear terms that if the leader did not direct his members to lock up, he would no longer be in a position to give anybody any orders because he would be immediately shipped out of state. The tenor of Warden Page's conversation got the leader's attention, and he directed his co-leader to advise their members to stand down and lock up. Let me make it very clear here. They only locked up because of the leader's directions; had he not given them that direction, we would have had to use force to get them to lock up. This typifies how the gangs often flexed their power through intimidation and threats and the balancing act that we had to do in order to ensure we effectively operated a safe prison.

The gang leader was still kept in segregation and we kept the facility on lockdown while we formulated plan B. We left the major's office and walked around the facility in each cell house gauging the mood and tone of the facility. We wanted to get a sense of whether or not we could take the facility off lockdown without experiencing further problems. We remained at the facility all day until late in the afternoon when the 3-to-11 shift came on duty. Traditionally, the 3-to-11 shift has less staff assigned to it to manage the facility than the 7-to-3 shift. Inmates know this and strategically choose to create most of their problems during this shift for that very reason. Instructions were given to the Shift Commander to allow each cell house to go to their dinner meal as scheduled to test the waters and see how they would respond. Upon giving the shift commander our instructions, we all left the facility with the exception of the duty warden. The duty warden and shift commander were to monitor the mood of the inmates as they went to chow by looking for signs that indicated this issue was over or at least over for now. Upon ending our walk-through, we didn't sense any glaring indicators that alerted us that we would be reporting back to the facility within minutes after the first group of inmates was let out to eat, but we did!

No sooner than I had arrived home and was about to open my front door, my pager started beeping. I looked at the number that flashed up on the screen and it was our numerical code that meant I needed to report to the facility ASAP! I quickly got back into my car and drove to the facility uncontested by the speed limit. Upon arriving the second time, I learned that we were facing the same situation that we had dealt with earlier that morning, only this time it was hedging on becoming more out of control. Once all of the administrative staff reported back to the facility, we convened in Warden Page's office. We discussed our plan for how we would approach this situation. We decided that we would pair up in groups of twos and go to each cell house to talk with representative leaders of this gang to assess their overall resistance to our orders to lock up. Additionally, we activated our tactical team to prepare for a use of force contingency encounter. We placed the facility on lock down so that only the inmates who were actually refusing to lock up were still out. In conversing with each cell house leader, we made our collective message quite clear to them that there would be less cooperative times ahead if their cooperation was not achieved immediately. The skill of conciliatory negotiating came into play and we achieved one of our finest crisis-avoidant moments during this potentially violent confrontation. We were able to exercise incredible tact in gaining their compliance without having to resort to force. But we were prepared to use force if they chose to force our hand. We demonstrated superb administrative diplomacy at a time when extreme violence was looming right in our faces.

After gaining control of the situation again, we turned our attention to the gang leader who was the key player in all of this. Warden Page had him brought back to the major's office and reminded him of their conversation from earlier that morning. Warden Page then made him aware that he, the leader, had just bought his ticket to Timbuktu. We contacted our assistant deputy director who had been kept abreast of the entire situation from the onset of the ordeal up until then. Upon being informed of this latest incident, the deputy gave us approval to immediately arrange for him to be transferred out-of-state. However, his transfer only bought us relief for a short-lived time because other gang-related issues were awaiting us just around the corner.

Gang activity is an ongoing problem in our maximum security prisons every day, and Menard certainly experienced its share of problems. In another incident that I recall, we had been on lockdown for more than a week due to a staff assault perpetrated by members of the Gangster Disciples. As a result of this assault, the tension became exceptionally high between staff and inmates, and it was unclear as to how long this level of hostility was going to last. As I alluded to before, when certain incidents occur, officials from our executive administration would become involved and personally come to the facility to offer their experience and guidance in helping us resolve the situation. In this case, Deputy Director Leo Myers paid us a visit to offer his insights and experience in dealing with gang-related matters.

Deputy Director Myers was a correctional veteran of 30-plus years and he was legendary within our agency. He operated from the old school philosophy of prison management, whereby strict control was the standard of operation and a tolerance of gang intimidation was not accepted. He was very seasoned in dealing with the gangs in our system and he was known for his no-nonsense approach to handling such matters. Upon his arrival to the facility, he was given a status report by Warden Welborn and he then requested to talk with the leader of the GDs. I, along with Superintendent Bonnie Gross, escorted the deputy to our West Cell House where the GD leader was housed. When we got there, Superintendent Gross instructed his unit captain to bring the inmate to his office. Gang leaders typically do not speak to administrative staff by themselves. They usually have at least one other member with them, and this meeting was no different. In addition to the leader being brought to the office, another ranking member was allowed to accompany him.

The meeting didn't last long and Deputy Director Myers was true to character. He was direct and to the point, but he listened very carefully to what the inmates had to say about the reason for the assault. Director Myers was concerned with their attitude toward staff and he wanted to understand clearly how they planned to conduct themselves once the lockdown was over. There came a point in the conversation where one of the inmates became cocky and told the director that as long as staff continued to provoke his members, he would give them permission to retaliate. This certainly did not resonate very well with the director. He sternly informed both members that if he had to call in the National Guard to help control his prison and protect his staff, that is exactly what he was prepared to do and that they would be the first two inmates on his list to be dealt with.

Being caught off guard by the director's response, they tried to downplay the tone of their threat. They told the director that they just wanted to be left alone and not be harassed by staff. They tried to reassure the director that whenever the facility did come off lockdown that he, the director, would not have anything to worry about from their gang, at least while they were still at Menard. The director responded by informing them that as long as they were at Menard, they would be held personally accountable for any assault on staff by any of their members and that they would truly regret it if they did. The leaders changed their rhetoric regarding the threat to harm staff and this seemed to have marginally appeased the director and the meeting came to an end.

We left the cell house and returned to the warden's office. The director briefed the warden about what happened in the meeting and gave the warden permission to gradually take the facility off lockdown over the next few days to test the waters. The management of a prison can be likened to that of a chess match. Prison officials and their staff and gang leaders and their members represent the pieces on the chess board. They each operate from a position of strength and they use strategic methods of engagement to achieve their end game. Wardens use negotiations, segregation confinement, lockdowns, transfers to other facilities, and use of force tactics as their strategic methods of engagement. Gangs use protests, intimidation, threats, and assaults as their strategic methods of engagement. The gangs had many pawns to sacrifice, and they were exceptionally good chess players. In this analogy, the playing surface of the chess board is represented by the prison facility itself. Each side is vying for the control of the other and one inadvertent move can cost the other a major loss and subject them to the rule of the other.

In this case, the GD leaders were outwitted by the director's power play move when he told them that he would do whatever it took to maintain control of his facility. This put the gang leaders in a position of checkmate. They knew that the director would make good on his word and that they could do nothing to counter-check his move; game over! Here again is another example of how the complex dynamics of prison life between those who operate the prison versus those who are confined to the prison vacillates within an intricate ritual of power, control, and survival. The director's checkmate gave us the opportunity to survive for another day, but when the game is played again there could come a day when we are put in checkmate and the inmates will control the asylum. This is how the game of prison chess is played—the strategies and tactics of implied force and control versus the strategies and tactics of intimidation and threats. Whichever player makes the more decisive moves will have the advantage of placing the other in checkmate, and the game will be over until the board is reset. We survived to play another day!

MANAGING INMATE PROTESTS

THE VIOLENT AND aggressive forms of protest that inmates engage in are the ones that the general public reads about most often. However, there are other forms of protest that happen almost daily that receive very little attention until they escalate into a larger problem. One of the more common nonviolent acts of inmate intimidation and protest is the hunger strike. The sensationalism that is usually given to this form of protest makes for a good media story, but very seldom does the media reflect the truth behind the protest.

And to offer a point of clarity, hunger strike incidents do not occur any more frequently in super maximum security prisons than they do in other high security settings. Advocates against supermax prisons try to embellish the perception that they do to help generate support for their cause to shut down these prisons. But let me just say that there is a hunger strike protest being declared by one or more inmates at any given time of any given day throughout prisons across the country. This is just an inherent fact of prison life. These protests, as a rule, are usually short-lived and last two to five days, but they have been known to exceed more than 30 days in duration in rare exceptions. There are a host of reasons why inmates engage in a hunger strike, but the underlying motive behind the majority of them is to manipulate correctional officials into a position of coercive bargaining.

I would be less than genuine if I were to portray that all hunger strikes are without merit. That would be simply categorically untrue. Some hunger strikes are based upon legitimate complaints and they serve to bring to the administration's attention errant situations that may need to be investigated and/or corrected. On the other hand, a great many of them are not grounded in merit. They are simply used to manipulate their situation for some kind of special conciliation. Hunger strikes are typically initiated because the inmate perceives that the administration is mistreating or neglecting his rights in some way. When I use the term *administration* in this example, I am speaking of the entire prison staff, correctional officers, non-security staff, and senior officials.

Inmates know that engaging in a hunger strike is a sure way to draw attention to themselves. More often than not, the issue that an inmate goes on hunger strike for is a result of his own poor choices and/or his unwillingness to accept certain conditions of his incarceration. For example, I recall where an inmate went on a hunger strike because he was placed on a meal loaf restriction. A meal loaf is a specifically prepared food entrée that is cooked in a meatloaf-type manner. It is intentionally designed to be undesirable to the taste (extremely bland), but it is nutritionally balanced and eatable for consumption. The inmate was placed on this restriction because he had refused to return his eating utensils after he had finished eating his meal. A cell extraction had to be performed to recover the items. Had he simply complied with the requirement to return the utensils after he had finished his meal, he would have never been placed on a meal loaf restriction. But, because he believed that we were denying him his legal right to eat a regular meal, he decided to protest by going on a hunger strike.

This is a common occurrence in prison. He wasn't intending to stay on a hunger strike for days on end; he just got pissed off and decided to use this form of protest as a way to cause us some grief. He knew that we could not discipline him for being on a hunger strike and that this was a safe way to protest without incurring any disciplinary trouble. Inmates will use medical services, quality of food, improper cell searches, staff harassment, protective custody concerns, and a variety of other reasons to justify going on a hunger strike. I will admit that there have been times when the abuses of these issues were uncovered as a result of a hunger strike protest, but on balance the hunger strike is an attempt to gain an unmerited privilege.

Individual hunger strikes are common in prison and are normally managed very well by correctional officials. They usually do not gain support from other inmates that the individual hunger striker hopes to gain support from. The individual hunger striker would like nothing more than to get several other inmates involved in his protest so, collectively, they can disrupt the day-to-day operation of the prison. And it is the mass hunger strikes that involve several inmates that cause great concern for prison officials. The public notoriety that their collective effort brings to the protest is extremely unwelcome by prison officials. When a mass hunger strike occurs, the entire facility, or at least the unit where the protest is occurring, is usually placed on lockdown. Dealing with a mass hunger strike requires a different level of prison management. Specific security protocols are implemented in order to keep the situation from escalating and to continue operating in an orderly manner. The main objective for correctional officials in this kind of situation is to prevent the mass protest from developing into a riotous situation. This requires the experience and personal involvement of senior facility officials to be acutely sensitive to the nature of the protest.

An example of this is a hunger strike protest that involved over 30 inmates in a segregation unit in New Hampshire State Prison in July 2010. The inmates went on a hunger strike because the unit was unbearably hot. The facility had been built in the early 1900s and was made of concrete and steel and did not have air-conditioning. The inmates' fans had been taken away a few days earlier because the fans were being broken and made into homemade weapons. The temperature became so intolerable that the inmates began flooding their cells in order to cool themselves. Prison officials recognized that there was some legitimacy to the inmates' concern about the high temperature and arranged for fans to be positioned in various parts of the unit to create some circulation of air. They still did not allow fans in the inmates' cells because of the security concern about breaking them apart to be used for weapons. This decision demonstrated that the administration was sensitive to the concerns of the inmates while at the same time balancing the greater concern for safety and security. Their actions prevented the situation from becoming more volatile and the inmates ended their protest after a week.

When inmates decide to engage in a prolonged hunger strike, they fail to factor into their decision the fact that they could kill themselves without ever intending to do so. Inmates have no intentions of killing themselves when they declare a hunger strike; however, that possibility does exist. What they are seeking when they protest in this manner is to receive some form of expected justice, to prove a point, to demonstrate some control over their world, and/or to intimidate the administration into giving them what they perceive is their entitlement. But the truth of the matter is, if they persist in prolonged days of not consuming proper nourishment, their bodies will begin to shut down, and this could cause some serious adverse health reactions that could prove fatal. The symptomatic effects of starvation will begin to develop and pose a serious health concern. This situation is exacerbated by the fact that many inmates have a history of substance abuse and poor health. Their bodies are much more susceptible to having complications as a result of a weakened health system. Consequently, the act of not eating for an extended period of time increases their potential to have a fatal outcome and therefore requires correctional officials to intervene.

The medical personnel in all prisons are bound by the Hippocratic Oath to preserve the life of an inmate equally as they would preserve the life of a civilian. They must obey this ethical standard requiring them to preserve life to the fullest extent possible. In fulfilling that oath, when an inmate has persisted in several days of a hunger strike, correctional officials must seek a court order to initiate a procedure called *force feeding*. This order is only authorized when an imminent life-threatening situation has been determined by a physician.

Force feeding is a medically administered procedure conducted by a facility doctor and assisted by the help of security personnel. It requires that a physician literally forces an inmate to consume nutritional fluids if he does not voluntarily do so. The great majority of times, when it reaches this point of intervention, the inmate complies on his own and consumes the fluids without having to be forced to do so. Once an inmate realizes that he will not be able to exploit his situation by continuing his protest, he ends his hunger strike. At that point, he will be placed on a medically prescribed regiment of nutritional intake to gradually elevate his health back to normal.

There are a couple of times that I remember where we had to force-feed an inmate to consume life-sustaining fluids. In each of those instances, the inmate never took his hunger strike protest to that extent again. Due to the serious legal ramifications associated with this form of intervention, we relied totally on our agency legal department to provide guidance for handling these cases. Central to their guidance was their responsibility to obtain the order from the court authorizing us to proceed with lifesaving intervention measures. I always found it interesting that many staff held the attitude that if an inmate wanted to starve himself to death, why should we interfere? Although we, the administrative officials, understood the nature of their sentiments, we were bound by a higher duty to ensure that proper care was afforded to each inmate to the greatest extent possible. To sustain an inmate's life when he does not regard his life in the same way is one of those unpopular responsibilities that many staff do not like but correctional administrators have to enforce. It is a responsibility that requires our greatest exercise of administrative due diligence and one for which we must fully demand from our staff.

Before an inmate is officially declared being on a hunger strike, he has to refuse eating all three meals for three consecutive days. This is to ensure that the inmate is truly declaring a hunger strike and not just playing games. This drastically limits their ability to manipulate staff and disrupt our operation. Many inmates will declare that they are on a hunger strike at one meal and then accept their meal at the next feeding. It is part of the games they play. At other times when an inmate would claim to be on a hunger strike, he would secretly receive food from other inmates on the unit and therefore not truly be on a hunger strike. Receiving food clandestinely made their claim of being on a hunger strike untrue and, in turn, made them less likely of being in any real medical jeopardy due to their false claim that they are depriving themselves of inadequate nutritional intake.

If an inmate missed eating three consecutive meals for three days, this also served to alert us that it was now time to involve medical staff in a more proactive management of the situation. When that happens, the inmate is required to be isolated in an individual cell and his vital signs are regularly monitored for symptoms of dehydration and other potential complications. During his quarantine, efforts are made by correctional officers as well as other administrative officials to persuade the inmate to end his hunger strike. Medical staff would educate the inmate on the adverse health effects caused by a lack of improper nutritional intake. He would be provided with such information to help him make an informed decision about continually depriving himself of food.

At other times, we would use a more subtle method to get inmates to end their hunger strike. We would push the food cart past their cell door so they could smell the aroma of the food, hoping to entice their hunger sensations. Particularly on the days when we served chicken, this would incite their hunger sensations so intensely that they would virtually break down their cell door and ask to be served a meal. But in more cases than not, after a member of the administration would talk with them about their complaint, they would usually end their hunger strike. They would then resume their normal routine and fade back into the everyday drama of prison life. Hunger strike episodes happen every day in our nation's prisons and I have yet to know of one that was fatal.

The Threat of Work Stoppages

Another form of protest that inmates engage in is work stoppages. Most prisons have some type of work assignments that inmates are allowed to participate in. These assignments ranged anywhere from custodial cleaning details to production work in small industry operations. For those of you who have the Hollywood image of inmates working in an old stuffy warehouse-like building making license plates or other products, which was true at one time, it's now more advanced and automated. As the gang presence increased in Illinois' prison system, more and more of our job assignments were filled by members of gangs. With the majority of our inmate workforce being dominated by gang members, the influence of their intimidation became a stronger leverage point for them to exploit the system. If the gangs felt as though the administration was not responding to an issue that they felt needed to be addressed, they could, and on a few occasions would, not report to their assignment until they had forced the administration to address their issue. Gang leaders would even go so far as to put the word out to other inmates that if they attempted to work in their place, they would be retaliated against. This intimidation tactic did not always work to their advantage because inmates could be transferred in from other facilities if necessary, but it did have an affect on how the issue was resolved.

As you might be able to imagine, when a work stoppage occurred it created a major disruption to the day-to-day operation of the facility. A stoppage did not occur very often, but when it did occur, our approach to dealing with the gangs had to be a well-thought out strategy because a lot would be riding on the outcome. These situations were extremely delicate, and if not handled correctly they could have far-reaching consequences for the facility. Keep in mind that our primary concern is to keep the facility operating normally, which means keeping people safe. Handling a work stoppage with the wrong approach could easily turn the situation upside down very quickly and prison officials could be faced with a very dangerous situation. The Attica State Prison is a prime example.

On September 9, 1971, an uprising by inmates at the Attica Maximum Security Correctional Facility in Attica, New York, occurred and ended four days later with a death toll of 39 individuals, 29 inmates and 10 correctional officers and civilian employees. This is one of the worst, if not the worst, prison insurrections in American history. Although this incident was not triggered specifically by a work stoppage, there were several other living conditions, educational concerns, and political issues that contributed to this protest. But what's important to understand here, is that the same approach of sensitivity and responsiveness to a work stoppage protest must be exercised in any protest. In the Attica incident this level of sensitivity did not happen.

The negotiations to end the siege by the Correctional Services Commissioner and other observers made up of state representatives, religious leaders, and newspaper editors were not successful, and the state police and National Guard were authorized to retake the prison. The outcome of that decision was a disastrous one. And without fail, if the element of sensitivity is left out of the equation when attempting to resolve a conflict and restore order in a prison, it will inevitably result in a violent outcome. These situations become even more unavoidable when the inmates have made up their minds to force the hands of prison officials. When this occurs, prison officials have no choice but to exercise a use of force to restore order, and that oftentimes ends up being deadly force. Prison life is extremely unpredictable and dangerous!

The concern about the quality of food has historically been a major area that has led to many work stoppages. I am quite sure you have heard about, read about, and even seen movies about inmates starting riots over food. Well, if there is one thing that will trigger a disturbance and cause a major protest, it is the quality of the food. Prison food as a whole is much like the food prepared in school cafeterias. The food items are usually lower-grade products and the food is usually not prepared very well. Notwithstanding that fact, most correctional institutions try very hard to ensure that their meals are prepared in the best of quality.

Correctional facilities hire civilian personnel with experience in culinary arts and dietary management to operate their kitchens. Although dietary managers are responsible for overseeing the operation of food preparation, they rely primarily on inmate labor to do the lion's share of preparing and cooking the meals. This is a major area of concern for prison officials because meals have to be prepared for hundreds of inmates and staff three times a day, every day of the year. Should an inmate or a group of inmates decide to tamper with the food or choose not to prepare the food, this would seriously disrupt the daily operations of the facility. A work stoppage involving this job assignment could cripple the operation of an institution for days and trigger a reason for the rest of the inmate population to become disruptive. One of the issues that the inmates at Attica protested about was the poor quality of the food.

Preparing good meals for large inmate populations is a very challenging undertaking and sometimes does not always meet the standard of preparedness that is acceptable. In all prison agencies, it is mandatory that a correctional official randomly sample each meal before the meal is served to the inmates. This is to ensure that the quality of the meal is acceptable to be served. There are times that I know of when a meal was not acceptable to be served and another meal had to be prepared and served in its place. Delaying a meal from being served at its regularly scheduled time is also a potential source for causing a protest. Inmates are so conditioned to the regimentation and routine of prison life that when their normally expected schedules get off schedule they become agitated and suspicious about the change in routine. And when it involves their meals being off schedule, they are very quick to start complaining and hassling staff. This is always an ongoing concern that correctional officials have to be mindful of and prepared to resolve quickly.

On the lighter side of this issue, special attention is always given to the preparation of the meals for the Thanksgiving and Christmas holidays. In the Illinois system, it is a priority that these two meals have all the trimmings of a traditional holiday meal and that the inmates receive larger portions of each serving than they normally would get. Contrary to the reality that prisons are a harsh and unforgiving place, there are a few moments in which the human element of a prison's shared collective condition rises to the surface and brings about a sense of humane goodness for staff and inmates. Preparing a special meal on these holidays is an effort by the agency to acknowledge the shared benevolent condition of humanity between staff and inmates, at least for a brief moment.

During my career, I have witnessed several incidents over the quality of food, and fortunately each situation was resolved without it resulting in a major problem. The peaceful resolution of these incidents had a lot to do with the ability of administrators and other staff to communicate effectively with the inmates. In many instances, making concessions with the inmates kept things from getting out of control. Showing a genuine effort to address their concerns played a major role in resolving the issues. A key element that helped us prevent various protests from getting out of control was our open responsiveness to the inmates' concerns, whether they were right or wrong in their perception of what triggered the problem. And we did what we had to do to protect the lives of everyone!

A DIFFERENT PERSPECTIVE

I AM GOING to shift the tone of this story for just a moment and talk about the non-security aspect of operating a prison. As much as I have spoken about the hardcore side of prison life, there is another side of correctional management that often receives very little mention relative to its impact on prison safety. It is an aspect of prison management that plays as much of a role in its success or failure as does the security aspect of its operation. It is the programmatic component of the rehabilitation aspect of prison management. I believe that what I am about to say, most hardcore correctional people will never admit as being the case. Be that as it may, it is my opinion, and I am confident that a study of the history of our nation's penal system would bear evidence to my position, that the most successfully managed prisons in this country have a strong programmatic component interfaced with its security practices. I will attempt to explain my position further.

I briefly mentioned in an earlier chapter Illinois' first African American Director of the Department of Corrections, Howard A. Peters III. What I didn't mention was his philosophy for managing a prison facility. He promoted a philosophy that advocated that a cleaner prison is a safer prison, and that having increased opportunities for inmates to improve themselves would enhance prison safety. He also advocated that prison administrators should recognize the *intangible positive qualities* of prison safety related to maintaining a high standard of sanitation and physical cleanliness.

Director Peters believed that this aspect of prison management combined with increased opportunities for inmates to learn and develop skills would make the issues of safety and security a lot less challenging to deal with. Maintaining a high level of security will always be the priority of the day in any prison and particularly in a high security facility. This is a fundamental prerequisite for good custodial supervision. However, he also believed that the enforcement of a high level of security could be reinforced by having a clean prison environment and by having increased opportunities for inmates to improve themselves while serving their time. I will offer the following example in support of this philosophy.

When I was initially assigned to Menard, I witnessed gang graffiti painted in virtually every cell and trash and debris were commonplace. Upon adopting Director Peters's philosophy, we instituted a campaign to paint the entire facility a neutral color, and we aggressively enforced higher sanitation standards. Once we gave the facility a sanitation facelift, we rigorously enforced the expectations of maintaining a clean facility. Having implemented this simple change in our operation, the inmates' attitude about their living conditions dramatically improved. They took ownership in keeping the facility clean and this took some of the edginess out of the normally tense atmosphere.

Don't misunderstand me. I'm not suggesting that our gang problems suddenly went away as a result of changing the expectations of what were acceptable living conditions, but what I am saying is that the tensions associated with the day-to-day problems that we experienced became less intense. The cleanliness of the facility seemed to have had a slight calming effect on the inmates and in turn produced a more cooperative and compliant attitude overall. When a facility experiences a less tense state of operation, it is less likely to have problems. This is one of the *intangible positive effects* of maintaining a clean facility that can be attributed to the management of a prison's overall safety and security. Prisons generally do not experience as much physical aggression and hostility among the inmate population when the facility is maintained at a level of clean decent living conditions.

I will now illustrate how programmatic services can be and are an integral component of prison safety. When I started in corrections in 1985 as a counselor, there were no programs within our agency addressing the issue of substance abuse. It was during the early '80s that the War on Drugs campaign enacted by President Ronald Reagan's Get Tough on Crime policy began to have its impact on Corrections. Laws were changed that allowed the simple possession of crack cocaine to be given stiffer sentences. This, in turn, led to an increase in prosecution of drug offenders and gave leverage to the courts to impose stiffer sentences against those who were the primary users and distributors of crack cocaine, young urban African American males. The "Three Strikes" law which permitted the court system to lock individuals in prison for accruing three or more convictions for longer sentences, and in some cases for life, also created an avenue for the judicial community to engage in an-all out assault on urban black youth. These laws were nothing more than strategic tactics by politicians to create the false impression that the government was winning the war on drugs, but what they actually were, were methods of control that legally gave the law enforcement community the authorization to engage this in practice.

As a result of these bias-laden forms of legislation, hundreds of young black males were locked up in prisons across the country and there was no formalized plan on how to deal with the aftermath. The mentality was simply to lock 'em up and throw away the key. The net result of this race-motivated strategy caused prison populations across the country to grow exponentially. This led to an explosion in the prison industrial complex that reaped the benefits of millions and millions of dollars in the construction of new prisons to house thousands of new felons. This enterprise became a cleverly disguised form of institutionalized slavery by which hundreds of young urban black males were locked up in our prisons all in the name of the War on Drugs.

In 1987, a colleague and very dear friend of mine had the foresight and fortitude to see the need for our agency to seriously address drug education and drug treatment within our prison system. She embarked on a mission to have frontline counseling staff trained to become certified substance abuse counselors. Her name is Donna Howell and, like me at the time, she too was a correctional counselor. Through her vision and tenacity, she was able to establish a certification program that trained correctional counselors to become substance abuse counselors.

Approximately 40 of us received training for two years in the field of substance abuse. And in 1989, we became the first group of correctional counselors in the Illinois Department of Corrections to become certified substance abuse counselors. The agency was now in a position to facilitate drug education in our prisons to better address the needs of our inmates. The growth and success of our agency's drug education and drug treatment programs can be attributed largely to Donna's efforts. Had it not been for her spirited commitment to make drug education and drug treatment an integral component of the programmatic services offered to inmates, Illinois' correctional system would not be where it is today with respect to this particular aspect of its operation.

Although much credit is deserving of Donna for her efforts to promote substance abuse education and treatment within our agency, I would be remiss if I did not also acknowledge the contributions of another outstanding colleague. Her name is Linda Dillion. Linda

Dillion was the third female ever to be appointed as a deputy director for the Illinois Department of Corrections, and she was the second African American female appointed to this position. She held various positions of responsibility throughout her career, not to mention a respectful tenure as a warden. She regarded programmatic services as an integral component of correctional management and promoted the importance of rehabilitation programs. She demanded quality performance from all departments that reported to her, and she was acutely devoted to her duty to serve. Her leadership and administrative guidance helped elevate the agency's Division of Program Services to a well-respected status. Donna's success can be attributed in part to the support given to her by Deputy Director Dillion. Deputy Director Dillion believed in the importance of drug education and drug treatment as well as the importance of other forms of self-improvement opportunities for inmates.

Recognizing the need to address drug abuse issues for our inmates prompted the agency to focus more attention on all areas of our rehabilitation programs. But having spoken on the issue of rehabilitation, this brings to mind the often asked question "Do prisons rehabilitate inmates?" My immediate and short answer is *no*! Inmates rehabilitate themselves, not prison. Prison in its true nature is designed to punish people, not rehabilitate people—albeit this philosophy is somewhat primitive and unconventional for our modern day social advancements. However, the real essence of this question is more complex and has multi-layered elements that demand a more explicit answer than my mere short coarse response.

In truth, all prisons, with the exception of a few specialized high security units, offer some level of self-improvement or rehabilitative opportunities for inmates. And contrary to media propaganda, most super maximum security prisons do so as well, although they do so under very restrictive conditions. The complexities involved in addressing the challenges associated with the rehabilitation of inmates is contingent primarily upon three prevailing factors: *the attitude that security staff have of inmates, the motivation for change by the inmate himself,* and *the security conditions by which a prison is able to be managed in a safe and controlled state.*

In other words, for programmatic services to be effective and thereby create a positive environment for rehabilitation to occur, there must be a supportive and cooperative relationship between program staff and security staff. Security staff must have buy-in to the understanding that the mere fact of providing educational opportunities to an inmate *does not* in and of itself lessen an inmate's punishment. Many security folks hold the jaded view of inmates that subscribes to the mindset that says, "Because they have been placed in prison, they are not entitled to be treated with any human decency and/or given any opportunity for restorative justice." The people who hold this view have what I call "the bread and water mentality." They genuinely believe inmates deserve nothing more than bread and water. There are many prison cultures where the mentality of a fair portion of their security staff harbor this debase mindset against inmates receiving any kind of self-improvement opportunity.

The fact of the matter is that the loss of an inmate's civil liberties and freedoms due to his incarceration is, in and of itself, his punishment. Imposing other artificial conditions such as limiting their opportunity to improve themselves through educational training only adds insult to injury. Establishing these kinds of barriers contribute to the undermining of an inmate's self-esteem whereby they no longer are likely to see themselves as worthwhile and the net effect is they lose all motivation to improve themselves. Unfortunately, there is a pervasive mindset within many prison cultures that reinforces the philosophy that "an inmate ain't got nothing coming," especially when it involves an opportunity for them to improve themselves through learning.

Rehabilitation is the desired outcome of inmates taking advantage of self-improvement opportunities that are made available to them. However, if the majority of the security staff does not buy in to this concept, they will continue to remain rigid in their views of inmates and continue to be reluctant to support efforts of rehabilitation. They will perceive it as an inconsequential and misguided endeavor and continue to approach their custodial responsibility from the perspective that *punishment* is to be the sum total of an inmate's incarceration. No more, no less!

Another issue that prominently factors into whether or not rehabilitation occurs in prison is that of *security and control*. Even if a prison could offer as many programmatic services as they wanted, if the management of that facility is constantly dealing with violent and disruptive situations, the inmate population would not have much of an opportunity to benefit from the programs offered. I will use Menard again as an example to illustrate my point.

In 1993, Menard was locked down for approximately 236 days of that calendar year because of the threat of inmate violence or actual inmate violence. Very little or nothing at all was provided in the way of programmatic services during that year. In 1994, we were on lockdown for over half of that calendar year and programmatic services were again impeded from being delivered because we concentrated our efforts on maintaining the safety and order of the facility. In 1995, we were locked down for at least two-thirds of that year. In October of that year, I participated in the Million Man March in Washington, DC. After attending the march, I was inspired to start a self-empowerment program for the inmates at Menard. The theme of the march was for African American men to engage in meaningful efforts to elevate our communities. As strange as this may sound, I viewed the predominantly African American inmate population at Menard as a community that could benefit from the principles articulated at the march.

Upon my return from the march, I began the groundwork to implement a lecture series for the inmates. The program was to be coordinated with professors from Southern Illinois University in Carbondale. Various subjects would be presented on a monthly basis to empower and elevate the consciousness of the inmates. This series was intended to supplement the few programs that were being offered and add to the overall process of their self-improvement/ rehabilitation. However, before any of this could come to fruition, an inmate was shot and killed at the Pontiac Maximum Security Correctional Center on January 12, 1996, and all of our maximum security prisons were immediately placed on lockdown. Our focus once again shifted to enforcing security and control and not on offering rehabilitative programs. This is a prime example of why rehabilitation in high security institutions is oftentimes viewed with a jaundiced eye when the competing factors for operating a prison in a safe and controlled state is placed in jeopardy.

To illustrate this even more, in April of that same year, our agency placed all of our maximum security facilities on permanent lockdown for an entire year. It was during this year, from April 1996 until April 1997, that we began the process of systematically taking control of our prisons and enforcing the control over the inmate population that was so desperately needed. The concern of offering rehabilitative programs became secondary to our agency's primary mission of operating safe and secure facilities.

There is no question that safety and security concerns will always take precedence in the day-to-day course of operating a prison. It should be that way, and it is that way. This aspect of prison management is deemed paramount in our high security facilities, and this heightened concern for safety was certainly the case for our four maximum security prisons, Statesville, Pontiac, Joliet, and Menard, during that period of time. They were the most problematic facilities in our agency, and between them they accounted for hundreds of lockdown days each year as a result of perceived and/or actual gang-related violence.

When a facility is locked down, there will be little or no self-improvement opportunities available for inmates. When this happens, the prison conditions become much more susceptible for problematic situations to occur. So, the answer to the often asked question "Do prisons rehabilitate inmates?" is tempered, in my opinion, by the set of circumstances for which a prison must operate. In other words, rehabilitation is predicated on whether or not a prison is operating in a controlled and safe enough state (for example, void of major day-to-day problems) so that inmates can have the opportunity to take advantage of the few programs that do exist. In addition to this, the prison culture established by the security staff must be such that they respect the role of rehabilitation programs and are willing to support the benefits of such programs. And lastly, the individual inmate himself must adopt the attitude that embraces the opportunity to improve his current and future condition through education and training. Otherwise, if these forces are not present, basic prison survival will continue to be the dominant element for how inmates do their time. And when this happens, inmates are forced to rely on their own wits to find ways to rehabilitate themselves, and unfortunately too few inmates demonstrate the mental discipline for overcoming those odds.

Over the last 15 years, and more specifically the last ten years, there has been a dramatic shift in the approach that correctional agencies have taken with regard to the issue of how inmates are being returned to society. Prisons, more than ever before, have become entirely too costly to operate. The overcrowded conditions that prison agencies are forced to deal with have heavily burdened taxpaying citizens. As a nation, we have spent over $60 billion during the last 20 years attempting to curb the impact of recidivism and its collateral effects. We obviously are not doing something right because we are grossly losing this battle. We will never be able to build our way out of the prison industry. As a consequence of this alarming crisis, correctional agencies are being forced to re-examine the way they do business and are being challenged to implement strategies to more effectively address this growing concern.

Many agencies have been forced to implement an early release plan for inmates in an effort to offset the financial expense of operating their prisons. Unfortunately, many of the inmates that are released are ill-prepared to successfully return to society and the cycle of re-incarceration is played out all over again. Over a decade or so ago, Illinois' prison agency focused on this issue through an initiative called pre-release. It was an effort designed to provide life skills preparation to inmates a few weeks to several months prior to their release. This was done so that they would be better prepared to obtain employment and deal with other needed services upon their release. Today, this is called prison re-entry. It's the same concept, just repackaged with a different marketing name.

Prison re-entry is nothing new because inmates have always been released from prison and returned to our communities. What is different now than in years past is that it has become a crisis of epidemic proportions for our society, and it is threatening, more so than ever, the fabric of our nation's public safety and economic growth. The basic principle of prison re-entry centers on the simple but highly evolving question "What role does the Correctional system play in preparing an inmate for his or her release back into our communities?" In other words, the question should no longer be "Do prisons rehabilitate inmates?" but rather, "How can prison agencies along with our communities *effectively* support and empower the successful transition of inmates back into our communities?" With the added pressures of the worst economic conditions that our nation has faced since the Great Depression, much attention has now been diverted to finding solutions to this most complex problem.

The implementation of job preparedness and skill development training programs in prisons, as well as outside of prisons, has taken on a much more urgent and critical tone. It has become more accepted now that self-improvement programs not only help prepare inmates for returning to society, but also help stabilize the order of prison life and contribute to the enhancement of both prison and public safety. More credibility has been given to the fact that when inmates believe that they have a chance to improve their conditions through different learning opportunities and skill development, they tend to steer away from the negativity that is so prevalent inside prisons. This also offers them the same kind of hope when they are in free society trying to stay out of trouble and improve their lives. They will be much more likely to put forth an effort to improve themselves if they believe that there is someone or some support service willing to help them make the change.

Having pointed out some of the ways in which programmatic services contribute to safer prison management, I hope I have provided you with a better understanding and appreciation for how such services play a significant role in helping maintain the safety and security of prison life. Unfortunately, the overcrowded condition of many of our nation's prisons makes it less conducive for programs to operate as effectively as they should in order for inmates to benefit from the expected outcome of rehabilitation programs. Regrettably, the disruptions that frequently occur in our high security prisons will continue to require prison management to focus on the safe management of the day-to-day issues of prison life and not on the societal benefits of rehabilitation.

SUPER MAXIMUM
SECURITY PRISON

THERE ARE APPROXIMATELY 25,000 inmates confined to super maximum security prisons in the United States. Tamms is just one of several supermax facilities nationwide designed to help manage the continued disruption of prisons by non-conforming inmates. Both the state and federal prison systems operate supermax prisons. The highest security prison in this country is a federally operated super maximum security facility located in Florence, Colorado. It replaced the super maximum security prison that was located in Marion, Illinois, after the Marion Penitentiary was downgraded to a lesser security facility around 2001. The criteria for confining inmates to these highly restrictive levels of custody include acts of violence and acts of disruption that pose a serious threat to the safety and security of an existing prison facility.

The argument put forth by advocates who are *against* the use of supermax prisons is that they are cruel and unusual methods of punishment, and that this type of confinement—*prolonged isolation*—will cause an inmate to lose touch with reality and therefore cause them to go crazy. In 1995, a federal court ruled after reviewing the conditions of Pelican Bay, the largest super maximum security facility in the state of California, that although the conditions of that prison "hover on the edge of what is humanly tolerable for those with normal resilience," the court *did not* find that this condition rose to the level of being cruel and unusual punishment. The notable exception to this ruling was for those inmates who are clinically diagnosed with a predisposition and/or who suffer from an acute mental illness. The court went on to cite that the conditions of a super maximum prison *did not* pose "a sufficiently high risk to all inmates of incurring a serious mental illness." In other words, the court was saying that when an inmate who is clinically diagnosed as *not* having a mental illness is placed in a super maximum security prison environment—thereby the inmate being considered *normal*—the inmate would not suffer from any significant life-threatening mental health deterioration any greater than he would in other high security prison segregation settings.

This was a critical ruling for the corrections community in that it allowed the continued practice of housing inmates in this level of custody; however, the court sternly cautioned against the practice of housing inmates with a mental health diagnosis in this level of custody. The court recognized the need for prison agencies to have a method by which to address very violent and problematic inmates while at the same time recognizing the potential for this kind of restrictive custody to be harmful to a certain class of inmates.

The argument put forth by those who advocate *for* the use of supermax prisons is that they provide a level of increased discipline that normal security custody does not offer, and it has a deterrent effect for assaults and violent behavior in the general population. Correctional officials must have a viable way to address serious violations such as assaults, escapes, and other serious acts that threaten the safety of staff and other inmates. However, in order for the deterrent effect of a supermax confinement to work effectively, correctional agencies must have a method of reintegration whereby inmates have some means of earning their return to a general population setting. It is the basic "carrot and stick" concept of reward and punishment. The problematic inmates are allowed to participate in normal congregate interactions with other general population inmates when their behavior conforms to appropriate and acceptable standards of conduct. On the other hand, should their behavior continue to demonstrate a disregard for the rules and the safety of others, they will continue to be subjected to the punishment of a restrictive confinement. For some inmates, this will end up being a very long time and, in some cases, possibly for the remainder of their incarceration.

With no disrespect intended nor an apology made to the human rights groups who are trying to champion the cause to shut down supermax facilities, the harsh reality and unfortunate consequence of managing violent and dangerous inmates confined in our overcrowded prisons is that they will always be subjected to this level of restrictive custody when safety deems appropriate, and the Illinois prison population is no exception. The question surrounding the placement of mentally ill inmates at Tamms was critically examined prior to and during its inception. When Tamms was opened, we instituted a very rigorous screening process that prevented facilities from trying to use Tamms as a dumping ground for their mentally and behaviorally challenging inmates. However, the philosophy of our agency at that time made allowances for exceptions to be made.

The agency reasoned that if an inmate who was clinically diagnosed with a mental illness, such as schizophrenia, bi-polar disorder, or major depression, clearly posed a significant security threat to our agency, he could be and most likely would be housed at Tamms. As a result of the agency's position on this issue, a specialized housing unit was designed in Tamms to provide intense mental health treatment for those few inmates who met this exception. In addition to the specialized treatment unit, our mental health staff was required to have more than the standard ratio of contacts with each inmate at Tamms. This requirement was put in place to ensure that the mental health of each inmate did not deteriorate to any concerning degree over time. If an inmate's mental health was determined to be of concern, he would be transferred to another facility that could best treat his condition.

The acting out of suicidal gestures, placing inmates on suicide watch, and using therapeutic restraints was no more frequent in our level of confinement than what was occurring in our other maximum security segregation settings. In most prisons, it is reported that anywhere from 10 to 16 percent of their population suffers from some form of clinically diagnosed mental illness. The findings of another federal court that examined the treatment of the mentally ill in the California prison system noted this observation: "*Mentally ill inmates who act out are typically treated with punitive measures without regard to their mental status . . . There is substantial evidence in the record of seriously mentally ill inmates being treated with punitive measures by the custody staff to control the inmates' behavior without regard to the cause of the behavior, the efficacy of such measures, or the impact of those measures on the inmates' mental illnesses.*" It was this concern articulated by the federal court that measured heavily in the establishment of our mental health protocol and the training of our custody staff for dealing with mentally ill inmates assigned to Tamms.

Our experience taught us that some inmates would feign a level of insanity or mental illness to avoid being punished for their misconduct. Inmates had learned that exhibiting this type of behavior would garner them a special kind of attention. When inmates acted out in this way, it was our professional obligation to ensure, to the extent that we could, the well-being of each inmate, and that included protecting them from hurting themselves, even if they were faking. Most inmates who engage in self-mutilating behavior do not concern themselves with the fact that their acting out will bring them negative consequences. These consequences would be things such as being placed in a room naked on suicide watch, having all of their personal belongings removed from their cell, being placed in therapeutic restraints for hours at a time, or being heavily sedated to control their self-destructive behavior. In their way of thinking, it was okay to engage in self-harming behavior because they were not harming others and, therefore, since they were not harming others, they did not believe they should suffer any consequences.

Considering the level of premeditation that went into their efforts to mimic being out of touch with reality, their suicidal gestures were more often than not determined to be an act of manipulation rather than a diagnosis of a genuine underlying mental illness. I have witnessed many incidents where inmates would engage in a variety of self-mutilating behaviors as a manipulative strategy to gain attention and/or attempt to earn a privilege. I recall one inmate who would repeatedly place foreign objects inside his penis trying to convince us that he was crazy. On the surface you would think that anyone who would do something like this was crazy, but the desire to manipulate a situation for a greater reward can become a very compelling strategy to use to achieve that reward, particularly when you have very little control of your environment, such as in a prison setting. And the end game to get out of Tamms was perceived to be a greater reward for all of the inmates assigned there.

I have seen inmates engage in some of the most bizarre behavior hoping that they could manipulate administrators into giving them what they demanded, which in the case of a few inmates housed at Tamms was a transfer back to a regular prison. They simply did not like the intense regimentation of the level of custody at Tamms. They would attempt almost anything to give the impression that they were suffering from a mental illness in hopes that we would send them to another facility. These illustrations are not intended to suggest that inmates do not commit legitimate acts of self-destructive behavior due to an underlying mental illness. That would be far from the truth. They were noted for the purpose of countering the more common perception and assertion that *all* inmates who engage in this kind of behavior in a super maximum security setting suffer from a mental illness. That is simply not true.

During the time that I was assigned to Tamms, which spanned almost seven years, we never had a suicide. This fact is noteworthy only to underscore the point that the conditions of a supermax prison do not necessarily contribute to an increase in suicides more than other high security segregation units. We had an excellent crisis team protocol in place whereby every staff person was trained in crisis intervention. This was a critical element of our management strategy that helped us be more effective in managing the complex behaviors of our inmates. We trained all staff to recognize basic signs and symptoms of the onset of depression and other mental health maladies. This equipped staff to respond more appropriately and in a timelier manner when those situations arose. Their training equipped them with the knowledge necessary to engage in preventive techniques of de-escalation until a more trained mental health professional could arrive to assess the situation for more appropriate intervention.

From the general public's perception, the concept of housing a person in a cell for virtually 24 hours a day for weeks, months, and even years probably seems extremely harsh, cruel, and inhumane. It is probably even harder for the layperson to imagine why such forms of incarceration are necessary. My response to this sensible and legitimate question is quite simple. Correctional officials are held accountable for the safe protection of all life inside prisons, and to that extent they must have the authority to impose reasonable measures of control over the inmate population that is deemed necessary in order to safely operate their institutions.

Super maximum security prisons are a by-product of our correctional system being inundated by sheer overcrowded conditions and rampant violence. Thus, they have now become the standard reasonable measure of control that correctional officials use as a management tool for dealing with their aggressive populations. As I have stated throughout the book, prison life is hard and oftentimes unforgiving. Correctional management is predicated on the premise that the prison population must be controlled in order for effective and safe living conditions to be accomplished. If the inmate population is constantly engaged in aggressive behavior that borders on being out of control, the reactionary response from prison officials will always be to enforce more restrictive measures of their custody. That's the natural and fundamental law of prison management. I'll share another story to help put this point in context.

On Easter Sunday, April 11, 1993, a maximum security prison in Lucasville, Ohio, became a tragic example of violent and uncontrolled behavior when a riot erupted and lasted for 11 days. The Southern Ohio Correctional Facility experienced the most tragic event that a prison facility can suffer—a riot that involves the taking of staff hostages and the loss of lives. Without going into any great detail about the incident, I'll just briefly mention some of the more glaring facts that are revealing. At the conclusion of the aftermath, five inmates and one correctional guard had been killed and $40 million in damages were incurred during this 11-day ordeal. There were many factors that contributed to this incident, of which I will not elaborate upon here. I simply mention this incident to add relevant context to the position of why super maximum security prisons are a necessary element of prison management.

A year after the incident, two warden colleagues and I visited Lucasville. We went there to learn of the reasons that led up to the riot and to learn of the new security methods that had been implemented to manage the facility more effectively. Several million dollars were invested in the restructuring of their operation. Top level administrators were replaced with new leadership, new security procedures were instituted, areas of the prison were redesigned to provide more secure housing, and the inmate population had been reduced to a more manageable size. This was a very costly lesson learned at the tragic expense of staff and inmate lives.

The general public must clearly understand that there is an extremely high cost for trying to protect the life of staff and inmates inside prison facilities. The public cannot have it both ways. They cannot expect correctional officials to provide a high level of protection for public safety and yet, at the same time, ask correctional officials to not use and enforce appropriate levels of control to do so, which is exactly what super maximum security facilities are designed to do. But, this is precisely what the advocates who are against supermax prisons seem to be implying.

They want correctional officials to protect the lives of those we incarcerate and to ensure the safety of the staff who provide the supervision of those we incarcerate. But yet, on the other hand, they seem to be asking correctional officials *not* to impose methods of prison management (such as supermax prisons) that help protect those that they claim they want to protect. Their position, in my opinion, is a contradiction and paradoxical dead-end argument. Until our criminal justice system begins to seriously deal with the complex issues of how persons are sentenced to prison and, consequently, how they are confined once placed in prison, correctional officials will continue to be faced with the extraordinary challenges of managing aggressive, violent, dangerous, and disruptive inmates. To that extent, super maximum security prisons will always be an essential element factored into the equation of how correctional officials manage this select group of problematic and dangerous inmates.

POLITICS AND VYING
FOR POWER

THE ILLINOIS PRISON system has a unionized labor force that has been part of their system for many years. Throughout those years, the union has fought to control the management of Illinois' correctional agency. Although there is a statewide contractual agreement established between the union and the Illinois Department of Corrections that clearly delineates the rights of both parties, the union has historically tried to undermine the agency's rights to govern their own operation.

Through years of filing grievances and having arbitration hearings, the union has attempted to finesse the language of the contract to position their ability to have more say in how the IDOC is managed. Much of their effort has been structured to favor the personal and/or political interest of their membership and not the betterment of the agency. It is my view that their one-sided agenda for coexisting has always been a major wedge that hindered establishing an amicable working partnership between them and the IDOC. Most correctional agencies do not have a unionized labor force and do not have to deal with union-related issues in order to manage their prisons or their personnel. And because of the autonomy that these agencies have with respect to independently managing their prison system, they operate with a different management perspective regarding how they deal with their workforce. They do not have to deal with some of the egregious forms of hyperbole that the union often creates for Illinois' executive directors and wardens when attempting to exercise their contractual rights to manage their facilities.

IDOC's relationship with the union can be described as the commonly portrayed antagonistic relationship that exists between most unions and management. Both parties attempt to coexist with a reasonable degree of respectful cooperation, but they harbor strong opposing views regarding how certain contractual matters are to be accomplished. These opposing views were often demonstratively expressed with verbal hostilities during monthly facility meetings, grievance hearings, or during negotiations of supplemental contracts and/or the statewide contract. There has been some modicum of conciliatory dialogue over the years, but on balance the relationship shares no love lost between one another.

During my tenure as a superintendent, as an assistant warden, and as a warden, I participated in numerous labor management meetings. And because of this, I can speak from direct experience and say with straightforward candor that 98 percent of those meetings involved some level of hostility expressed by the union toward management. I can recall many instances where labor meetings were reduced to shouting matches and the union members got up and walked out. During a meeting where I was serving as warden of Menard, a regional union leader openly stated to me that I was "out to get staff" and that he was not going to tolerate that from me. This was nothing more than verbal posturing to look impressive in front of his members. He was simply playing to his membership to remain favored for his future election term. He knew I had no agenda to "get staff," but nonetheless it was these kinds of propagandized statements and false insinuating comments that kept communication between wardens and union members from more productive outcomes. I made it very clear to him that I was not out to get staff as he alleged, but reinforced to him that if any staff person did not abide by contractual policies or our departmental rules, I would most definitely hold them accountable; simple as that!

These kinds of antagonistic confrontations were, and I suspect still are, common occurrences in many of the facilities throughout the agency. Each correctional facility has their own local union to mediate issues specific to that facility, but each local union is accountable to the larger statewide organization. Each local union has their own union president, vice president, and union stewards, and each union reports to a regional representative for advice and counsel. There were times when union members would have their moments of dissension within their own ranks, but they would always put their differences aside when it came time to negotiate against management.

Many of our disagreements ended up being decided at third-level grievance hearings or through arbitration. And sad to say, we (management) lost more than our fair share of those disagreements. The union's influence was, and probably still is, widely established in many circles. As a result of their influence, we often came up on the short end of the dispute. Many of the arbitrators that were selected to conduct our arbitration hearings were pro-labor sympathizers, and this was certainly not by accident. Union reps frequently tried to intimidate wardens with threats of filing unfair labor practice claims in an attempt to force wardens into conceding to their demands. It was the blatant disrespect that they showed for management's right to operate our institutions that led to many of our uncompromising disputes.

One example of the uncompromising position that they often took is when they demanded that certain levels of discipline imposed against an employee be either reduced or removed from an employee's file, even though the employee was unquestionably in violation of misconduct. If a compromise was not reached, the union would threaten to file, and in some cases did file, an unfair labor practice claim. Many union leaders believed they ran the show, and at times they did! However, because I was committed to managing my facility as I determined best for its overall operation and not based on the terms dictated by the union, I was frequently challenged with grievances.

Most union representatives had a hard time accepting stern opposition from any administrator, and the ones that I personally dealt with had an even harder time accepting it from me. Although my white warden colleagues held the same position that I did regarding how we managed our facilities and also caught much grief from the union, the fact that I was an African American administrator gave cause for many union members to deal with me from the jaded perspective of racism. I'll offer another case in point.

In 2004, President Obama was at that time campaigning for the nomination to be appointed as an Illinois Senator. During his campaign tour, he was scheduled to make an appearance at a statewide fair that was held in a small town in downstate southern Illinois. I was the warden of Menard at the time and was experiencing a tremendous amount of opposition from the union. There were many issues that I inherited when I was assigned to Menard, and my approach in dealing with those issues did not endear me to the union's liking.

It was customary for political figures that were campaigning for elected office to visit select prisons throughout the state. This was done to demonstrate their support for the work that correctional employees did, but also to gain the political support of the union. The American Federation of State, County, and Municipal Employees (AFSCME) has one of the largest labor forces in Illinois, and their membership makes for a strong constituent base for any political official who receives their support.

Menard is also the largest correctional facility in Illinois and had various unique features related to its operation, such as a Death Row Unit and several prison industry operations. Because of Menard's prominent status within Illinois' prison system, our agency wanted to arrange for Obama to visit Menard during his campaign while visiting the state fair. When my local union learned of the agency's attempt to have Obama visit Menard, they vehemently protested. Their protest was not in opposition of Obama, but was in opposition of me. Because of our differences and their dislike of me, they strongly fought against his visit. I am more than convinced that had I been a Caucasian warden, the union would have never protested. And needless to say, they got what they wanted; Obama never visited Menard during his campaign.

The politically correct explanation for why he did not come to Menard was that he had a conflict in his schedule. However, I knew that that was smoke and mirror talk. Due to having a few connections of my own, I learned first-hand from someone involved with arranging the visit that their protest was in opposition of me. I was informed that the union pressured the agency with threats of not participating in the reception if they allowed Obama to come. The agency did not want to create any more issues with the union concerning Menard and be subjected to potentially embarrassing media coverage as a result of the union not participating in his welcome, so they compromisingly gave in to the union and chose to forgo Obama's visit.

My instincts were that the union simply did not want an African American warden of the largest prison in the state to meet with a prominent, up-and-coming African American political figure as was Obama at the time. The prospect of me meeting him apparently intimidated them in some way, and they protested very vehemently to keep our meeting from happening. This is but one example of many situations that reinforced for me that my ethnic difference was the primary reason for the union's staunch opposition to me.

My management style was no doubt an anomaly for many union representatives, and they had a hard time dealing with that. We certainly didn't share many of the same principles of management, and most wardens I knew operated with the same philosophy of management that I did. We operated from the perspective that the union had little say in how we managed our prisons. However, the difference was the latitude that some wardens were extended because of how those wardens did or did not go along with the union's demands. I fundamentally differed with the union's expectation that wardens simply relinquish their managerial rights. I would not acquiesce into making conciliatory concessions to give up certain management rights solely to appease the union. I managed based upon our contractual agreement and administrative policies, not based upon the backroom good ole boy philosophy of "I got your back and you got mine." Under that scenario, if something were to go wrong or it wouldn't work out as we agreed, they would have thrown me under the bus. I knew it and they knew it. I wasn't going to be placed in that lose-lose situation. So, because I would not acquiesce to their way of doing business, we were at odds more often than not.

In other efforts to demonstrate their opposition, some union members spread accusations that I did not care for the safety and well-being of staff. Well, was it true that I would aggressively attempt to discipline any staff person that violated institutional rules when such violations placed the facility in jeopardy and/or involved the mistreatment of inmates? The answer is *yes*! That was my charged duty as the warden. Had I not addressed the misconduct of staff, the safety of the entire facility would have been compromised by my willful indifference and negligence. Had that been the case, I would have been rightfully labeled as not being concerned for the safety and well-being of staff, but that was not the case.

Some union members even went as far as to play the reverse racism card by accusing me of not liking white people and claiming that I was a racist. These accusations were nothing more than a ploy to create negative propaganda against me in an effort to intimidate me into becoming more conciliatory to their demands and their way of operating. It is my opinion that all of this was designed to provide a smoke screen distraction to mask the truth of why many of them were in opposition of me. I wasn't the only warden who differed with the union, so it wasn't just my management style that got under their skin. They will never openly admit (maybe a few die-hards will) that my skin color was the primary reason for their strife with me. This element of contention existed throughout my administrative career because of the pervasive racist mentality that existed among a select group of narrow-minded union members.

At other times they tried to create the perception that I was more of a supporter of inmates than I was for them. This was their rallying cry to keep antagonistic sentiments stirred up in an effort to undermine my authority and discredit my leadership. They based their accusations on incidents where they disagreed with how I chose to handle certain situations. They wanted me to take a more punitive approach when deciding what consequences should be imposed against an inmate or a group of inmates when an incident occurred. They did not concern themselves with whether or not fair and impartial judgment was used in making the decision. They just wanted a negative outcome to happen regardless of the elements of fact. In their minds, an inmate didn't have anything coming, so whenever there was an opportunity to impose disciplinary actions against an inmate, they believed we should do so without impunity, regardless of what was fair. This was a reckless and dangerous way of thinking that I simply did not buy into.

Many of them also took exception to the fact that I held staff accountable for their misconduct, and I'll offer another example of this. During my first week as warden of Menard, in June of 2004, I placed several staff on administrative lockout due to an investigation of staff misconduct. Prior to my assignment there, the Internal Affairs Division for the agency had been conducting an external investigation of an alleged inmate assault by staff. Upon reviewing the information presented in the preliminary investigation report, I concurred with the investigator's recommendation that the staff identified as being involved should be immediately removed from the facility until the investigation was completed.

The preliminary findings strongly implicated staff in assaulting an inmate and conspiring to conceal that fact. Union members quickly seized this opportunity to fuel their accusation that I was out to get staff. There was a strong anti-inmate mentality held by a representative core of the security staff and my actions of locking out staff reinforced for them that I supported inmates and not staff. They openly expressed their sentiments that inmates didn't have anything coming and that my actions were traitorous. They conveyed the attitude that they could use their authority however they saw fit regarding an inmate's treatment. That was a very dangerous attitude to have, and that way of thinking usually led to someone getting hurt. Because I never bought into that way of thinking, several union members tried to peg me in the category of supporting inmates and being against staff. Well, to set the record straight, if doing what was *right* is considered supporting the inmates and not staff, then I plead guilty.

Union members could never legitimately claim that I did not appropriately discipline inmates when such actions were warranted. During my 11-year tenure as an administrator, I was responsible for sanctioning the placement of many inmates in segregation confinement, restricting many of their privileges, and even being involved in putting an inmate to death. These actions are certainly not indicative of someone who favored inmates over staff. If an inmate was not compliant in his conduct, I ensured that he was dealt with accordingly. However, if an inmate was entitled to receive a certain privilege, I would equally ensure that he received that privilege unconditionally. In a few cases that warranted so, I mitigated the severity of a disciplinary sanction that could have been imposed. I used my administrative discretion in weighing the circumstances of each situation because inmates were not always entirely at fault in every incident. Fairness to me meant weighing all sides of the situation and not operating entirely from the position of blind authority and unregulated control.

There were some staff who believed that because I was black and the majority of the inmates were black that I would automatically side with the inmates. Those staff who were in opposition of me attempted to create this false perception to justify their efforts of being contrary to my authority. It wasn't that I was an ally of black inmates simply because of our ethnic commonality, because when you examined the truth of the situation, the majority of inmates that I disciplined were black. I wouldn't look upon that as demonstrating any biased allegiance to them solely on the fact that we shared the same racial makeup. When black inmates got out of line and violated the rules, I held them accountable. However, did I try to ensure that the discipline that was imposed against them was fair and consistent? Yes I did. I simply refused to accept the mentality of some staff that an inmate didn't have anything coming. I would not allow inmates to be mistreated in order for me to garner favored approval of a few wayward staff. I didn't need their approval to do my job. They simply needed to understand that I expected them to do theirs and to do it properly, or there would be consequences if discovered otherwise. By doing their job properly, we would all be safer. It was those staff who regarded inmates as being unworthy and treated them as such that made it more dangerous for all of us who worked there.

The union's presence in the IDOC added a very unique dynamic to how the agency operated their prisons. They frequently created unnecessary opposition against wardens and agency executives when efforts were made to execute or enforce policies that were intended to provide equitable management of staff and inmates. The contentious adversarial approach that the union uses in vying for control is likened, in my opinion, to the intimidation and threat approach that the gangs employ. The only difference is the union doesn't use shanks and knives like the gangs do; they use their political influence.

The Influence of Politics

Talking about the union's efforts to exert their influence on the management of the IDOC brings to mind the dramatic change that our agency underwent after Illinois had its governor's election in 2002. During that election year, the now-impeached Governor Rod Blagojevich was elected as the first Democratic governor of Illinois since 1977, over 26 years. The incumbent governor at that time was George Ryan, the leader of the Republican Party in Illinois. The AFSCME union, which represents the majority of the state's correctional employee workforce, supported Blagojevich during his campaign.

With AFSCME's support, combined with other constituencies throughout the state, Blagojevich was elected Governor of Illinois in a landslide. Most Illinoisans were fed up with Governor Ryan's cronyism and were desperately seeking a change. Governor Ryan's unpopularity made it very easy for Blagojevich to capitalize on the state's desire for change. His youthful charm and charisma blindsided a lot of people, including me. However, looking back with the benefit of 20/20 hindsight, Governor Blagojevich's election turned out to be the beginning of a tremendously disastrous and regrettable term of leadership for many Illinoisans and, specifically, for many of my correctional colleagues.

Shortly after Blagojevich became governor, many of the top officials in the Department of Corrections were fired. The director, several deputy directors, and other top-ranking administrative staff were issued their walking papers without so much as a thank you.

This political power play demonstration was neither unexpected nor uncommon in Illinois' style of politics. The deep-seated resentment that had developed between the Democrats and the Republicans over the preceding 26 years was well established, and the headhunting campaign that ensued was highly anticipated. Now that the Democrats were in office, they were going to make up for the past 26 years of being subservient to the Republicans. The outcome was an all-out political melee against any Republican or Republican associate who had a prominent position in government. Heads were being chopped off left and right, and many Republicans were running and ducking for cover.

What made this administration different from previous administrations was the extent to which they selectively targeted individuals who would be fired. They went several layers deeper into the personnel ranks of corrections to terminate individuals, which was unprecedented. Historically, the upper echelon of the administration, such as directors, deputy directors, and wardens, and occasionally an assistant warden would be fired. But not only did Blagojevich's administration fire ranking executive officials, he gave tacit approval to his newly appointed executive staff for the IDOC to fire seasoned correctional personnel below the ranks of assistant wardens. This included superintendents and other staff. This was in direct response to the union's influence that they had now gained because of Blagojevich's election. Many local state government positions were now filled with persons tied to the Democratic Party. This gave the union a stronger relationship with local officials and they were more than anxious to exert their newfound power. Let me make this perfectly clear. Almost everyone who was fired was either a member of, had allegiance with, were perceived to be loyal to, or had at one time or another been associated with the Republican party.

At the time of Blagojevich's appointment as governor, I was the warden of Tamms and one of my assistant wardens was fired for those very reasons. The union for my facility did not like my assistant warden at all, and they jumped on the chance to get him fired. It wasn't his performance, it wasn't his lack of ability or experience, and it wasn't his lack of commitment to serve the agency that caused him to lose his job. It was simply retaliatory politics! The union didn't like him and they got him out. He was replaced by a correctional officer who had less than seven years in the system, and he was a Dietary Food Supervisor before his political appointment. Imagine, if you will, the highest security facility in the state being managed by this level of experience, a food supervisor. It was an administrative disaster waiting to happen. And when the truth about his inexperience came to light, he summarily relieved himself of his position within about a year or so later because he couldn't handle the responsibility. But unfortunately, the damage from his inexperienced leadership had already been done.

Everyone who was fired was fired without regard for their years of service or without regard for the concern of the agency's continued level of competent management. There was no way for the agency to replace the years of experience, wisdom, and leadership that had been lost because of the firing of so many seasoned individuals. The firing of these individuals was purely politically motivated. It had nothing to do with the person's performance as a correctional professional. And quiet as it may be kept from the general public, those of us who were eyewitnesses to the carnage that resulted from this political witch hunt know for a fact that the union played a major role in determining who got hired and who got fired.

It became so blatant and appalling that several of my warden colleagues filed a class action lawsuit against Governor Blagojevich for their unjustified termination. Unfortunately for them, their lawsuit did not receive proper consideration; they lost their appeal. The only justice that they received came far too late and long after the damage had been done to their professional and personal lives. Their justice came in 2009 when Governor Blagojevich was impeached from office and faced the possibility of going to prison himself.

For my colleagues who suffered the loss of their careers during his administration, this was poetic justice. Since that time, Governor Blagojevich was found guilty of 17 counts of political and criminal malfeasance, and in December 2011, he was sentenced to 14 years in prison, a befitting end for someone who took advantage of his position of power and caused so much grief to befall upon the lives of so many.

To give you a little more insight as to the extent to which some of my colleagues suffered as a result of the political vindictiveness that became rampant, I will share two stories that are representative of this game of power and retaliation. Kim Bagley was a warden who had obtained several years of experience with the agency, but on October 1, 2003, she and two other wardens were fired. Their firings were greatly influenced by members of their local union who had connections with local and state Democratic officials. Union members will never publicly admit the influence that they had in getting these individuals fired, but the record will bear evidence of several prison administrators being terminated beginning shortly after Blagojevich was elected into office and throughout much of his term. The political climate during that time was so cutthroat that revenge, payback, and defamation of a person's character were the modus operandi for those who had come into power. Because the union had backed Blagojevich during his campaign, they gained significant political influence as a result of his appointment as governor, at least as it related to the Illinois Department of Corrections.

When Kim and another warden colleague were let go, neither she nor he had enough time in the system to retire and begin receiving their pension. As a result of not having a job and needing to continue to work, they both sought other employment opportunities. Kim got hired with a company that provided prison contractual consulting services to foreign countries, and my colleague found work as car salesman. Kim's first assignment required that she go to Iraq to assist with a project there. While on a bus tour of the area, her bus was ambushed by insurgents and she was shot in the head and killed. In my colleague's case, his drastic loss of income as a car salesman created a significant financial hardship for him, which affected him and his family for several years afterward. The point of these stories is simply to highlight the unfortunate suffering that many of my colleagues experienced for nothing more than petty politics. Had Kim not been fired for vindictive political reasons, she would have never been in Iraq and therefore would not have lost her life prematurely. She would most likely still be alive today! And as for my colleague, he probably would not have experienced the financial hardship that he and his family suffered.

These are just a couple of the situations that resulted from the political melee caused by the unwritten but widely accepted policy of the governor's administration which declared that the hunting season for political opponents was now open. Other colleagues suffered in other personal ways as well and were also adversely affected by the vindictiveness of this political juggernaut. No one in the governor's administration or in the union will ever accept any collateral responsibility for the role they played in Kim's death. The governor can conveniently hide behind the jurisprudence loophole that Kim's appointment as a warden is done at the discretion of the governor (and in her case it was Governor George Ryan) and there is no justification needed by a governor for firing a political appointee. From the pragmatic and practical perspective of knowing how political appointments happen, this is a factual reality. The governor is politically insulated from being personally responsible for hiring or firing certain governmental positions. He delegates that authority to the director of each agency. Although Governor Blagojevich did not personally fire Kim, nor did he personally know her as far as I know, his tacit collusion with the union's political influence created the circumstances that led up to her firing and, in my opinion, indirectly to her death.

Let me be very clear here. It was common knowledge among the correctional community in Illinois that the decision to fire Kim and others like her was made solely on the basis of political vindictiveness influenced by the special interests of the union. There were certain individuals targeted for various reasons of retaliation. The climate was such that they could use their political hunting license with impunity. None of my colleagues were fired on the basis of poor performance or lack of committed effort. It was pure politics! It is my personal belief that Kim would still be alive today had they not played politics with her life and fired her for the horrid reason of vengefulness.

Because of this antagonistic style of political management, an atmosphere of uncertainty, instability, and leaderless direction was created within our agency. And to add insult to injury, which made this whole situation even more difficult for me to tolerate, was the fact that Kim and other high-ranking administrative staff were replaced with inexperienced and less than competent people. The agency was becoming dangerously ill-fitted with status-seeking persons rather than being equipped with experienced, qualified correctional leaders. The writing of an agency's internal implosion was clearly plastered all over the wall.

As for my situation, I was not concerned about being fired for political reasons because I had traditionally voted as a Democratic since I was of voting age, and I did so in this case as well. However, what I will say is that I deeply regret having cast my vote for Governor Blagojevich. He turned out to be a colossal failure in integrity and trust for his constituents. I became extremely disillusioned by the unwarranted firings and rampant vindictive demotions of so many of my colleagues for nothing more than the politics of who was in power. It became a very vile atmosphere to work in.

And to add further insult to injury, I became even more disillusioned witnessing how competent and experienced correctional professionals were replaced with inexperienced political appointees.

The majority of the appointees had no clue how to effectively manage a large, complex correctional agency such as ours, and this made it increasingly more difficult for me to accept the direction that our agency was headed. In truth, we had no direction. The union began blatantly flexing their influence even greater than before because they now felt they had the unconditional support of political leverage from the top down. They seemed to have become punch drunk on their newfound power and were unfazed about who got hurt by their unscrupulous efforts to ruin people's lives.

The inexperience and naive understanding that many of the new appointees had regarding how to manage a large and complex correctional agency would have far-reaching consequences throughout our system. The infrastructure of our operating procedures began to lose their effectiveness because of poor leadership and mismanagement of established practices. Our new management took for granted and/or ignored the precedents of the agency's well-established methods of operating. This created an atmosphere that allowed the undermining influence of the union to become more and more invasive into the day-to-day operations of how wardens managed their facilities. It had gotten to the point where most wardens, if not all of us, were having more problems with our staff than we were with our inmates.

As I mentioned earlier, during my last tour of duty at Menard, the union and I were at odds quite a bit. In one particular situation that I recall, a member of the union chose to demonstrate his dislike of me by putting a degrading slogan on the license plate of his truck. The slogan was an image of a little boy pissing on my name which was to be interpreted as "Piss on Hinsley." I cared nothing about the slogan because he had a right to voice his opinion about me. The First Amendment of the Constitution gives him that right. But, when he chose to park his truck on state grounds displaying the license plate in full view, that's when the situation became an administrative matter. As far as I was personally concerned, he could have displayed his license plate all around the world or anywhere else for that matter. It was just that trivial of an issue to me. But when he decided to park on state property as a state employee, that is when it became an issue of inappropriate and unacceptable conduct.

It was no longer just about him disrespecting me specifically, because had he chosen to put another employee's name in place of mine, I would have taken the same course of action on their behalf as well. I initially gave him the option to park his truck across the street off of state property. I never told him that he could not have the slogan on his truck because that was his personal right to do so. However, I did advise him that I was not going to allow him to park his truck on state property if he insisted on keeping the slogan displayed on his truck. To make a long story short, he chose to continue parking on the prison grounds and, consequently, I disciplined him for his misconduct. And as usual, the union filed a grievance against the discipline he received and they were successful in getting his discipline reduced at a third level grievance hearing.

Our agency has an administrative body that is designed to represent wardens at these hearings on behalf of our management rights. Many times our representatives would cave in to the pressures of the union at these hearings, and they did so in this case as well. Our representatives would call their acts of compromise mediation; we, the wardens, called it what it was, selling out. In essence, the authority that was given to wardens to exercise appropriate discipline against staff for their misconduct would be undermined by the very people who were supposed to support us. The failure by our representatives to consistently support the disciplinary and/or administrative actions that we imposed against staff was a frequent occurrence that wardens experienced. Our ability to effectively manage our prisons was being subverted by our own people. This only served to reinforce for the union that there were no limits to their efforts to control how our prisons operated. All they needed to do was continue their intimidating tactics using their political leverage and they would get just about whatever they wanted. And they were very quick to flaunt their newfound sense of power in the face of wardens and our upper management.

I clearly recall how some members of our executive management would repeatedly impress upon wardens that we needed to become more "*union friendly.*" This was our executive management's politically correct way of telling us that we needed to cooperate, stop making waves, and go along with basically whatever the union wanted. This edict became even more evident to me during a meeting that I and a few of my warden colleagues were involved in with our new Chief of Operations, Salvador Godinez.

I was the warden of Menard at the time and was experiencing my fair share of contentious issues with my local union, as were other wardens. One of the topics on his agenda was Union/Management Relations. When he finished explaining to us the position of compromise and conciliation that he expected us to acquiesce to in order for us to become union friendly, he made a closing comment that was indelibly imprinted upon my mind. He stated, and I quote, "If you can't be a team player then you need to get off the team." Here was a senior executive administrator insinuating to his senior facility administrators that if we were not willing to appease the union, then we needed to start looking for another line of work.

In addition to taking his comment to heart, I considered it to be insulting and a disrespectful affront to all wardens in our agency. Of all the employees working in our agency, wardens were the one group of individuals that he should have been supporting the most, not the union. We were committed to the equitable and fair management of our facilities, and the union was committed to the self-interest of their membership. I interpreted Chief Godinez's comment to mean that if we didn't appease the union in every way they requested, we would not receive support from our executive leadership, he being one of them. Each of us at that meeting, as well as the wardens who were not present, had given our devoted commitment to serving the agency for the best interest of the agency. For him to suggest that we needed to step down from our positions as warden if we were unwilling to allow the union to have as much say in how we managed our prisons as they (the union) wanted was totally absurd! This was a blatant insult to our professional integrity and leadership. It seemed to me that he simply wanted us to go along to get along. His statement became the significant turning point and a defining moment for me which led to my decision to tender my services with the agency.

His statement reinforced what I and other wardens had been noticing gradually happening between our new executive leadership and the union. A co-opted relationship had formed whereby we, the wardens, were told in so many words that we had better cooperate with the union or else we would not receive the administrative support that we had customarily received from previous managements when dealing with union-related matters. In other words, we would be hung out to dry and left on our own if we continued to challenge the union. This had become a lose-lose situation that wardens were faced with simply because our executive leadership had become beholden to the political influence of the union. Our effectiveness as administrators was severely undermined by our administration's tacit approval of the union's invasive efforts to manage our agency. It had reached a point for me where I could no longer accept our administration's co-opted style of managing our agency and, regrettably, this style of management became the standard mode of operation for the agency and it also became the downfall of our agency.

This area of contention was a non-negotiable point for me, and I was not going to change the way I conducted business with the union. Insisting that staff adhere to the rules, insisting that staff treat inmates respectfully, and insisting that management maintain the right to operate our prisons as we deemed necessary were the principles for which I would not back away from. With that being the case, I decided that it would be in my best interest to separate myself from this train wreck before it happened. It wasn't the fact that I couldn't deal with the petty issues brought forth by the union; I had been doing that all the while and would continue to deal with them. It was the fact that I no longer had confidence in our executive administration to stand committed behind their wardens and support us against the behest of the union when those challenging moments would come. And they would come!

The writing was now on the wall. Our administration was willing to squander the leadership experience of seasoned wardens just to appease the union. With that understanding now made very clear by Chief Godinez, I made the decision right then to opt out from being relegated to the position of an administrative puppet, and I respectfully tendered my services with the Illinois Department of Corrections on December 31, 2004.

As I look back over those times and reflect on the conditions of what was occurring, I am confident that I would make the same decision now. It was an atmosphere of sheer unbridled pandemonium relative to wardens not having any true say in managing their facilities. We were expected to be puppets on a string or act like Pavlov's dog when the bell rang, and I didn't respond well to either of those scenarios. Was I loyal to the agency? Absolutely! But I refused to be subjugated to operating at the direction of an organization whose principles of management seemed to be leading the agency into a polarizing maelstrom. I had no trusting sense that our administration was going to reverse their way of operating with the union, so I made the decision that it was best for me to leave and I left on my own terms. And it's my understanding that it is still this way today and may be even worse.

To add credence to my point about our executive management's unwillingness to support their wardens, three days after I retired from the agency, one of my warden colleagues was fired from the Centralia Correctional Center on January 3, 2005, because he refused to play by union politics and acquiesce to being union friendly. The management of our agency was under imminent siege from the political influence of the union. We were facing an internal collapse of our infrastructure because of a complete lack of strong leadership from our executive administration. The Illinois Department of Corrections had now hit one of its lowest points, if not the lowest point, ever in its illustrious history of providing strong managerial leadership of its operations. This is a sad but true commentary for what was once a progressive and competent agency.

20

WHAT DOES THIS ALL MEAN?

I AM QUITE sure that what I have attempted to explain in this book may not resonate entirely with all who read it and therefore it may require further study for some to help put this into its proper context. For there is no easy way to convey the tremendous life-threatening pressures and varied complexities that correctional officials and their staff face every day while managing a prison. It is literally a life or death situation for both staff and inmates alike in many of our overcrowded prisons. This aspect of prison life is oftentimes not spoken about publicly and usually goes unmentioned until a sensationalized incident happens, such as Attica, Lucasville, Pinckneyville, or other prison incidents across the country.

The complexities involved in the multi-layered dynamics that impact our system of control over a person's freedom are more than the average person can and will ever fully understand. The fundamental purpose of prison is to protect the common good of society from those who take advantage of society's vulnerabilities and innocence. But bear in mind that our cultural social structure has contributed greatly to the plight by which many persons, and particularly the poor and persons of color, have become entrapped by the institutionalization of a capitalistic system of the haves versus the have-nots, not to mention the racial discrimination that has been a fundamental and perpetual practice of American society.

I have attempted to provide a rare and realistic glimpse of what takes place behind the walls of our nation's prisons and, more specifically, behind the walls of the Illinois prison system for which I had the privilege to work for almost 20 years. What I had to say is from my own experiences and represents my own perspective. I do not claim to be a definitive expert in the field of criminal justice or prison management; however, I assertively profess that I have a unique insight into the inner workings of our prison systems through my personal experience, from being an entry-level staff person to becoming a senior level administrator. This experience affords me the latitude to express my point of view freely and candidly and from a perspective not experienced by a large facet of our society. My point of view is certainly open to criticism and opposing views; however, in taking the liberty of speaking my truth as I believe it to be, I will briefly reiterate some of the perspectives that I have offered heretofore.

The War on Drugs campaign during the early '80s and '90s greatly contributed to the overcrowded conditions in our nation's prisons. This led to increased violence within our prisons and became a major contributing factor why many prison systems implemented super maximum security prisons as a way to help manage their agencies. Illinois was no exception. The rampant violence and incessant disruptions that occurred in our prison facilities had simply become out of control. We desperately needed to reverse the trend of who was running our prisons and put the administration back in control.

Significant progress toward regaining control of Illinois' maximum security prisons occurred during the middle '90s and early

2000s. This is when we introduced new security methods and implemented different management strategies throughout our maximum security facilities. The implementation of our supermax prison in Tamms, Illinois, was one of many managerial strategies that were introduced in our effort to restore order and regain control in our prisons. And with all due respect to the advocates who oppose this form of prison management because they claim that super maximum security prisons are a form of cruel and unusual punishment, they have *failed*, in my opinion, to offer one credible solution to offset the real life day-to-day challenges of dealing with disruptive, violent, and problematic inmates. They simply cry foul against the use of highly restrictive measures of control that prison officials exert over their most dangerous and problematic inmates. And they do so without giving probing consideration to the complex dynamics that impact the prison culture that is heavily influenced by the overcrowded conditions of persons who have predatory and violent tendencies.

Prisons as a whole are a negative place. To that end, these negative environments inherently require harsh responses and demand restrictive methods of control to maintain order when such behavior becomes a threat to their safe operation. The Tamms Super Maximum Security Correctional Center was one of our management tools created for handling the overt negativity that many of our problematic inmates repeatedly engaged in.

The gang presence in Illinois' prison system during the time I worked there, and even today, is quite pervasive within their prison facilities. The level of sophistication and prevalence of gang activity continues to demand that the agency's security methods be proactive, firm, and decisive; otherwise they will lose the leverage of control that has been established over many years through blood, sweat, tears, and litigation. Unfortunately, the lack of strong, consistent administrative leadership over the past 10 to 12 years has eroded much of that leverage. Need I remind Illinois of Superintendent Robert Taylor and other staff who have been seriously injured and brutally killed by gang members during a time when the gangs were running our asylums? I need not say any more in defense of supermax prisons; the agency's history should speak for itself. However, it's a matter of whether or not the powers that be will listen and take heed of the lessons learned from history. I just pray that Illinois' prison system does not have to relearn those lessons the hard way.

Although I have devoted much of my commentary to the security aspect of how prisons operate and the survival elements of prison life, I would be remiss if I did not comment on the programmatic infrastructure that serves as the balancing force that helps keep the operation of prisons stabilized. Security is the primary emphasis for operating a prison and rightly so, but as I alluded to earlier, the most secure and effectively operated prison will always have a significant programmatic component interfaced within its operation. Even in highly secured, closed custody prisons such as a supermax prison, there is a recognized need to offer some level of programmatic services. Most prison officials will tell you that integrating educational and self-help programs into their daily operation greatly enhances the quality of safety within their facilities. However, if a facility is frequently on lockdown due to ongoing disruptions and/or gang-related activity, the availability for programs to be offered will be greatly diminished. Therefore, the opportunities for rehabilitation to occur will be of little consequence.

Additionally, programmatic resources, or a lack thereof, are inexplicably tied to the amount of budgetary funding allocated to each agency. As more and more agencies face a reduction in their budgets, more and more programmatic services will be reduced and in some cases eliminated altogether. Over the past 15 to 20 years, there have been several significant events that have occurred that have reinforced why programmatic services are a necessary element that must be included in effectively managing prison culture. These events are far too complicated to address in my closing summary. However, I will state in a broad sense that the War on Drugs, the Truth In Sentencing Law, our overcrowded prison conditions, and the increased violence in our prisons have collectively contributed to the need to re-examine the issue of rehabilitation within our prisons.

Now that our nation is facing an epidemic with regard to inmates being ill-prepared to return to our communities and successfully transition into society, a committed effort by the federal government has been initiated that focuses on the overarching concern of prison re-entry. With the passing of the Second Chance Act in April 2008, which authorized $300 million to be awarded to states and their respective correctional agencies for developing comprehensive collaborative strategies with community-based organizations to address prison re-entry, programmatic services in prisons are gaining more support for the role they share in helping stabilize the prison environment. But even more than that, these services are now receiving greater attention for the role they play in preparing inmates to be better equipped to stay out of prison and helping curb the revolving door of recidivism. We still have a very long way to go to get where we need to be, but this commitment is a step in the right direction.

I spoke very briefly about the unionized labor force that plays a major role within the Illinois Department of Corrections. I spoke of this aspect of Illinois' prison management for the sole purpose of enlightening the general public about the tremendous influence that the union has on the operation of Illinois' prison system. Should the union be instrumental in and have a voice in creating better working conditions and wages for the members of their organization? The answer is an absolute *yes!* And should the union fight for and stand up for safe working conditions for their membership? The answer is still an absolute *yes!*

However, should the union be allowed to make administrative policy—albeit unofficially through political influence—and have tacit authority to manage our agency? The answer is an emphatic *no!* Should they be involved as an equal partner in deciding the day-to-day operation of our facilities? This answer is also an emphatic *no*! But unfortunately, their political influence has become so invasive in how Illinois' prisons are operated that they routinely determine which administrative personnel will get hired or fired and which policies will or will not be implemented.

Our administrative leadership was basically held hostage by the political influence of the union, and the ransom that they demanded from the agency was for us to give up complete control over how our prisons would be managed. There were many situations where policy and/or personnel-related matters that wardens and senior executive officials wanted to be implemented were prevented from occurring because of the union's opposition. During my exit interview with the director of the agency at the time of my retirement, he confided in me that there were many senior level positions filled by the powers that be that he was not privy to prior to them occurring. He further stated that he would learn of them only after a decision to appoint them had already been made. Individuals were being appointed to high paying, responsible positions solely at the discretion of the union's influence and without the director's input or concern.

If the union did not agree with a particular matter, in many cases that situation would not happen. For years, there has been a tenuous history between the ASFCME union and the Illinois Department of Corrections competing for hierarchy of the agency's management. It is my opinion that from the time of Governor Blagojevich's election in 2002 until the present day, the union's influence has reached an unprecedented level of power in Illinois with respect to the day-to-day operation of its prisons. Because of their unabated involvement in the day-to-day management of Illinois' prison facilities, the union had and may very well still have, a stifling affect upon wardens' and executive officials' ability to ensure the efficient operation of their prisons. That, my folks, is a very vulnerable and dangerous position for a correctional agency to be in.

I also talked about the controversial issue of the death penalty. Is the death penalty constitutional and should it be prohibited altogether? Illinois answered that question with the signing of legislation into law by Governor Pat Quinn on March 9, 2011, banning the death penalty in their state. Nonetheless, as I stated before, I believe that a society's authority to impose the sanction of death against another human being is preempted in divine law. And because of this belief, I firmly support the use of the death penalty. And as I also said previously, I am acutely aware of the historical and factual evidence that most persons who are currently on death row and who are sentenced to death by execution are disproportionately African American men. However, it is not the action of taking someone's life per se that I struggle with most; it is the improper application of the law of justice against an individual who has been assigned this fate that is of greater concern to me.

Malcolm X once stated, "*I am for truth no matter who truth is for, and I am for justice no matter who justice is for.*" When the system of justice that we practice continues to be influenced by biased, self-serving, and discriminatory methods of judicial jurisprudence, the administration of the death penalty will continue to adversely impact people of color and those economically disadvantaged. It is not the principles of law that are improper per se; it is the actions of those who misuse the principles of law that are improper. Tragically, innocent people and persons who cannot ensure a quality defense will always be the victims of this judicial imbalance. However, it is my belief that if the true principles of the law of jurisprudence are exercised without such bias and discrimination, the true intent of the law of judicial jurisprudence will prevail more often than not. Therefore, if the process of proper justice renders a sanction of death for a person's violation of another person's human life, then the integrity of fair justice that we all are entitled to receive will be upheld for the good of society.

I am totally convinced that there are human beings that will inflict harm to other human beings as often as they can get away with it. I have walked among many of them and certainly have read about others. It is this type of individual, in my opinion, that if found unequivocally guilty of the premeditative and wanton act of taking the life of another person, should summarily forfeit their right to remain on this earth and as a consequence, their life can be legally and justifiably taken. The penalty for one who violates the human rights of another to peacefully coexist without fear of harm from others should be severe and of equal consequence when the violation of that right is heinous and reprehensible. The premeditated and wanton act of murdering someone is reprehensible to me!

When presented in its raw truth, the stark reality of prison life is not a pleasant notion to talk about, but we *must* talk about it if we are to change the way we currently operate. Although 98 percent of the people who are placed in prison eventually get released, the emotional, psychological, spiritual, and, in some cases, physical scars that result from their experience are immeasurable in terms of human suffering and the immense collateral consequences that result from it. Prisons are an unfortunate and an unavoidable reality of our human condition. Regrettably, persons who experience this degrading and dehumanizing circumstance are fraught with the challenges of how to offset the adverse affects of such a negative experience. The internalization of the negative effects of prison life is usually suffered in silence by the individual, but the repercussions of their suffering are manifested in society in more ways than one. We may never ever fully comprehend the extent of their suffering, nor the extent of society's collateral consequences.

Do many individuals survive the harshness of prison life and overcome the negative impact that it has on their life? The obvious answer is *yes*, because there are many stories that can be told to attest to this triumphant accomplishment. My brother is one of them. However, there are far too many individuals who have not been so fortunate. With that being the reality, the more critical question to ask ourselves is, "At what cost and to what degree of sacrifice are we, *society*, willing to help an individual achieve this redeeming act of triumph against the odds of such stigmatized and prolific adverse conditions?" Please do not be misled by the misconception that this is an individual who lives in someone else's neighborhood and not in your own neighborhood. For if you were to just look around, you'd probably see this individual living in your own neighborhood, and possibly even in your own family. The collateral effects of the criminal justice system touch us all, but the choice to be involved and make a difference is yours!

Prison life . . . the good, the bad, and the ugly!

APPENDIX I

THE ILLINOIS DEPARTMENT OF CORRECTIONS

Perspectives

Illinois Department of Corrections

News for and about IDOC　　　January - February 1998　　　Volume 21 - Number 1

IDOC...Past-present-future
Building upon our legacy

See related articles - Pages 2, 4 and 8-15.

Howard A. Peters
Director 1991-1995

Peter B. Bensinger
First IDOC Director 1970-1972

Allyn R. Sielaff
Director 1973-1976

Kenneth L. McGinnis
Director 1990-1991

Director
Odie Washington

Charles J. Rowe
Director 1977-1978

Michael P. Lane
Director 1981-1990

Gayle M. Franzen
Director 1978-1980

The future looks gray fo

FROM THE MINUTE NEW INMATES WALK INTO A PRISON, GANGS INFLUENCE HOW THEIR LIVES ARE GOVERNED

Maximum-security institutions are patrolled with shotguns.
A guard stands on a catwalk in Pontiac's south cellhouse.

Illinois' prison system

A MATTER OF TIME

Too many inmates

MANY OF THE PROBLEMS FACING PRISONS CAN BE TRACED TO THE DARK WORLD OF DRUGS

'NOTHING CAN PREPARE YOU FOR DEALING WITH AN INMATE HAND TO HAND'

Originally published in The State Journal-Register, *Springfield, IL. Reprinted with permission.*

245

BOOT CAMP AND PROBATION ARE AIMED AT REFORMING INMATES — AND SAVING MONEY

New arrivals at boot camp are almost jovial as they're herded out of a DOC van. Their smiles vanish, however, during a two-hour hazing session—their introduction to Impact Incarceration Program.

Two inmates carry the "motivation" log as punishment for fighting. For two days they must carry the log, which weighs about 100 pounds, everywhere—even to the showers.

An inmate who asked to leave IIP sits near his bed, which sports a "quitter" sign. The sign on the wall reads, "It is characteristic of wisdom not to do desperate things." The inmate rejoined the program.

Originally published in The State Journal-Register, *Springfield, IL. Reprinted with permission.*

May 9, 1996
SECTION TWO

COUNTY JOURNAL

State Says It Will Get Prison Cell Curtains Down

It's An Old Problem That Has Bothered Guards For Several Years

"There's not an agreement. We don't need an agreement to take the curtains down."

That's how Department of Corrections public information officer Nic Howell sums up the issue of makeshift curtains in cells at Menard Correctional Center.

The employees' union and higher-ups in the department are still at odds over the issue, however.

Both sides agree the curtains should come down, but the union says it's not being done.

Guards and other correctional employees have campaigned to have blankets and other makeshift curtains in cells removed since they create a danger to employees and, in some cases, the inmates themselves. Last month, representatives of the American Federation of State, County and Municipal Employees Union (AFSCME), the union which represents the correctional officers, announced that an agreement had been reached to take down the curtains. That announcement was made during a visit to the prison by Stat Representatives Terry Deering and Kurt Granberg.

AFSCME field representative Steve Joiner of Chester says, however, the plan to remove the curtains has stalled.

"Apparently our agreement has broken down," said Joiner. "They started taking down curtains in the (segregation) unit at Menard and the prisoners started causing trouble. They haven't even begun to take them down in the general population."

This file photo from March, 1986 shows that obstacles placed inside cells was a problem back then. At the time, guards were complaining about how the practice made their work more dangerous.

Howell said there never was an agreement between the department and the union. He adds, however, that taking down the curtains is a policy which the department will pursue throughout the state system.

"The curtains are going to come down, starting in the segregation units and going right down the line," says Howell. "This will take some time, but it's going to happen and it's going to be complete. It has to be consistent. You can't have one guy taking them down on one shift and someone else come right back in and give them back to the inmates."

Deering and Granberg had included the curtain issue in legislation which called for more guards and tighter security at the state's prisons. That legislation is still pending in the general assembly.

Originally published in Randolph County Journal, *Percy, IL. Reprinted with permission.*

249

The Southern

ILLINOISAN

www.thesouthern.com   SATURDAY, MARCH 4, 2006   Vol. 113, No. 63 50¢

Inmate killed at Big Muddy

BY MATT ADRIAN
SPRINGFIELD BUREAU

SPRINGFIELD—An inmate at Big Muddy Correctional Center died after a fight with another prisoner, marking the second major incident of violence within the Illinois prison system in the last 17 days.

The death comes as the Blagojevich administration and state government's largest employee union square off over understaffing within the state prison system.

Gerald Donaldson, 64, died Thursday at St. Louis University Hospital after an altercation with another inmate on the sidewalk outside the high-medium security prison's commissary. The prison, located near the Jefferson County community of Ina, is still was locked down Friday evening.

The incident is being investigated by the IDOC and the Illinois State Police, said Dede Short, a spokeswoman for the Corrections department.

When the investigation is completed, it will be forwarded to the Jefferson County state's attorney to review whether charges will be filed.

Donaldson was serving a 19-year prison sentence after being found guilty on multiple charges such as aggravated criminal sexual assault and

INMATE: *Killed at Big Muddy Correctional Center*

kidnapping in Cook County. The man was charged with luring six children between ages 7 and 12 into an abandoned building in 1993. Donaldson's projected parole date was Nov. 20, 2013.

There hasn't been an inmate homicide in the state prison system since fiscal year 2004, when the agency reported three murders, Short said.

This is the second violent incident to occur within the state prison system in the last 17 days. On Feb. 14, a female food service worker was allegedly sexually assaulted by an inmate in the Jacksonville Correctional Center.

The incidents come as the American Federation of State, County and Municipal Employees union has raised concerns that the prison system is understaffed.

Anders Lindell, an AFSCME spokesman, said having additional staff "may have minimized the incident or kept it from happening."

Short defended the department's handling of the situation.

"I think that it's irresponsible to claim staffing had anything to with this incident," she said.

Originally published in The Southern Illinoisan, *Carbondale, IL. Reprinted with permission.*

Pinckneyville prison condition warrants study

OUR VIEW: We need to know more about the conditions at Pinckneyville Correctional Center before the Dec. 14 violent incident.

It's rarely a good sign when prisons are in the news, especially when the news is reported at the top of the front page. Silence and a scarcity of news reports are better signs a prison is operating safely and effectively.

Such has not been the case at Pinckneyville Correctional Center, beginning with a mid-December violent incident and continuing this

week with investigative reports from our state bureau chief, Kurt Erickson, about underlying conditions at the prison that may have been contributing factors.

Here are the facts:

A prisoner, 37-yer-old Alonje Walton of Chicago, was shot and killed by law enforcement Dec. 14 after he took the prison librarian, a 62-year-old woman, as a hostage and held her captive for seven hours.

It was reported Tuesday inmate assaults against prison workers at Pinckneyville have increased at an alarming rate, according to statistics from the Illinois Department of Corrections. Assaults on staff members averaged 21 per year between 2000 and 2008 but spiked to a total of 41, for an increase of 95 percent, in fiscal year 2009.

In Wednesday's paper, Prison Union President Randy Hellman linked the Dec. 14 violent attack to the segregation capacity of the prison being cut in half. Hellman said space previously used to segregate troublesome inmates from the rest of the population was instead used to accommodate prisoners being transferred to Pinckneyville because of budget related downsizing at other institutions.

If you've been reading the reports, you may not yet know the specific corrections that need to be pursued but likely have decided Pinckneyville Correctional Center needs a top-to-bottom review of the entire operation. A comprehensive, objective study is needed to look at each aspect of the prison operation—including inmate profiles, staffing levels, staffing experience, inmate population and security measures.

Here are some of the questions we'd like to see answered:

Are the inmates being transferred to Pinckneyville suitable for the confinement in a medium-security prison, or are they being moved within the system solely to meet budget expectations?

Why does Pinckneyville have an incident of attacks on staff that is nearly three times higher than at comparable institutions, such as Lawrence Correctional Center in Sumner and Hill Correctional Center in Galesburg?

What efforts were taken to determine the reduced number of segregation beds at Pinckneyville, a total of 2014, is appropriate for the specific prison population? We appreciate the explanation from DOC spokeswoman Januari Smith that the prison's segregation unit's capacity of 214 is in line with comparable institutions, but it evades the real issue. We'd like to see a deeper explanation.

Was it reasonable to allow staffing at Pinckneyville to decrease to the current total of 394, down from 520 in 2006, while the inmate population grew from 2,159 to 2,241 during the same time period? Perhaps it is possible to safely confine greater numbers with fewer workers; what are the specifics of how it is being done?

And, finally, what more can DOC officials tell us about Alonje Walton being housed in the general population of the prison instead of segregation before the Dec. 14 incident? Hellman suggested if the prison's segregation unit had not been downsized, Walton may not have been allowed back in the general prison population within four months of being caught with a homemade weapon.

This is not just a matter of importance to Southern Illinois and to the people who are personally attached to the staff and prison population at Pinckneyville. We respect their desires for safety and security for their loved ones—it is the expectation for all prisons—but also want to ensure any warning signs identified in the Pinckneyville investigation are quickly communicated to the state's other correctional centers.

This is a matter of statewide importance. The Dec. 14 incident in Pinckneyville may represent the tip of an iceberg. Once all the facts are known, it may be possible to safely and effectively chart a course away from disaster.

Originally published in The Southern Illinoisan, *Carbondale, IL. Reprinted with permission.*

APPENDIX II

MENARD CORRECTIONAL CENTER

The maximum security Menard Correctional Center along the banks of the Mississippi River

Unit Superintendent

South Uppers Gallery

"Real men" behind bars

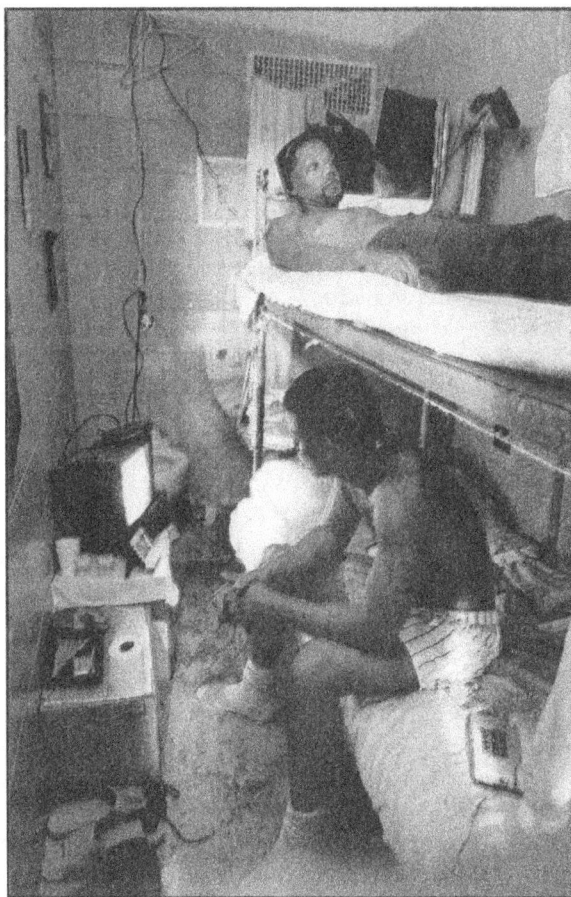

Two inmates share a run-down cell at Menard Correctional Center.

Sunday, December 31, 1995

▶MENARD CORRECTIONAL CENTER

Warden hopes to

By Thomas Beaumont
The Southern Illinoisan

An idea can become a vision with the addition of one simple ingredient: inspiration.

For Charles Hinsley, the assistant warden for programs at the Menard Correctional Center in Chester, that inspiration came from the faces of a million black men in Washington, D.C., last fall. With the program he is trying to organize, Hinsley hopes to transplant some of that inspiration to the inmate population at the maximum security prison.

Early last year, Hinsley got the idea to try to have lecturers from Southern Illinois University at Carbondale come to the prison to talk to the inmates as a way of encouraging them to strive for more.

"I had been thinking about it since January 1994, but I only got involved in trying to push this program after I attended the Million Man March," Hinsley said.

"It was just that after participating in the march, I began trying to pride a means—to provide an atmosphere—of something positive inside the walls. So I just took my idea from that."

What Hinsley is trying to put together is a regular series of lectures that appeals to a wide variety of interests to allow the inmates to have a chance to hear how they can improve themselves and even consider plans for when their release comes.

"We would like to show them what makes this world work, give them a glimpse of something other than the world in which many of them operate." He said. "Hopefully it will enlighten a few others and get them to focus."

The Million Man March, Hinsley said, "was a tremendous event. You really can't adequately describe it in words."

In an atmosphere that he described as enthusiastic, peaceful and spiritual, the march itself and the day of speakers encouraged those in attendance to cherish unity and responsibility to family and community, Hinsley said.

"Bottom line: It just felt good," he said. "And when you feel good, you want to make others feel good."

Hinsley said carrying the message back to the prison is part of what he can do to transfer the positive energy from the march to the inmates.

'inspire' inmates

The lectures would be on a variety of topics, which would be determined by the professors who are willing and available.

"Whatever professors I can get involved we will consider," Hinsley said. "Science, education, you name it, business, government, wherever I can get the support for the program."

Hinsley said that the plan comes at a time when funding for the prison's community college program has been sharply cut.

"Inmates can get involved in correspondence courses," Hinsley said. But unfortunately we had to cut back on our college program through Rend Lake College. That's something that has gone on in the past."

For now, Hinsley is trying, not so much to allow every inmate a chance to earn a college degree while at Menard, but to enlighten and inspire large groups.

"This is just something to let the inmates be exposed to something of a more positive nature," he said.

Some inmates have attended lectures during February's Black History Month observation, Hinsley said, but he would like to make this series more permanent and available to more inmates.

In the past, the response has been that about 40 or 50 of the prison's roughly 2,500 inmates attended the lectures. "I would like to expand on that," he said.

Hinsley is planning to circulate a questionnaire to get a feel for the level of interest among the inmates, but his sense is that it will be well-received.

Originally published in The Southern Illinoisan, *Carbondale, IL. Reprinted with permission.*

Belleville (Ill.) News-Democrat   Wednesday, October 11, 1995

'The Pit': At Menard, life is as hard as the nearby bluffs

Associated Press

CHESTER—Those who live there call it "The Pit," as apt a description as any for Illinois' largest maximum-security prison and the limestone bluffs towering above it on two sides.

For many of the 2,600 inmates at Menard Correctional Center, the nickname covers more than the geography. Menard, after all, is not a nice place.

"Sit down when shots are fired," warn signs posted all over the prison mess hall. Dangling from the ceiling are large sheets of white plywood with small dents left by a guard's warning shots.

"This place is a death trap, if you really want to know the truth about it," said Andre Jackson of Chicago, serving eight years for robbery. "I wouldn't wish Menard on my worst enemy."

Warden Thomas Page and his guards wouldn't go quite as far but agree the 117-year-old prison along the Mississippi River can be very dangerous.

Five guards have been killed on duty since 1965. Assaults by inmates on both guards and other inmates are common. One of every three prisoners is a convicted murderer.

"You've heard the expression, 'We live day-by-day'? Page said. "Well, it's hour-by-hour over here."

Overcrowding has turned a difficult job into an explosive one; Menard's aging structures were designed to hold only 1,612 inmates.

"It's not built for modern-day criminals," Assistant Warden Roger Cowan said.

Menard was made with stone carved from the 30- to 40-foot bluffs to its east and south. Although the 41-acre prison's tall, razor-wire-topped walls are sound, keeping the electricity and plumbing working is a never-ending challenge, Cowan said.

Menard is like a tiny village with its own water treatment plant, laundry, store and clinic. In its factories, the best-behaved inmates are paid to make brooms, towels, cigarettes and other items. The prison even has a 2,400-acre farm, where prisoners raise hogs and cattle.

Atop one bluff sits a somber-looking castle where 56 condemned me wait. While their fate may be depressing, their view of the wide Mississippi below is breathtaking.

Nearby, a $14 million cellhouse under construction will house another 150 prisoners.

Just as a visitor grows complacent, Page points out: "The location of our towers is excellent. There are very few blind spots. You're normally under a gun just about everywhere you go here."

Page 10   Springfield, Illinois   THE STATE JOURNAL-REGISTER

Menard Penitentiary Warden Tom Page stands outside the Condemned Unit, aka Death Row, at the prison near Chester. There are currently 56 inmates residing in the unit. Unlike the rest of the jammed prison where nearly all inmates are double-celled, death row inmates have their own cell, where they are confined 23 hours a day.

Menard living measured 'hour-by-hour'

Overcrowding turns a difficult job into an explosive one

By FRANK FISHER

THE ASSOCIATED PRESS

CHESTER—Those who live there call it "The Pit," as apt a description as any for Illinois' largest maximum-security prison and the limestone bluffs towering above it on two sides.

For many of the 2,600 inmates at Menard Correctional Center, the nickname covers more than the geography. Menard, after all, is not a nice place.

"Sit down when shots are fired," warn signs posted all over the prison mess hall. Dangling from the ceiling are large sheets of white plywood with small dents left by a guard's warning shots.

"This place is a death trap, if you really want to know the truth about it," said Andre Jackson of Chicago, serving eight years for robbery. "I wouldn't wish Menard on my worst enemy."

Warden Thomas Page and his guards wouldn't go quite as far but agree the 117-year-old prison along the Mississippi River can be very dangerous.

Five guards have been killed on duty since 1965. Assaults by inmates on both guards and other inmates are common. One of every three prisoners is a convicted murderer.

"You've heard the expression, 'We live day-by-day'? Page said. "Well, it's hour-by-hour over here."

Overcrowding has turned a difficult job into an explosive one; Menard's aging structures were designed to hold only 1,612 inmates.

"It's not built for modern-day criminals," Assistant Warden Roger Cowan said.

Menard was made with stone carved from the 30- to 40-foot bluffs to its east and south. Although the 41-acre prison's tall, razor-wire-topped walls are sound, keeping the electricity and plumbing working is a never-ending challenge, Cowan said.

Menard is like a tiny village with its own water treatment plant, laundry, store and clinic. In its factories, the best-behaved inmates are paid to make brooms, towels, cigarettes and other items. The prison even has a 2,400-acre farm, where prisoners raise hogs and cattle.

Atop one bluff sits a somber-looking castle where 56 condemned me wait. While their fate may be depressing, their view of the wide Mississippi below is breathtaking.

Nearby, a $14 million cellhouse under construction will house another 150 prisoners.

Just as a visitor grows complacent, Page points out: "The location of our towers is excellent. There are very few blind spots. You're normally under a gun just about everywhere you go here."

Welcome back the real Menard, where a guard recently was hospitalized after a prisoner threw hot water in his face. It's the prison where guards have found hundreds of homemade knives, made from such mundane items as paint rollers, yard sticks and typewriter parts.

In the prison's 26-bed clinic, one inmate sleeps in the hall because no room is available. Overcrowding is forcing 75 percent of Menard's prisoners to share cells. So far, the most aggressive inmates live by themselves, but Page worries that won't last.

A tour along the prison cells is purposely kept at a quick pace and under a concrete walkway to avoid the cartons of milk, food, urine and feces launched by prisoners above. High along a wall, a guard toting a shotgun stares from an enclosed catwalk.

Inmates thrust small mirrors through the bars so they can see anyone approaching. Profanity fills the rancid-smelling air.

Sgt. Brian Thomas, who was smacked in the face by an inmate a few years ago, accepts the risks that come with the job. But he tries not to talk about his work when he gets home.

"My wife doesn't really like to hear about it that much," Thomas said.

Originally published in The State Journal-Register, *Springfield, IL. Reprinted with permission.*

THURSDAY, MAY 9, 1996   RANDOLPH COUNTY HERALD TRIBUNE

COMMUNITY

No Inquest Date Set Yet In Menard Inmate's Death

An inquest date has not yet been set for a Menard Correctional Center inmate who died April 29.

The death of Antwan Walker, 22, is being investigated by the Randolph County Coroner's Office as a potential homicide. Walker was found with a swollen face, which may have been caused by trauma to his head.

Walker was serving a six-year sentence for a Cook County conviction for unlawful manufacture and delivery of a controlled substance and aggravated discharge of a firearm. He was sent to Menard Correctional Center on April 19, 1995, and was to be release in 1999.

Originally published in Randolph County Herald Tribune, *Chester, IL. Reprinted with permission.*

Menard Holds Memorial For Officers Slain In Duty

Menard Correctional Center held a memorial on Tuesday night for officers killed during duty at the prison. Attending were about 50 family members of the slain officers and a few Menard guards.

Killed on Nov. 23, 1965 were: Lt. Lewis Paul, 36, who began his career with the DOC on April 7, 1957; George Wilson, 62, who began his employment May 1956; and Lt. Arthur Kisro, 45, who began his employment Nov. 17, 1952.

These three men were killed during a riot in the dining hall during the evening meal. A Molotov cocktail was thrown into the tower and blinded the guard. Inmates armed with knives then rushed the other guards. Four inmates were found guilty of the three guards' murders.

Joseph J. Cushman, 52, started work at Menard Correctional Center September 19, 1963. Cushman was found murdered at the correctional center's farm on Oct. 24, 1982. Cushman was killed when trying to prevent an inmate's escape. Davis was charged with murder.

Cecil Harbison, 30, began working at the Menard Correctional Center on May 4, 1984. He was attacked from

Assistant Warden Charles Hinsley, left, presents the memorial

behind by Inmate William Crews during a disagreement as the lines were returning from eating. Crews received the death penalty.

The death of a peace officer occurs about every 57 hours.

A prayer was given before the dedication by Assistant Warden Charles Hinsley, who expressed his appreciation for the officers who gave their lives for their jobs. A memorial flag was then presented by its unfolding. The flag is to be flown on the anniversary dates of the Menard Correctional Center staff who lost their lives while working and when the American and State Flags are flown at half-mast.

After the ceremony, the family members were given a tour. On Wednesday evening, a tactical unit demonstrated a hostage taking situation.

Originally published in Randolph County Herald Tribune, *Chester, IL. Reprinted with permission.*

How far should prisons go to accommodate the religious life of inmates?

By Mohammed El Nawawy
For The Southern Illinoisan

Worship opportunities still exist for sincere prisoners, officials say

The Menard Correctional Center in Chester is restructuring its security measures, and one part of that process is the reassignment of inmates to cellhouses according to their levels of aggression.

"We separate the more aggressive inmates from the rest of the prison population to keep those inmates from victimizing and influencing the least aggressive ones," Charles Hinsley, assistant warden for programs, said.

Another goal is to reduce the number of inmates in any one place at one time.

There shouldn't be more than 100 inmates in one place at one time. That way, we would have smaller numbers to deal with, and if a situation or disturbance takes place, it would be easier for us to manage," Hinsley said.

The prison chapel is one of the central locations where inmates from all the cellhouses gathered on a particular day when a service or activity was conducted, Hinsley said.

"The chapel was being misused by those large numbers of inmates. Instead of actually being used as a place for worship, it was used for fights, gang activities and drug trafficking," he said.

Jeff Becherer, a correctional officer at Menard, remembers an incident in which two gangs got into a fight and a stabbing took place just outside the door of the chapel.

"This is the only violent incident I can remember that stemmed from inside the chapel," Becherer said.

Hinsley said the system was changed "to put an end to illegal activities at the chapel."

> The chapel was being misused by those large numbers of inmates. Instead of actually being used as a place for worship, it was used for fights, gang activities and drug trafficking.
>
> **CHARLES HINSLEY, Menard assistant warden**

"Now, inmates from each cellhouse have a particular weekend during which they can attend the chapel," he said. "This has reduced the gang effect and the number of inmates we have to supervise."

He added that all chapel services are videotaped and aired on the institutional television for the inmates who didn't have a chance to attend. Menard also offers religious study groups where the inmates go to chapel to study their faith once a week.

Prison chaplains also play a vital role in the religious and spiritual lives of inmates.

"I help the prisoners, pray with them and cry with them in their hard times," Steve Keim, a Protestant chaplain at Menard, said. "This gives me the same satisfaction a pastor gets with his congregations."

Thomas Castellano, associate professor in the department of administration of justice at Southern Illinois University at Carbondale, said inmates might not trust their chaplains if they believe they are co-opted by the prison system.

According to Castellano, chaplains are recognized differently by different wardens.

"If the warden feels favorable toward the chaplain, he'll provide him with more local power and authority, leading to better religious services for the prisoners," Castellano said.

Keim said many prisoners are very sincere about faith. "Those prisoners' relationship with God turns the bitterness, anger and rage in their hearts into kindness, responsibility and peace."

However, others are not serious. They join a religion to use the privileges of going to chapel and socializing with other prisoners, Keim said. He believes that inmates who don't have faith have a tougher time dealing with incarceration because they have nothing to fill the void in their lives.

Inmates differ in how they view the chaplains.

Andre Banks, 33, is a Christian inmate who has been at Menard since 1991 for a murder and attempted murder.

"The chaplains' main concern is to pick up their paychecks every month," he said. "They are tools for the authority."

He said the chaplains are always regarded by the prison's administrators as significant sources of stability and security inside.

"If there's a lot of demoralization, alienation and hostility among the prisoners, an effective chaplain can serve as an intermediary between the administration and the inmates," Castellano said. "This way, chaplains can help reduce tension and can control violent and volatile prison settings."

Keim, who has been at Menard for two years, is one of five chaplains representing Protestant, Catholic, Moslem and Jewish religions.

"I'm here because I believed God placed me here. This is what my life is for. I deal with men who are no different than myself other than they've tragically done something in their lives."

However, Michael Drabing, 42, a Catholic inmate who has been in Menard for 21 years, considers his chaplain "a friend with whom I can discuss my religious and personal matters," he said.

Van Buren, another Protestant chaplain who has been serving at Menard for 14 years, said some inmates refuse chaplains.

Buren said he believes that about 60 percent of the religious inmates don't continue to be religious or spiritual after being released.

According to Buren, 40 percent of the inmates in Menard are religious. Among those 40 percent, two-thirds are Protestants and one third belong to other religions.

Originally published in The Southern Illinoisan, Carbondale, IL. *Reprinted with permission.*

Local

THE SOUTHERN ILLINOISAN FRIDAY, JULY 16, 2004

Union: Warden mal

CHESTER—Union representatives of Menard Correctional Center employees say Warden Charles Hinsley is more concerned with being liked by the inmates than worker safety.

The complaint came from American Federation of State, County and Municipal Employees representatives and prison guards following an inmate assault of a guard Monday at the facility. Menard union President Peggy Sauer said officer Eric Pasquino suffered serious damage to his face, when an inmate allegedly punched him in the east cell house of the prison.

Union members and workers criticize Hinsley for not locking down the facility after the event, but Illinois Department of Corrections officials said they have confidence in how the warden handled the situation.

Sauer said she has a problem with what she called a disregard for employee security.

"It was the warden's judgment call to call (the assault) an isolated incident," she said. "But, when a staff member gets assaulted like that you don't run business as usual."

Kevan Plumlee, AFSCME staff representative, said the situation doesn't represent a good start for Hinsley, who replaced Eugene McAdory Jr. in May.

McAdory was fired from the prison, following the filing of two lawsuits alleging sexual harassment among staff members and neglect and abuse of inmates.

Plumlee told a crowd of correctional officers gathered in front of the facility Thursday wearing orange ribbons in support of Pasquino that Hinsley is going to allow the inmates to get away with too much.

"The new warden is more worried about what the inmates think about him, rather than the safety of the employees," Plumlee said.

CHUCK NOVARA / THE SOUTHERN

Kevan Plumlee, staff representative for AFSCME Council 31, says union members are concerned about safety at Menard Correctional Center.

ing Menard unsafe

Edward Mayo, a 20-year guard at the prison, said he and other employees of Menard were disturbed by an incident in which they allege they saw Hinsley doing pushups with an inmate one day in June.

"It kind of shocked me he came out in the yard doing push-ups with inmates," Mayo said.

He said in a maximum security prison, with more than 3,500 inmates, there never is a totally safe place to work, but Mayo said he'd like to see stricter action taken by the administration when incidents like Monday's assault take place.

Hinsley declined to comment and referred questions to Illinois Department of Corrections spokesman Sergio Molina.

Molina said the department has been concerned about the leadership in Menard for some time, but it placed Hinsley as warden of the prison to ease those worries.

"We placed Chuck Hinsley there because we have all the confidence in his experience," Molina said.

He said it was Hinsley's call whether to lock down the prison after the attack. Molina said he trusts the warden made the best decision for the incident.

"There is no cookie-cutter approach to these situations, despite some who would like to see that," Molina said.

Molina said each assault in an IDOC facility is reported to the central office, and while Menard, like other prisons, has its share of incidents, he said nothing about it stands out.

"We understand there is the potential for this type of incident everyday," he said. "We don't see it everyday, and I think that is a testament to the employees and leadership. But you can't expect it to never happen."

Originally published in The Southern Illinoisan, Carbondale, IL. Reprinted with permission.

271

APPENDIX III

TAMMS CORRECTIONAL CENTER

Task Force Opens Way For Super Max

'TAMMS IS NOT A PLACE YOU WANT TO BE'

On the job already: *Prison Warden George Welborn stands in the execution chamber of the Tamms supermax prison, which will be used for all executions in the state after the first of the year.*

▶TOUGH PRISON IN FINAL PHASE

Word is out

By Pete Rosenbery
The Southern Illinoisan

Illinois' super-maximum-security prison is still weeks away from opening. But it appears that "the word" is out on the Tamms Correctional Center.

In his talks with wardens of maximum-security prisons in the state, Tamms Warden George Welborn has learned that inmates already are asking if they are being ticketed for Alexander County.

"I think in some sense we are already driving home the message: Tamms is not a place you want to be," Welborn said last week.

Some of the state's most violent and troublesome inmates will begin arriving at the 520-bed prison early next year, likely in January or February.

Work continues on the final phases of the $73 million prison. It also will be the site for all of the state's executions.

Tamms will have 480 beds for inmates in general population and another 40 beds for inmates in a pre-

274

transfer unit. An inmate who is ready to leave Tamms will receive counseling for a few weeks before he is transferred.

Inmates will stay for at least a year before they are considered for transfer back to another prison to continue serving their sentence. And Corrections Department officials will first review the case and determine if circumstances have changed that would allow the transfer.

Originally published in The Southern Illinoisan, *Carbondale, IL. Reprinted with permission.*

Tamms Correctional Center

■ **Location:** Alexander County.
■ **Type:** Super-maximum security.
■ **Open:** Early 1998.
■ **Cost:** $73 million.
■ **Average annual cost per inmate:** $31,000 to $35,000.
■ **Projected inmates:** 520.
■ **Projected employees:** 350, including 250 correctional officers.

Operations Warden Chuck Hinsley stands at the master control panels of one of the cell blocks at the new facility.

Southern Illinois Prison Committee

SPECIAL EDITION - OPENING OF TAMMS SUPERMAX PRISON - 1998

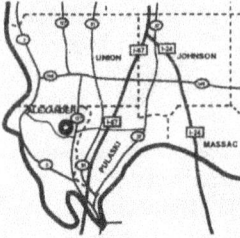

SIPC Southernmost Illinois Prison Committee

• Alexander County • Johnson County • Massac County
• 'Pulaski County • Union County

P.O. Box 529 -:- Anna, Illinois 62906 -:- 618-833-8407

January 1998

AN OPEN LETTER TO THE COMMUNITY
OF SOUTHERNMOST ILLINOIS

The opening of the Tamms Super Max. Correctional Facility is a proud
landmark for the Southernmost Illinois Prison Committee.

This event is neither the end or the beginning of what SIPC hoped to
accomplish when it was established in 1993. It was and is the goal of
SIPC to work in partnership with the Illinois Department of Corrections
to bring quality employment to this area. This ideal has been realized
through hundreds of construction jobs in the past few years and will
continue to benefit the area many, many years in the future with jobs at
the Super Max. and Work Camp.

SIPC did not bring the Super Max. to Tamms, it was merely the coordinating
group which voiced the desire of the entire region. SIPC did not donate
the money for the land, surveys or numerous projects, it was the money
of individuals, banks and other organizations which SIPC served to gather
and distribute. Everyone in the five county area served by SIPC deserves
the credit for bringing this project to where it is today. The volunteers
of SIPC are only happy that they could be there to help.

Again, thanks for the support.

Sincerely,

Jerry L. Reppert
Chairman

ILLINOIS
DEPARTMENT
OF
CORRECTIONS

Jim Edgar
Governor

Odie Washington
Director

P.O. Box 400, 200 E. Super Max Road / Tamms, IL 62988
Telephone: (618) 747-2042 • FAX: (618) 747-2062 • TDD: (800) 526-0844

WARDEN'S COMMENTS:

Approximately four-years ago I was appointed as Warden of the Tamms Correctonal Center. Much has happened during this period of time. In June 1995, the Tamms Minimum Security Unit, which houses 200 inmates and employs 85 people, opened and began providing public work crews throughout the area. These inmate work crews have performed a variety of valuable tasks to communities and will continue to do so.

In the very near future, the Tamms Closed Maximum Security Facility will begin initial occupancy. Once it is completely phased in, the CMAX will house approximately 500 maximum security inmates and employ 350 staff members. The hiring and training of staff has been in process for several months and will continue into the Spring. The Tamms Closed Maximum Security Facility has a unique mission and is an integral component in the Illinois Department of Corrections' ongoing plan to deal with disruptive, violent inmates. Reducing staff assaults and protecting the public is an I.D.O.C priority. The design, construction and operation of the Tamms CMAX will give us much needed administrative flexibility that was previously not available.

The primary emphasis during the design phase of the CMAX was security. First, this means security for our Correctional Officers who will be required to perform the difficult job of dealing with the inmates on a day-to-day basis. Every attempt has been made to build a prison that will maximize the safety of staff. Small, self contained housing units, which minimize staff/inmate contact, was the goal given to the project architect. I am pleased to say that this goal has been met! Along with established procedures regarding the escorting of individual inmates, and extensive training, the housing units will give our security staff ample opportunity to protect themselves. Second, the Tamms Closed Maximum Security Facility was designed to protect the public. The design of the facility, deployment of correctional staff and specific security procedures will enhance our ability to protect the public. I can assure you that every effort possible will be taken to protect the community.

As the opening of this facility draws near, I would like to take this opportunity to thank several people who have been instrumental in this process. First and foremost, I want to thank Governor Jim Edgar for his commitment and vision to the philosophical concept behind this prison. In addition, the members of the Illinois General Assembly need to be commended for the support shown during the past four years. Director Odie Washington, Deputy Director David Watkins, Deputy Director Karl Becker, Assistant Deputy Director Mike Neal and Assistant Deputy Director Michael O'Leary all have provided significant contributions to the vital policy making decisions that are critical to the success of this new and unique facility. Mayor Walter Pang, Mr. Jerry Reppert, Don Denny and all the members of the Southernmost Illinois Prison Committee are to be commended. On countless occasions over the past few years, I have asked for help and advice from them and never have been disappointed. Thanks.

George C. Welborn, Warden
Tamms Correctional Center

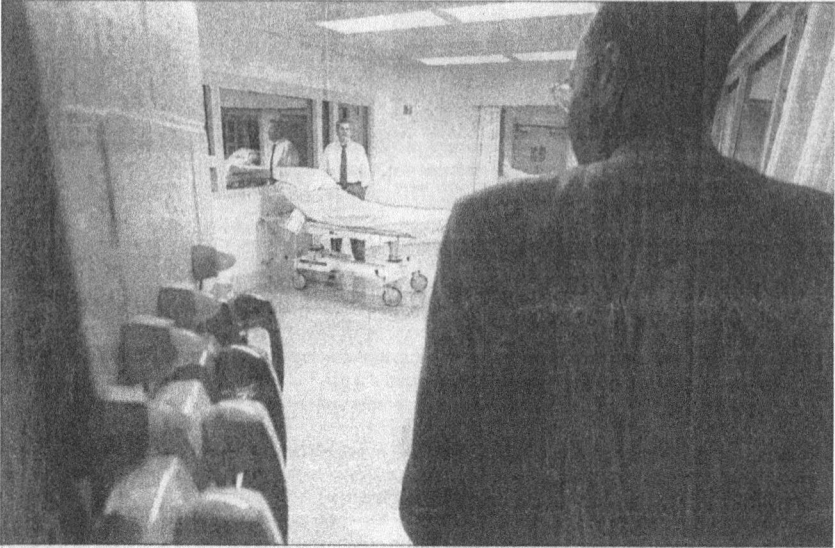

FRED ZWICKY/Journal Star

On Nov. 18, Peorian Willie Enoch is scheduled to be the first person executed in the death chamber at Tamms Correctional Center. The only people who Enoch would see in his final moments—other than his own reflection—are Warden George Welborn, who stands by the gurney where lethal chemicals are administered, and assistant warden Charles Hinsley, who will write down his final statement.

Death'sDoor

Find out what's in store for Willie Enoch, the first to be executed at the Tamms supermax prison

By PHIL LUCIANO
of the Journal Star

TAMMS—Condemned murderer Willie Enoch soon could spend his last earthly moments staring into his own eyes, watching himself die.

No Peorian has been executed in a half-century. But all signs indicate that on Nov. 18, Willie Enoch will break that string and become the first inmate to die in the state's new death chamber, which boasts a modern design aimed at streamlining executions.

"We tried to create an efficient process," says Warden George Welborn. "And I think we've succeeded."

Because of a twist in the layout of the new chamber, Enoch would lie strapped in a gurney before a wall of one-way mirrors through which witnesses can see in, but he cannot see

Originally published in The Southern Illinoisan, *Carbondale, IL. Reprinted with permission.*

278

Warden mum on debate

Pekin native in charge of Tamms prison keeps his opinion on capital punishment to himself

By PHIL LUCIANO
of the Journal Star

How does Warden George Welborn feel about capital punishment? Don't bother asking.

"Even my wife doesn't know if I'm in favor of the death penalty," says the native Pekinite, who now runs the supermax prison in Tamms, home of the state's new execution chamber. "I've never told anyone."

Welborn, 51, has observed executions but has never overseen one himself. That will change Nov. 18, when he will stand at Willie Enoch's side and direct the Peorian's death.

Welborn, a 1965 graduate of Pekin High School and recipient of a master's degree in public administration from Illinois State University in Normal a decade later, often talks about the philosophy of the death penalty with

Pekin High School graduate George Welborn, now the warden to oversee executions at Tamms Correctional Center, says his feelings on capital punishment are not important. "We didn't judge this inmate," Welborn says. "We didn't sentence this inmate. The law says we must execute this inmate."

his assistant warden, Charles Hinsley. Their feelings sound ambivalent.

"We didn't judge this inmate," Welborn says. "We didn't sentence this inmate. The law says we must execute this inmate.

"I don't feel our feelings about the death penalty are important. We feel it's part of our job."

Adds Hinsley, "You cannot allow your personal feelings to influence the case. It would cause you to become unfocused. And you would have to be in focus because it's a very serious responsibility."

They say they recognize the heinousness of the crimes that push men onto death row. Still, in that their job duties involve taking lives, they take pause.

"I would ask the most ardent death-penalty advocate, the ones that say, 'Let me pull the switch,' to come here and see what the staff goes through. It's not a pretty thing," Welborn says.

"The bottom line: there's a human element there, a connection. You're taking a healthy human being from a cell. And in a few minutes, he's going to be dead."

Welborn expects protestors at Tamms' first execution, and has designated a demonstration area near the prison entrance. He says he's unsure how many will show up, but will deploy a heavy contingent of police officers—even though most recent execution protests have been peaceful.

"My priest will be there," Welborn says with a slight grin. "Nothing personal, he insists."

SUNDAY SOUTHERN

www.southernillinoisan.com

© The Southern Illinoisan   SUNDAY, JULY 2, 2000   Volume 108-No. 184

SPECIAL REPORT

Tamms Super-max

Does the maximum-security prison work?

Provided photo

Is Super-max prison a deterrent for violence?

By Richard Goldstein
The Southern Illinoisan

When Gov. Jim Edgar announced he would support the bill in 1993 authorizing construction of a super-maximum security prison, he said it was necessary to calm the rest of the prison system. It would remove the most violent, and deter the rest with the threat of being sent there.

Prison violence in Illinois spiked in fiscal year 1996, which began July 1, 1995, and has been falling steadily ever since.

The Legislative Research Unit says that in fiscal year 1996 there were 1,108 attacks on staff in maximum security prisons. In fiscal year 1999 there were 413 attacks on staff.

Debby Lippincott, staff representative for the American Federation of State, County and Municipal Em-

The Southern Illinoisan, SUNDAY, JULY 2, 2000

VIOLENCE IN PRISON
Attacks by inmates in Illinois Maximum Security Prisons

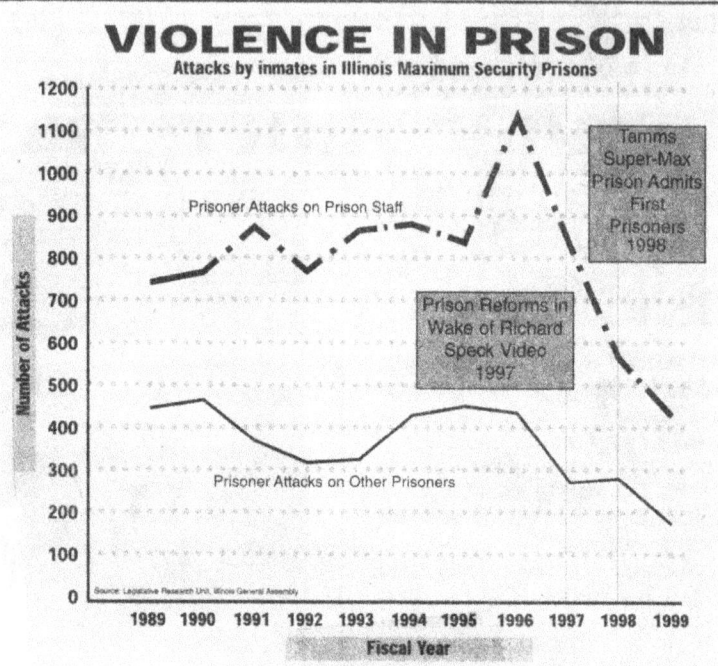

ployees Council 31 in Marion, gives Tamms much of the credit.

"It has made a big difference. It means that there's truly repercussions for an inmate assaulting a correctional officer," Lippincott said. "It's made the prisons a much safer place to work in these days."

Attacks by inmates against inmates have dropped less sharply but also are down.

"A lot of old time convicts say, 'Don't quote me, but thank God for Tamms; people don't want to go there,'" said Charles Fasano who visits prisons regularly to assess conditions as a staff associate for John Howard Association, a prisons watchdog group in Chicago.

Originally published in The Southern Illinoisan, *Carbondale, IL. Reprinted with permission.*

SPECIAL REPORT

Tamms Super-max

It's not a wonderful life

By Richard Goldstein
The Southern Illinoisan

Last night, at about 5 p.m. when correctional officers opened the 271 chuck-holes on cell doors in the Tamms super-maximum security prison, they slid through trays holding dinners of turkey ham, great northern beans, tomatoes and okra, a lettuce salad, bread and angel food cake.

These morsels followed a lunch of black bean burger with gravy, cooked cabbage, potatoes and carrots, a lettuce salad and bread and cookies, according to the Illinois Department of Corrections.

This was the menu available to all except prisoners punished with meal loaf—an oven-baked hamburger-vegetable mixture that looks like a meat loaf and which an independent observer likened to the flavor of squash.

"The food is good here. I have no complaints about the food," said inmate Larry Foutch. When he spoke, the 34-year-old Effingham man had

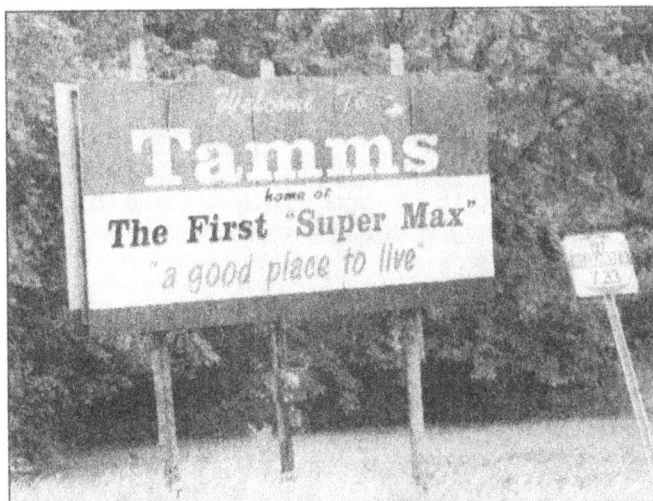

For tough customers: Tamms' inmates have the fewest privileges in Illinois. The harsh conditions are justified as necessary to control the system's 'worst of the worst.'

283

lasted three weeks into a hunger strike protesting prison conditions and policies.

Foutch, convicted of a 1984 Marion County murder, was sent to Tamms for alleged gang ties. He was one of three inmates who survived 33 days on water. When the strike started May 1, more than half the inmates skipped at least one meal.

The hunger strike bought state attention to the two-year old prison, which specializes in solitary confinement.

Inmates are in their cells all but an hour each day, when they exercise in a larger concrete-walled room partially exposed to the sky. For privileged inmates, exercise is followed by a 20-minute shower five days a week.

Through demands issued when the hunger strike began, prisoners asked that the department give clearer rules for leaving Tamms and returning to the general prison population. They asked that the administration rescind a "gang renunciation" policy they said put their lives in danger by forcing them to snitch on other prisoners as a condition for departure.

They also echoed federal lawsuits asking that mentally ill prisoners be removed from the prison, and that meal-loaf be ended as a punishment.

The Department of Corrections says the prisoners inside Tamms richly deserve these depravations because of gang activity or violent behavior in other prisons.

Corrections spokesman Nic Howell said no changes have been made at the prison in response to the demands.

So for now, life goes on the same as ever in the Tamms super-max, where

Originally published in The Southern Illinoisan, *Carbondale, IL. Reprinted with permission.*

◆ Tamms: Isolation in more ways than one

Continued from Page One

correspondence).

It's the Jerry Springer problem, Corrections spokesman Nic Howell explained.

"If we let you in, we'd have to let everyone else in. It would become a security issue. We would have to devote a lot of time in ushering news media and entertainers around Tamms," Howell said.

Howell mentioned talk show host Jerry Springer, known for his rowdy daytime segments.

A consequence of shielding information about Tamms and other super-maximum security prisons nationally may have been to dampen scholarly support for the super-max as a means for controlling prison populations.

The first modern use of a super-maximum security prison came in 1983 at the Marion federal penitentiary, where inmates were locked in their cells 23 hours a day. The lockdown was a response to the murder of two guards in separate incidents on the same day in 1983.

During the 1990s the federal government and states built scores of super-max prisons.

But among corrections scholars, the super-max idea is often referred to as a "solution in search of problem," as in a 1998 study by Roy D. King of the University of Wales.

Castellano said, "There is no rigorous scientific evidence that super-max prisons are effective in accomplishing their goals."

Rep. Thomas Dart, a Chicago Democrat and chairman of the House Prisons reform committee, says the public has a right to know about its $65 million "tool."

"Outside of security concerns, I don't see why we shouldn't be able to look into exactly what taxpayers are getting for their money," Dart said. "Hiding stuff in my opinion has never worked to the advantage of anybody other than the people who have reason to be hiding."

Dart noted, however, that director Donald Snyder informs lawmakers more readily than his predecessor, Odie Washington.

Far far away

It may be difficult to get information about the Tamms super-max, but it is also difficult to get to the super-max.

Most Tamms prisoners are from the Chicago area. For their visitors, the prison lies in one of the remotest sections of Illinois, within sight of the Mississippi bluffs of rural Alexander County.

The location and the restriction on visits contribute to the scarcity of visitors, says a prison watchdog group.

Visitor log books from a May weekend show nine to 11 visitors per day to the 271 inmates. Some prisoners are restricted to one visit per month.

A 1999 report issued by the John Howard Association, which monitors Illinois prisons, criticizes the placement of Tamms in a remote location and says visits by relatives often improve inmates' behavior.

Charles Fasano, director of monitoring for the John Howard Association, who has visited Tamms as part of a team assessing conditions, summarizes the attitude of corrections officials toward secrecy.

"Outsiders in general and particularly the media are sort of a pain," he said. "It's a lot of work, so none of these places want to be totally open. And if you're going to clamp down on it, where are you going to clamp down on it? Your most secure facility."

Originally published in The Southern Illinoisan, *Carbondale, IL. Reprinted with permission.*

What's the bottom line on super-max prisons?

By Richard Goldstein
The Southern Illinoisan

Super-maximum security prisons are expensive, as everyone will tell you.

Since it opened in 1998, media and private studies have reported the cost of housing each inmate in the Tamms super-max at about $35,000 a year. The writers say Illinois Department of Corrections officials told them so.

That would be about twice what it costs to house an inmate for a year in a state maximum security prison.

But an analysis of the budget as part of an investigation into the operation of the state's 2-year-old prison suggests that the $35,000-a-year figure is about half the actual amount.

Unlike the rest of its maximum-security prisons, the Department of Corrections doesn't publish the per-inmate cost of its super-maximum security prison in Tamms.

The reason offered by Corrections spokesman Nic Howell is that there is no separate budget for the super-maximum security prison. The Tamms budget combines the super-max prison and its companion minimum-security work camp, which contains 200 prisoners.

But there is a way of estimating the operating costs of the super-max prison.

The work camp operated for two years before the super-max prison opened; the last was fiscal year 1997. By subtracting the fiscal year 1997 operating budget from the fiscal year 2000 budget, an approximate super-max budget can be estimated.

Using this method, the approximate super-max budget in fiscal year 2000 was $20.8 million. Dividing that figure by 271—the number of super-max prisoners in May—equals about $77,000.

Comparable figures for state's maximum security prisons are about $20,000, according to the Department of Corrections.

Charles Fasano, director of monitoring for the John Howard Association, a prisons watchdog group, said another $5,000 to $15,000 per prisoner should be added to the annual operating cost of any recently built prison to account for the cost of financing its debt.

Because the super-max was relatively expensive to build—$65 million out of $73 million for the Tamms complex—the debt service is likely to tilt toward the high end, he said.

That could push the annual cost toward $90,000 per inmate.

Howell said that no matter the cost, the super-max is worth it because the department believes it reduces violence in the prison system.

If the super-max were full—using all its 520 beds—its per-inmate costs would be closer to what the department has advertised since it opened.

But Fasano's group, for one, favors the Department of Corrections' policy of running a half-empty super-max prison, the only one with so many free beds in the system.

"We're giving them pats on the back for that," Fasano said.

A report on Tamms issued last year by the John Howard Association says the empty beds allow a more judicious use of the facility.

Originally published in The Southern Illinoisan, *Carbondale, IL. Reprinted with permission.*

Tamms Correctional Center

200 East Super Max Road
P.O. Box 400
Tamms, Illinois 62988
618-747-2042
618-747-2062 FAX

Rod R. Blagojevich, Governor
Roger E. Walker Jr., Director
Deann Benos, Assistant Director
Ian Oliver, Executive Chief
Salvador Godinez, Chief of Operations
Charles L. Hinsley, Warden

**Tamms Correctional Center
C-Max Entrance**

MISSION STATEMENT

The Tamms Closed Maximum Security Facility (C-Max) has been designated and designed to house the Illinois Department of Corrections' most disruptive, violent and problematic inmates. Inmates approved for placement at the Tamms C-Max will have demonstrated an inability or unwillingness to conform to the requirements of a general population facility. In addition, inmates who have manifested a negative influence on the safety and security of the Illinois Department of Corrections, or may have perpetrated criminal activity that threatens the community may be transferred to the Tamms C-Max. The Tamms C-Max will provide extra high levels of security and restrict or eliminate privileges permitted at other Illinois Department of Corrections' general population facilities. Inmates transferred to the Tamms C-Max may be required to stay for a minimum, pre-determined length of time. Positive behavior, willingness to conform to stated rules and regulations, or a change in the circumstances surrounding the rationale, among other matters, will be considered in determining whether an inmate returns to a general population environment.

GOAL STATEMENT

The goal of the Tamms C-Max is to improve the quality of life, safety, and day-to-day operation of other Illinois Department of Corrections facilities and to enhance the safety of staff, inmates and the public.

Charles L. Hinsley, Warden

On behalf of the Illinois Department of Corrections, I welcome you to Tamms Correctional Center.

Administration

The current administrative staff consists of two Assistant Wardens: Sam Riley, Assistant Warden for Operations and R. Shelton Frey, Assistant Warden for Programs. In addition, Greg Gossett serves as Unit Superintendent at the Minimum Security Unit.

The facility has a full time staff consisting of 389 employees at both the MSU and C-Max.

APPENDIX IV
PERSONAL

Boy's Club of Asheville, 1974–1976. Sitting on left, Chuck Hinsley; third from the left, Coach Larry Grant.

AB–Tech Basketball Team, 1976–1978

Atomics' 'Find'

Hinsley Has Tech's Lead

By KEITH DUDLEY
Citizen-Times Correspondent

Last year, A-B Tech's head basketball coach, Jim Rhea, went to the Asheville Boys Club to observe one of the players on the team that had won several tournaments in Tennessee.

The player that Rhea found, Chuck Hinsley, is not only the leading scorer for the Atomics this season, but he's second in scoring in the Western Tarheel Conference.

"There was a lot of potential there," Rhea said. "It didn't take us very long to invite Chuck to A-B Tech."

Hinsley is averaging 18.8 points a game for the Atomics, has 83 steals in 16 games, and he's second on the team in assists, averaging 3.6 an outing.

When the 5-foot-11 guard came to A-B Tech, he had only one year of basketball experience, playing his sophomore year at Asheville High. But, this was no barrier for Hinsley.

"He's got real desire to play the game," Rhea. "Chuck usually stays after practice and shoots foul shots. If the who team had his desire, we'd be 17-0 this year."

Hinsley's desire can best be observed on the court. In his last three outings

against Montreat-Anderson, Davidson Community College, and Isothermal Community College, he scored 26, 20, and 29 points. In an earlier contest with Isothermal, he spurred the Atomica to an 84-81 victory with 10 steals, 12 rebounds and eight assists.

But playing good basketball requires a desire both on and off the court.

Hinsley takes the city bus to school and practices everyday. During the snowfalls of the past weeks, he walked one and a half miles to reach the bus routes in order to get to practice.

"Chuck has really improved since he started the season," Rhea said. "His strongest points are his speed and quickness. If you turn your back on him, the ball will be gone."

"I try to practice everyday," said Hinsley. "Except for Sundays, when I rest up. When we don't practice at A-B Tech, I practice at the Elizabeth Street Community Center gym. "I need to work on my defense," Hinsley added. "If my defense is going okay, my offense just follows. I like the man-to-man defense best, there's more chances to steal."

"Hinsley hopes to get an offer from a four-year school. He's on a one-year program at A-B Tech, doing his study in Heating and Air Conditioning, a study that will not transfer to the four-year schools. Since Hinsley has played one year of his eligibility, he could only play three years at a university.

"I'd settle for three," Hinsley noted. "If I don't get an offer, I'll stay at A-B Tech on another program. When I get out, I'll work out on my own, and try it as a free agent with professional ball."

A-B Tech Wins, 77-72

Atomics Trim Cavaliers

Chuck Hinsley scored 18 of his game-high 23 points in the first half Thursday night as A-B Tech built a 16-point half-time margin en route to a 77-72 victory at Montreat-Anderson College.

The meeting between two-year schools in Buncombe County seemed headed for an early decision when A-B Tech took a 45-29 advantage at the end of the first half. But the Cavaliers, who have now lost their last 14 games, came back in the second half to give the Atomics a run for the win.

Montreat-Anderson steadily chipped away at the A-B Tech margin in the second half, closing to within four points, 74-70, with three minutes left. However, the Atomics' effort at ball control, attempting to run out the clock, paid off.

The victory boosted A-B Tech's record to 5-8 while the Cavaliers dropped to 1-14.

Following Hinsley in the scoring department for A-B Tech was Lionel Gash with 17 points. Kenny Ball scored 14.

Montreat-Anderson was led by Denorris Nichols' 17-point performance. Tim Edwards was close behind with 16 and Kevin Shaffer got 14.

The Cavaliers travel to Lee-McRae College in Banner Elk Tuesday for their next outing while A-B Tech will be at home Saturday night against Isothermal Community College.

Hensley Leads Atomics' Win

Chuck Hinsley fired in 26 points to lead Asheville-Buncombe Tech to a hard-fought 92-86 victory over Southwestern Technical Institute on the Atomics' home court Friday night.

The two teams battled to a tie, 48-48, at the half and Southwestern Tech took a 74-72 lead at the end of three quarters. However, key goals by Hinsley and Mike Grant staked the Atomics to a six-point spread which they never relinquished.

Grant scored 20 for the Atomics, now 2-7, while Kenny Ball added 18 points.

Jay Yeargin led Southwestern Tech with 28 points.

Articles originally published in Asheville Citizens-Times, *Asheville, NC. Reprinted with permission.*

ASHEVILLE-BUNCOMBE TECHNICAL COMMUNITY COLLEGE

K. Ray Bailey, *President*

340 Victoria Road
Asheville, NC 28801
Telephone (704) 254-1921
FAX (704) 251-6355

December 11, 1997

Mr. Chuck Hinsley
82 Golpen Rd.
Carbondale, Illinois 62901

Chuck:

It was great to hear from you yesterday. I assembled a few stats from the 1976-77 and 1977-78 school years. I hope you enjoy seeing what you did.

1976-77:   **Won 14, Lost 12**

Most points in a game (34) by Chuck Hinsley against Brevard College
Highest season scoring average (20.8) points by Chuck Hinsley
Most points in the season (521) by Chuck Hinsley
Most assists in the season (114) by Chuck Hinsley

1977-78:   **Won 15, Lost 13**

Most points in a game (30) by Chuck Hinsley against Surry Community College
Highest season scoring average (19.3) points by Chuck Hinsley
Most points in the season (503) by Chuck Hinsley
Most assists in a game (12) by Chuck Hinsley
Most assists for the season (133) by Chuck Hinsley

I'm sorry we didn't keep more stats but remember we had very few statisticians.

Good Luck,

Jim Rhea

Atomics' Leader ??-?8

Hinsley Gets Juco Chance

By MILES D. MORGAN
Citizen-Times Sports Writer

Chuck Hinsley didn't let being cut for two years at Asheville High stop his playing career.

But through a lot of determination and desire, the 5-10, 155-pound guard was given a shot at making the A-B Tech team by coach Jim Rhea.

He made good on Rhea's decision to keep him. In the past two years the sophomore has led the Atomics in scoring with a 21.0 average and a 19.8 average.

Hinsley is 24 points shy of becoming A-B Tech's all-time career scorer and this season he has already broken the school record for assists with 143 and steals with 147. Hinsley has scored 1,011 career points and has tossed in 494 points in 24 games this season in leading the Atomics to a 15-12 record.

Reflecting on his career, Hinsley said, "I wasn't about to let being cut at Asheville stop me. In the two years I was cut I went out and played for the Boys Club of Asheville's basketball team.

"I wanted to continue my career and was lucky enough to be given a tryout by coach Rhea. He didn't cut me and I've been happy playing for A-B Tech ever since."

Concerning his final year as an Atomic, Hinsley noted, "I felt I could have done better—average-wise. But this year we've had better shooters and I've had to give out more assists.

"I like to shoot the ball but I felt I had to be a team player because that is important and I knew it."

Hinsley feels the strongest point of his game is speed. "My speed has enabled me to get past a slower opponent on offense," he said. "On defense, it has allowed me to set an opponent up to steal the ball or force the turnover.

"I would like to improve on my defense," he added. "This is the weakest part of my game. I've tried to work on it. I have a habit of reaching around and I still do it some now."

"Chuck is the best all-around player we've had at A-B Tech in eight years," said Rhea.

"He's a hard worker, too," added Rhea. "He has a real good attitude about the game and stays before and after practice working on his game.

"Chuck's not playing high school basketball made him have to work. He has overcome a lot of the basic fundamental mistakes that he did not have a chance to learn about in high school."

Hinsley has three things on his mind now—he wants to win the upcoming Western Tarheel Conference tournament beginning Thursday, he wants to play senior college ball and he wants to graduate.

"I do feel like I can play senior college ball and I would like to play at either Winston-Salem State of UNC-Charlotte.

"Over the past years I've seen how the coaches at these schools have done with their basketball programs. They run a lot and shoot a lot and that's my style. Also, I feel like the coaches at these schools have good backgrounds."

As for the tournament, Hinsley explained, "I feel like we can take it. I sprained my ankle recently but I'll be ready. We do have the talent. It's just a matter of us putting it together. I know that, if at all possible, I will give it 120 percent."

Originally published in Asheville Citizens-Times, *Asheville, NC. Reprinted with permission.*

Winston-Salem State University basketball team, 1978-1980. Chuck Hinsley, # 32, appears fourth from the left on the second row.

SOUTHERN ILLINOISAN

The road to grocery s

By Dave DeWitte
Of The Southern Illinoisan

Southern Illinois University-Carbondale graduate student Charles Hinsley has no reason to believe a Monday morning stop at a local market for some groceries would be anything other than normal.

But before Hinsley had returned home the morning of Dec. 10, he had been held at gunpoint, handcuffed and taken into police custody for questioning.

SIU-C police say the incident involving Hinsley at Arnold's Market south of Carbondale shortly before 10 a.m. Monday morning was to all outward appearances an armed robbery in progress. An SIU-C police officer reportedly took Hinsley, a black male, into custody after he observed a car driven by another black male idling outside the market.

Hinsley, 27, says he had ridden his bicycle to the apartment of a female friend who was out of town to pick up her mail. On the way back to his apartment, located across U.S. 51 from Arnold's Market, he decided to stop for groceries. Picking up a carton of milk, a Polish sausage and a small set of fingernail clippers, he went back outside to his bicycle.

As he approached the bike, he was surprised by a voice from behind commanding him to "move away from the bike, put down the bag, lay face down on the ground and spread your arms and legs wide," he said.

Hinsley was released about 20 minutes later with an explanation for being detained, he said, but not before being forced to lie on the ground in a spread-eagle position, being handcuffed and taken to the SIU-C police department for questioning. At one point as an officer kneeled beside him, he said, a pistol was held less than a foot from his head.

Authorities searched for, and located, the man in the idling car with out-of-state plates. Neither he nor Hinsley knew each other. The driver also was released after questioning.

Now Hinsley is considering legal action against the department.

"I was humiliated in public. I was discriminated against and I was unjustly accused of a wrong I did not commit. There was no probable cause whatsoever," he said of the incident.

Hinsley believes the fact that both he and the car's driver were black was the main factor which triggered suspicion on the part of the officer. He was not satisfied by the explanation offered by the officer who detained him.

"He said I was in the wrong place at the wrong time," he said.

However, SIU-C Police Capt. Carl Kirk said the steps taken by police officer Mikey Thomas, who initially detained Hinsley, were the same steps any "reasonable and prudent" police

ɔre may lead to court

officer would have taken under the same conditions.

"He exerted control on what appeared to be an armed robbery," Kirk said.

Kirk said the critical point in the incident was when the man in the idling car reached toward the waistband of his pants. He said the officer's view was obscured at the man's waist level, preventing him from seeing if he had a gun. The man in the car drove off and the officer moved to take Hinsley into custody.

"He (Thomas) did just exactly what he should have done if I'd been standing there supervising," Kirk said. He said Thomas' swift actions might have greatly lessened the chances of someone in the store being killed if the incident had turned out to be an armed robbery.

Rob Sims, a cashier at Arnold's Market, said the driver of the automobile previously had been in the store buying a toothbrush. He did not know the driver, Sims said, but knew Hinsley as a regular customer.

Sims said he was not asked if the store had been robbed or was being robbed until after Hinsley was taken away.

"In my opinion, the police were totally jumping to conclusions," Sims said. "They didn't ask anybody any questions at all. They just arrested a guy and hauled him off."

Kirk said Thomas' explanation for the incident was plausible. He said Hinsley's suggestion that the race of the two men was any kind of factor at all was false.

Charles Hinsley: 'Wrong place a the wrong time'?

"All the necessary requirements were present to cause a reasonable and prudent officer to believe a robbery was coming down," he said.

Although he was not physically harmed in the incident, Hinsley said he plans to pursue the matter in court. He does not plan to seek a big monetary settlement, he said, but feels the actions of the police should not be allowed to go unchecked.

"Too many things like this go uncontested," he said. "I'm going to follow it through and I hope something can be done."

Originally published in The Southern Illinoisan, *Carbondale, IL. Reprinted with permission.*

301

ILLINOIS
DEPARTMENT
OF
CORRECTIONS

HOWARD A. PETERS III
Director

Vienna Correctional Center / P. O. Box 200 / Vienna, Illinois 62995 / Telephone (618) 658-8371

M E M O R A N D U M

DATE: October 15, 1991

TO: Charles L. Hinsley
          Correctional Casework Supervisor

FROM: Warden Rod Tally

SUBJECT: Appreciation

On this first anniversary of the opening of the Impact Incarceration Program, I want to congratulate you on your contributions to the program. You have every reason to be proud of your personal contributions to the collective success of the program.

Your dedication is very much appreciated and I hope you continue to grow and enjoy what is a unique program in the Department of Corrections.

cc: Personnel File

RT:FB:cd

Asheville native gets prison post

Charles Hinsley

Charles L. Hinsley, son of Mr. and Mrs. Isaiah Tutt of Asheville, has been appointed assistant warden of programs at the Menard Correctional Center, a maximum security prison in Chester, Ill.

Hinsley graduated from Asheville High School in 1976.

He earned a B.A. degree in psychology from Winston-Salem State University in 1982 and a Master of Science degree from Southern Illinois University in Carbondale, Ill., in 1990.

Appointed warden

Charles L. Hinsley, son of Mr. and Mrs. Isaiah Tutt of Asheville, has been appointed assistant warden of programs at the Menard Correctional Center, a maximum security prison in Chester, Ill.

Hinsley graduated from Asheville High School in 1976 and earned a B.A. degree in psychology from Winston-Salem State University in 1982 and a Master of Science degree from Southern Illinois University in Carbondale, Ill., in 1990. He is a certified substance abuse counselor and a member of the National Association of Blacks in Criminal Justice.

HOUSE OF REPRESENTATIVES
WASHINGTON, D. C. 20515

January 18, 1994

JERRY F. COSTELLO
TWELFTH DISTRICT ILLINOIS

Mr. Charles Hinsley
C/O Menard Correctional Center
Menard, IL 62259

Dear Charles:

Congratulations on being appointed as
Assistant Warden for Programs.

This is an honor for which you can truly be
proud.

Charles, if I can ever be of assistance to
you or your family in any way, please do not
hesitate to contact my office.

Sincerely,

JERRY F. COSTELLO
Member of Congress

JFC/kac

North Carolina General Assembly
House of Representatives
State Legislative Building
Raleigh 27601-1096

REP. NARVEL JIM CRAWFORD
15 EDGEMONT RD
ASHEVILLE, N.C. 28801

February 22, 1994

Mr. and Mrs. Isaiah Tutt
146 S. French Broad Avenue
Asheville, NC 28801

Dear Mr. and Mrs. Tutt:

Congratulations on your son Charles's
appointment to the position of assistant
warden of programs at the Menard
Correctional Center. I know you and your
family are extremely proud of him.

I am especially aware at this time of the
contributions individuals such as Charles
make toward improving public safety for our
citizens. Please give my best wishes to
him as he begins his new job.

Sincerely,

Narvel Jim Crawford

www.ingramcontent.com/pod-product-compliance
Lightning Source LLC
Chambersburg PA
CBHW060026030426
42334CB00019B/2194